Obesity among Poor Americans

Obesity among Poor Americans

Is Public Assistance the Problem?

Patricia K. Smith

Vanderbilt University Press   NASHVILLE

© 2009 by Vanderbilt University Press
Nashville, Tennessee 37235
All rights reserved

13 12 11 10 09   1 2 3 4 5

This book is printed on acid-free paper
made from 30 percent post-consumer recycled content.
Manufactured in the United States of America

Library of Congress Cataloging-in-Publication Data
Smith, Patricia K. (Patricia Kay), 1959–
Obesity among poor Americans :
is public assistance the problem? / Patricia K. Smith.
p. ; cm.
Includes bibliographical references and index.
ISBN 978-0-8265-1635-0 (cloth : alk. paper)
ISBN 978-0-8265-1636-7 (pbk. : alk. paper)
1. Obesity—United States—Etiology. 2. Obesity—
Social aspects—United States. 3. Poverty—Health
aspects—United States. 4. Public welfare—United
States. I. Title.
[DNLM: 1. Obesity—etiology—United States.
2. Poverty—United States. 3. Public Assistance—
United States. WD 210 S656o 2009]
RC628.S6415 2009
362.196'3980086942—dc22
2008024088

To my parents,

who provided a healthy

and loving environment

Contents

Acknowledgments

My family, especially my husband, Richard, has given me great encouragement in writing this book. My writing group (Carolyn Kraus, Lora Lempert, Maureen Linker, and Jackie Vansant) and my colleague Michael Twomey provided invaluable help by diligently reading and critiquing various versions of several chapters. The College of Arts, Sciences, and Letters at the University of Michigan–Dearborn supported this research with a course release, which is the only financial support I received for this project. My teachers in the public schools of Casper, Wyoming, and at the University of Wyoming provided the educational foundation, intellectual guidance, and encouragement necessary for me to successfully pursue an academic career. Thank you all.

Introduction

Critics have argued that public assistance reduces work effort, discourages marriage, and encourages nonmarital births. Now some claim that public assistance also causes obesity. For example, Douglas Besharov, of the American Enterprise Institute, testified before a congressional committee that he thinks the Food Stamp and National School Lunch programs contribute to weight gain and obesity among participants (Besharov 2003). He recommended that food stamps be cashed out so recipients aren't forced to spend benefits on food.

For a while, I dismissed Besharov's claims as yet another conservative attack on the poor and on any federal attempt to assist them. But a question kept nagging me: what if he's right? Allocating scarce public resources to programs that encourage a condition associated with several health problems and reduced labor market outcomes would indeed be a waste and would contradict the goal of helping the less fortunate lead healthier, more productive lives. If assistance programs contribute to weight gain, then we need to figure out how to reform them in ways that reduce this unintended consequence while still preserving the social safety net. If they don't, then reforms based on the belief that public assistance encourages weight gain could weaken the social safety net without conferring any health benefits.

Good public policy with respect to public assistance requires that we determine whether current programs cause obesity. Understanding the relationship between poverty, public assistance, and obesity may also contribute to the federal goal of reducing health inequalities (U.S. Department of Health and Human Services 2002). Like all economists, I'm interested in the efficient allocation of scarce resources, in this case public resources. However, economics alone can't unravel the complex relationships between public assistance, obesity, and poverty. I began working with anthropologists on the connections between poverty and obesity to broaden my perspective (Smith et al. 2006), and as a result I developed a firm conviction that an interdisciplinary approach to this topic is vital. Consequently, this book reviews research not just from economics but from other fields of study as well, especially anthropology, medicine, nutrition, psychology, and sociology.

Why Worry about Obesity?

Some researchers argue that despite current public concerns about obesity in the United States, not everyone finds high body weight problematic. Anthropologists note that in many cultures fatness signals prosperity and is considered attractive (e.g., Popenoe 2005; Powdermaker 1997; Ritenbaugh 1982). Brown (1991) succinctly explains the relationship between resources and the cultural meanings attached to body size: "American ideals of thinness occur in a setting in which it is easy to become fat, and preference for plumpness occurs in settings in which it is easy to remain thin. In context, both standards require the investment of individual effort and economic resources; furthermore, each in its context involves a display of wealth" (49). Historians Hillel Schwartz (1986) and Peter Stearns (1997) document changes in the social interpretation of obesity over time within the United States. Both note that Americans' attitudes toward fatness changed from positive to negative around the turn of the nineteenth century. Stearns argues that this change began as an upper- and middle-class reaction to growing consumerism and personal freedom. People became uncomfortable with expanding freedoms, particularly for women, and needed some new method of restraint. The upper classes found moral superiority in demonstrating self-control through thinness. Indeed, in the United States and other developed nations, thinness has become a status symbol, while obesity is often interpreted as a sign of laziness and lack of self-control (Oliver and Lee 2005). In addition, feminists argue that cultural pressure to be thin is a means of social control over women. An undernourished woman preoccupied with her weight is less likely to have the time and energy to challenge male domination (Chernin 1981; Wolf 1991). Sociologist Steven Shapin summarizes the change in attitudes toward the obese more bluntly: "It's hard to avoid the conclusion that fat became ugly when the poor became fat" (2006, 78).

Although class and gender undoubtedly influence attitudes toward body weight, there are still good reasons for policy makers to worry about rising obesity in the United States. Economic interest in body weight arises from obesity's substantial economic costs, in terms of both direct medical costs and indirect costs from lost labor productivity

(Colditz 1992; Sturm 2002; Tucker et al. 2006). The obese face a greater risk of many medical conditions (American Obesity Association; Dietz 1998; Visscher and Seidell 2001; Wyatt et al. 2006) and have lower life expectancies (Flegal et al. 2005; Fontaine et al. 2003). Wolf and Colditz (1998) estimate that the total costs associated with obesity constituted 6.8 percent of our nation's medical spending in 1990.[1] Finkelstein et al. (2003, 2004) put the share at 9.1 percent in 1998; they also find that the annual medical costs of overweight and obesity in 1998 ran between $52 and $75 billion and that roughly half of these costs were paid by Medicare and Medicaid, which raises concerns about obesity among those participating in these federal programs. Thorpe et al. (2004) estimate that the rise in obesity and the increase in medical spending on the obese explains 27 percent of the growth in real health care spending from 1987 to 2001.

Some researchers contend that these figures overestimate the true costs because they don't believe that excess body weight increases morbidity or mortality. Instead, they argue that the associated diseases are caused by factors correlated with obesity (Angell and Kassirer 1998; Ernsberger 1989; Gaesser 2002; Oliver 2006). For example, obesity and dental caries are positively associated (Al-Zahrani et al. 2003), but no one thinks body fat causes cavities—dietary patterns cause both cavities and weight gain. Similarly, some argue that body fat doesn't cause cardiovascular disease and diabetes; rather, poor diet and lack of physical activity cause both weight gain and disease.

Research by Flegal et al. (2005) addresses the issue of mortality. Using the nationally representative National Health and Nutrition Examination Survey (NHANES), the authors find that being overweight is not associated with excess mortality, but obesity is.[2] Although evidence of an association is strong, this is not definitive proof of causation. Whether obesity causes mortality hinges on whether obesity causes disease. For some diseases there is solid evidence that obesity is causal, while for others there is some debate. Currently, there is consensus in the medical community that obesity can cause osteoarthritis (e.g., Felson and Zhang 1998; Lievense et al. 2002), through stress placed on weight-bearing joints, and endometrial and breast cancers, through elevated estrogen levels (e.g., Kaaks et al. 2002; Eliassen et al. 2006). According to a 2007 report from the World Cancer Research Fund and the American Institute for Cancer Research, there is also convincing evidence that obesity increases the risk for cancers of the esophagus, pancreas, colorectum, and kidney. There is also good empirical evidence that obesity contributes to sleep disturbances (Lawrence and Kopelman 2004), pregnancy complications (ACOG 2005; Smith et al. 2007), and asthma (Beckett et al. 2001; Tantisira and Weiss 2001).

Our understanding of whether obesity plays a causal role in cardiovascular disease is evolving. There are case studies in which increased physical activity and dietary changes have reduced the incidence of cardiovascular disease without substantially reducing body weight—for example, Finland's North Karelia Project (Puska et al. 1995). However, recent developments in metabolic research suggest that excess adipose tissue and its accompanying secretions can lead to disease, notably diabetes and atherosclerosis. Rather than simply being an energy storage system, fat tissue can be thought of as an endocrine organ with considerable influence on metabolism (Trayhurn and Beattie 2001). Problems occur when fat cells can no longer store additional incoming nutrients and the fat "spills over" into tissues like the liver and muscles (Unger 2003; Ronti et al. 2006). Thus, while it is true that some fat in and of itself is not harmful, too much poses serious medical problems, and obesity is a marker of such over nutrition.[3] The Social Security Administration regards obesity as a causal factor in disease processes, stating that "it commonly leads to, and often complicates, chronic diseases of the cardiovascular, pulmonary, and musculoskeletal systems" (2000).[4]

The reported figures could underestimate the costs of obesity, as they sometimes don't include losses associated with disability and depression, and generally omit injury in vehicular accidents. Economists Burkhauser and Cawley (2004) present evidence that obesity can lead to disability, while Mustillo et al. (2003) and Stunkard et al. (2004), research teams made up predominantly of psychologists and psychiatrists, present evidence that obesity can contribute to depression. Finally, physicians report that the obese are more likely to incur serious injury and die in automobile accidents (Mock et al. 2002; Zhu et al. 2006), and child safety experts estimate that nearly 300,000 heavy children under seven years old would have a difficult time finding a car seat appropriate for their weight (Trifiletti et al. 2006).[5] Estimated costs of obesity may also be too low because methods to determine the value of lost productivity rely on lost wages (Kuchler and Ballenger 2002). Thus, nonpaid work—for example, homemaking—is not included in the estimates of obesity's indirect costs. Because there is strong evidence that obesity causes four serious medical conditions (osteoarthritis, cancer, sleep apnea, and pregnancy complications) and growing evidence that excess adipose tissue can damage the cardiovascular system and raise the risk of diabetes, I believe the health costs associated with excess weight are serious enough to warrant our attention even though we can't precisely estimate them.[6]

Public health costs are not the only cause for concern, however. Obese individuals face substantial personal costs as well: stigma and discrimination (Puhl and Brownell 2001), higher unemployment and lower wages (Cawley 2004b), lower wealth (Zagorsky 2005), and decreased likelihood of marriage (Gortmaker et al. 1993). Public programs intended to help the less fortunate should not contribute to such personal difficulties.

Finally, if assistance programs cause obesity, they might inadvertently impede the desired goal of moving participants into financial self-sufficiency. Size discrimination in the labor market can reduce the chance of securing a job and thus moving from welfare to work. If the government seeks to help the poor support themselves through their own labor, any features of public assistance programs that contribute to obesity would be counterproductive.

Theories of Obesity, Poverty, and Public Assistance

The economic theory underlying concerns that public assistance promotes obesity is straightforward: more cash or food stamps enable recipients to buy and consume more food. In addition, welfare's work requirements may reduce the amount of time available for food preparation, and the once-a-month payment schedule may distort food intake patterns in a manner similar to binge eating—"feasting" when benefits arrive and "fasting" toward the end of the month when benefits run out. Yet alternative models offer equally compelling explanations of why public assistance and obesity might be related. For example, it could be that obesity leads to welfare receipt by harming one's physical and mental health, which in turns adversely affects one's ability to earn sufficient income. Or perhaps poverty leads to public assistance receipt via eligibility requirements and simultaneously to obesity by encouraging consumption of lower cost, calorie-dense foods, creating a spurious correlation between the two. Or perhaps something else, such as physical disability or mental illness, causes both poverty and weight gain.

Thus, we have four models of how public assistance programs and obesity could be related. Each of these four models suggests different public policies (Table 1). For example, if the "Public Assistance Causes Obesity" model is correct, then to reduce obesity we should consider policies such as restricting the types of foods that can be purchased with food stamps, subsidizing recipients' purchase of healthy foods, offering cash instead of food stamps, and requiring recipients to take nutrition and health courses. But if in fact poverty causes public assistance participation and obesity, then those policies will probably fail. Instead, appropriate policies include efforts to increase poor people's access to education, job training, healthy foods, and opportunities for physical activity.

Goals for This Book

Because policy recommendations vary—sometimes dramatically—across models, we must carefully examine all of the available evidence in order to determine which model or models best explain the observed associations between obesity, poverty, and public assistance. Only then will we have a sound theoretical foundation for formulating successful public policy. Thus, this book reviews evidence from a variety of disciplines and determines the extent to which each of these four basic models is actually helpful in explaining the relationship between public assistance and obesity—that is, which of the models garners substantial empirical support. When possible, this review focuses on findings from large, nationally representative samples. However, there are many situations in which researchers are only able to study small samples from specific geographic locations.

Much of the empirical research seeking to test the theories linking obesity, poverty, and public assistance suffers from the same methodological problem: large barriers to conducting double-blind, random experiments, which are the gold standard for detecting causal patterns. For example, it is illegal to deny anyone with the specified qualifications from receiving benefits in an entitlement program, so researchers can't randomly assign some poor people to a control group that gets no benefits. This book focuses on studies that employ sound statistical techniques to adjust for the problems associated with nonexperimental design. Because many of the causal patterns we need to identify simply can't be proven conclusively, we must rely on whether the best available research consistently finds statistically significant associations predicted by the causal pattern under scrutiny.

Outline of the Book

Chapter 1 describes and quantifies the observed relationships between poverty, public assistance, and excess body weight. The descriptive

Table 1. Selected policy implications of the four models

Model 1:
"Public Assistance
Causes Obesity"
	• Limit types of foods covered by
	  Food Stamp Program
	• Subsidize purchase of healthy foods
	• Offer cash instead of food stamps
	• Distribute benefits more than once a month
	• Require nutrition and health courses
	  for public assistance recipients

Model 2:
"Obesity Causes
Public Assistance"
	• Require good nutrition and
	  health education in schools
	• Devise legislation to protect the obese from
	  size discrimination in the labor market
	• Reduce or eliminate government supports for
	  high-calorie, low-nutrition fats and sweeteners
	• Provide safe public recreation areas and
	  subsidize exercise equipment and facilities
	• Restrict advertising of high-
	  calorie, low-nutrition foods

Model 3:
"Poverty Causes Both
Public Assistance
and Obesity"
	• Expand antipoverty programs, such as job
	  readiness training and placement programs
	• Offer nutrition and health courses
	  to low-income adults
	• Increase access to healthy foods and facilities
	  for physical activity in low-income areas
	• Provide mental health services to the
	  poor to reduce the adverse impact
	  of stress on health behaviors

Model 4:
"Factor X Causes
Both Public
Assistance and
Obesity"
	• Domestic abuse: Offer counseling to
	  those suffering from abuse and expand
	  programs to reduce domestic violence
	• Impatience, or lack of future orientation:
	  Develop programs to encourage patience
	  and discourage impulsiveness
	• Disability: Increase health care and
	  rehabilitation services for the disabled

evidence suggests that public assistance participation is positively associated with adult, but not childhood, obesity. Of course, associations don't prove causality, so Chapters 2 through 5 consider each of the four models in turn to see whether the evidence supports or refutes the hypothesized causal patterns. These four chapters follow a similar format: first, I lay out the model's basic theoretical structure, and then I review the available empirical research to see whether the model is supported. Chapter 6 summarizes the findings and reviews policy recommendations.

1

Trends in Obesity, Poverty, and Public Assistance

The first step toward understanding the relationship between public assistance and obesity is to quantify it. This chapter presents descriptive statistical evidence documenting the associations between poverty, public assistance, and obesity. First, I'll present the general trends in obesity prevalence, and then I'll disaggregate the rate of obesity by socioeconomic status and ethnicity. Lastly, I'll review trends in public assistance to begin to uncover the relationship between public assistance programs and obesity among the poor.

Obesity Trends

Concerns about an "obesity epidemic" pepper the popular media, and with good reason. The prevalence of obesity among both adults and children in the United States has risen spectacularly in the past few decades (Ogden et al. 2006). In 1998 the federal government adopted the World Health Organization's definition of adult obesity: a body mass index (BMI) of 30 or higher (Kuczmarski and Flegal 2000).[1] For a woman who is five feet four inches tall to be considered obese by this standard, she would have to weigh at least 175 pounds. A six-foot-tall woman like me would have to weigh at least 221 pounds. BMI has some limitations as a measure of obesity; most notably it doesn't distinguish mass associated with fat from that associated with muscle. Thus, among highly muscular individuals BMI can indicate obesity when body fat is actually not excessive. In addition, there is growing evidence that the location of fat matters to health, with abdominal fat being more highly predictive of cardiovascular disease (Yusuf et al. 2005). Nevertheless, BMI is a useful gauge of excess body fat in populations because it is easily measured and correlates with adiposity. More precise measures of body fatness and distribution are expensive to apply to large samples but can be used for diagnostic purposes if BMI indicates that a particular individual may be carrying an unhealthy amount of body fat (Hubbard 2000).

Since the late 1970s the share of obese adults has doubled, rising from about 14 percent to 32 percent (Figure 1.1). This general pattern holds whether we look at the National Health and Nutrition Examination Survey (NHANES) or other large, nationally representative data sets such as the Behavioral Risk Factor Surveillance System (BRFSS) and the National Longitudinal Survey of Youth (NLSY).[2] Among children, the prevalence of obesity has tripled (Figure 1.2).[3] Furthermore, the extent of children's obesity, measured as the percentage of children whose BMI exceeds the relevant age-gender-specific obesity threshold, has increased even faster than the prevalence rate (Jolliffe 2004). All the evidence shows that we as a nation are getting fatter; there is no controversy regarding this point. There is also widespread scientific agreement as to the general cause of rising obesity in the United States and other developed nations. Such a quick and large increase in obesity can't be explained only by genetic changes; instead, changes in our environment interacting with our genetic adaptations to survive frequent famines are the source of the problem (Bogin 1999; Cutler et al. 2003; Hill and Peters 1998; O'Keefe and Cordain 2004; Smith et al. 2002).

Figure 1.1. Percentage of U.S. adult population that is obese, based on NHANES data

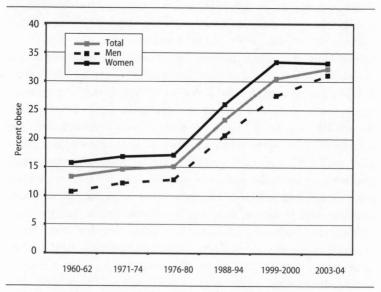

Source: National Center for Health Statistics 2005, table 73; Ogden et al. 2006.
Note: Data are for individuals ages twenty to seventy-four with a BMI of 30 or more.

Figure 1.2. Percentage of U.S. children ages two to nineteen who are obese, based on NHANES data

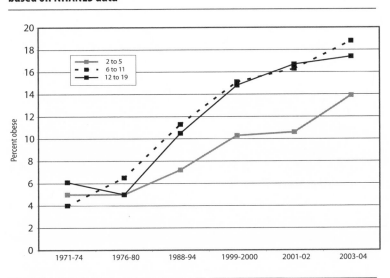

Source: National Center for Health Statistics 2006, table 1; Odgen et al. 2006.
Note: Data are for individuals ages two to nineteen with a BMI at or above the ninety-fifth percentile on the age-gender adjusted distribution.

Obesity Prevalence by Socioeconomic Status

Researchers describe the relationship observed between general health and socioeconomic status (SES) as a gradient, because as income and status rise incrementally, measures of health increase in a stepwise fashion. On average, within developed countries, those lowest on the SES scale exhibit the poorest health, those in the middle have better health, and those at the top are the healthiest. This gradient appears across a variety of measures of SES and health for children (Case et al. 2002) and adults (Marmot 2004; Smith 1999). Since general health follows a social gradient, it seems likely that obesity does too.

Hurricane Katrina may have raised public awareness of obesity among the poor. One television viewer explains that as she watched the news coverage of victims being rescued she "was struck by how many of these people were overweight and obese" (Kufahl 2005). In the course of analyzing obesity trends, however, researchers have long observed that in the United States, and other developed nations, the prevalence of obesity, especially among women, tends to rise as SES falls (e.g., Garn

Reprinted by permission of Rick McKee

and Clark 1976; Sobal and Stunkard 1989; Wardle et al. 2002).[4] This general relationship is becoming more well-known, as indicated by the political cartoon shown here.

Recent studies suggest that the strength of this association may be diminishing. Zhang and Wang (2004) show that in nationally representative data from the NHANES, the relationship between adult obesity and SES as measured by educational attainment has weakened since the early 1970s. Maheshwari et al. (2005) also use the NHANES to compare obesity prevalence in 1971–1974 and 2001–2002, but they measure SES by income quartiles and find similar results (Table 1.1). For both time periods, obesity is most prevalent in the lowest income group and decreases as income rises. For example, in 1971–1974, 22.5 percent of the poorest quarter of Americans were obese compared to only 9.7 percent for the richest quarter. However, the rate of increase in obesity prevalence between 1971–1974 and 2000–2001 is greatest among the upper income levels: 176 percent in the top quartile versus 44 percent in the bottom. These two studies confirm the inverse relationship between income and obesity, but they also suggest that it is dissipating over time because the rich and middle class are catching up.

Analyzing the NHANES obesity data by poverty status rather than by income quartiles produces similar results: poor adults present higher obesity rates, but the difference in the prevalence of obesity across pov-

Table 1.1. Adult obesity prevalence by income quartile

Income quartile	Obesity prevalence, 1971–1974 (%)	Obesity prevalence, 2001–2002 (%)	Change (%)
Less than $25,000	22.5	32.5	44
$25,000–$39,999	16.1	31.3	94
$40,000–$60,000	14.5	30.3	109
More than $60,000	9.7	26.8	176

erty status has become smaller since 1971–1974 (Figure 1.3).[5] Miech et al. (2006) use the NHANES to examine trends in obesity among adolescents. They find no difference in obesity prevalence among poor and nonpoor children ages twelve to fourteen in the four waves of data. Among children ages fifteen to seventeen, however, the prevalence is growing faster among poor than nonpoor children. In the most recent wave (1999–2004), 23.3 percent of poor fifteen-to-seventeen year olds were obese compared to 14.4 percent of their nonpoor counterparts.

While public assistance receipt could theoretically lead to higher obesity rates among the poor, it can't explain the greater acceleration in obesity prevalence among nonpoor adults. It's also unclear why public assistance would affect the BMI of twelve-to-fourteen year olds and fifteen-to-seventeen year olds differently. Perhaps public assistance has little to do with obesity among the poor; instead, the poor may simply be canaries in a coal mine, their health suffering from environmental changes before others feel the impact.

The Obesity-Poverty Relationship by Gender and Ethnicity

The relationship between SES and obesity varies not only across time but also across gender and ethnicity. The positive association between excess weight and income is most pronounced among women. A U.S. surgeon general's report notes that women with incomes below 130 percent of the poverty line are about 50 percent more likely to be obese than women with higher incomes (U.S. Department of Health and Human Services 2001). If we analyze the NHANES data to show the difference in obesity prevalence by gender, we see that obesity is actually

Figure 1.3. Obesity prevalence by poverty status

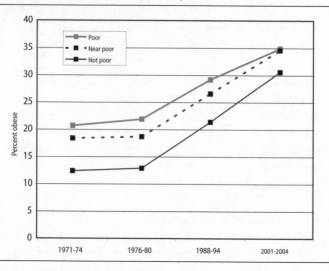

Source: National Center for Health Statistics 2007, table 74.

a bit less prevalent among poor than nonpoor men, but much more prevalent among poor than nonpoor women (Figure 1.4).[6]

When we break down the poverty-gender-obesity relationship by ethnicity, we see that poor black and Mexican American men exhibit less obesity than their wealthier counterparts (Figure 1.5). By contrast, obesity prevalence among poor white men noticeably exceeds that of their wealthier counterparts. The elevated prevalence of obesity among poor women relative to the wealthiest women is most pronounced among white women (40 percent versus 23 percent) and is also noticeable among black women (46 percent versus 40 percent).

Physician and sociologist Virginia Chang and epidemiologist Diane Lauderdale use four waves of the NHANES data to examine changes from 1971 to 2002 in the relationship between SES and obesity in the six different gender-ethnicity groupings depicted in Figure 1.5 (Chang and Lauderdale 2005). They measure SES as the poverty-income ratio (PIR), or the ratio of family income to the official poverty line. A PIR of less than one indicates official poverty, a PIR of between one and two defines the near poor, a PIR of between two and four indicates middle income, and a PIR of greater than four indicates high income. They find a consistent inverse gradient between PIR and obesity among white women over the thirty-year observation period, although the rich-

Figure 1.4. Obesity prevalence by gender and poverty status, 1988–1991

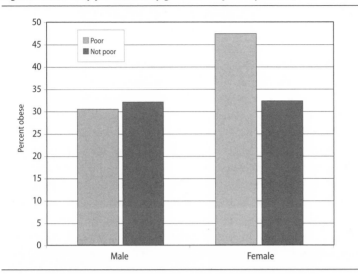

Source: National Institutes of Health 1998, table III.A.3.d.

Figure 1.5. Obesity prevalence by poverty status, gender, and ethnicity, 1999–2002

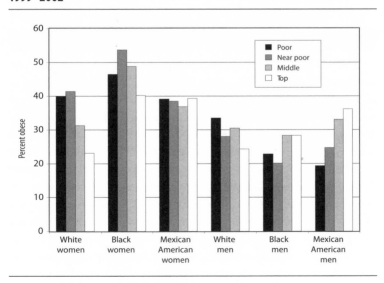

Source: Chang and Lauderdale 2005.

est white women now have a slightly higher rate of obesity than did the poorest women in the 1970s (23.1 percent versus 21.4 percent).

For the other five groups the PIR-obesity gradient is not consistent over time. Among black women, the inverse relationship between obesity and PIR holds except at the highest PIR levels in the latest two waves of data. Among wealthier black women there appears to be a positive association between PIR and obesity from the late 1980s on. For Mexican American and black men there is evidence of a positive gradient in the later sample waves; obesity prevalence rises as PIR rises. These results suggest that the socioeconomic gradient in obesity varies across gender-ethnic groups and has been changing over time.

Like Maheshwari et al. (2005), Chang and Lauderdale also find evidence that the rate of increase in obesity prevalence is not necessarily highest among the poor. For white women the rate of obesity increased most among the near poor (22.6 percent) and least among the wealthiest (13 percent). Similarly, among Mexican American women, obesity increased the most among the near poor; however, it increased the least among the poor. For black women and men, obesity rose fastest among the wealthiest. This pattern was most dramatic among the men, with an increase of 21.5 percent among the richest and only 4.5 percent among the near poor. Among Mexican American men, obesity prevalence grew most among the middle income group (11.1 percent) and least among the poorest group (–3.1 percent).

Trends in Public Assistance That Could Influence Obesity

Why would poverty tend to positively affect the weight of women and not men? What is it about poverty that places women, particularly white and black women, at greater risk of obesity? Some researchers note that women constitute the majority of adults receiving cash benefits from Temporary Assistance for Needy Families (TANF) and food benefits from the Food Stamp Program (FSP).[7] Furthermore, white women make up the bulk (46 percent) of household heads participating in the FSP (Poikolainen 2005). Some speculate, therefore, that public assistance programs cause recipients to over-consume calories and gain weight, which accounts for the gender differences in the poverty-obesity association. For example, American Enterprise Institute Fellow Douglas Besharov argues that our public assistance programs are feeding the poor "as if they're starving" when more likely they are overweight (Besharov 2002).

In 2003 Besharov repeated his concerns before a congressional hearing (Besharov 2003) and presented quantitative evidence from the third wave of the NHANES data set to support his claim (Table 1.2). These data show that both poor and nonpoor people consumed more calories, on average, in the period 1988–1994 than in the period 1971–1974, but that the rate of increase in calorie intake was greater among the poor. For example, mean caloric intake increased by 12.2 percent among poor women compared to about 9 percent for nonpoor women. Furthermore, the rate of increase in calorie consumption was somewhat higher for poor women (12.2 percent) than for poor men (11.5 percent).

The problem is that these data don't distinguish between the poor who actually participated in public assistance programs and those who didn't. It could well be that some aspect of poverty other than public assistance caused the changes in respondents' eating patterns. Furthermore, the mean calories consumed by the poor in the latter time period don't generally exceed the National Research Council's Recommended Dietary Allowances for adults (2,900 for young men; 2,200 for young women). In short, these data do little to make the case that public assistance causes recipients to become obese.

Three more-recent studies produce descriptive evidence that focuses on obesity among welfare recipients rather than the poor in general, which will help us begin to distinguish the impact of public assistance from that of poverty. First, Cawley and Danziger (2005) find that the

Table 1.2. Caloric intake by respondents ages one to seventy-four years in the 1971–1974 wave of NHANES and ages two months and older in the 1988–1994 wave

	Mean caloric intake, 1971–1974	Mean caloric intake, 1988–1994	Change (%)
Male	2,393	2,517	5.18
Female	1,618	1,764	9.02
Poor Male	2,108	2,350	11.48
Poor Female	1,575	1,767	12.19
Nonpoor Male	2,434	2,575	5.79
Nonpoor Female	1,624	1,770	8.99

Source: Besharov 2003.

rate of morbid obesity (BMI of 40 or higher) among white female welfare recipients in one Michigan county is three times the rate for white
women nationally. However, the rate of morbid obesity among black
female welfare recipients in their sample does not differ from that of a
nationally representative sample. Given the limited geographical scope
of this study and the fact that Michigan's obesity prevalence ranks in the
top seven nationwide, these results may not be representative of the nation as a whole.[8]

The other two studies examine obesity rates among public assistance
participants in nationally representative data sets. Fox and Cole (2004)
use the NHANES-III (1988–1994) to compare average BMI and the
prevalence of excess weight among children ages two to nineteen years
old across three groups: food stamp participants, income-eligible nonparticipants (that is, children who are poor enough to qualify for the
program but are not enrolled), and higher-income (ineligible) nonparticipants. They find no statistically significant difference in BMI or the
risk of being overweight between food stamp participants and income-
eligible nonparticipants. Among young adults, both food stamp participants and income-eligible nonparticipants exhibit mean BMIs that
meet the standard definition of overweight (BMI of 25 to 29.9). However, there is a statistically significant difference between average BMI
among adult food stamp participants (28.3) and income-eligible nonparticipants (26.9), with the difference mostly associated with women.
Furthermore, the prevalence of obesity (BMI of 30 or higher) among
women food stamp participants exceeds that of income-eligible non-
participant women (42 percent versus 30 percent). These results suggest
that there may be something about food stamps independent of poverty
status that is associated with greater body weight among women.

Smith and Zagorsky (2006) use another nationally representative
sample, the NLSY, to see whether obesity is more prevalent among
adult welfare participants than nonparticipants. Their analysis shows
that from 1981 to 2000 the obesity rate among those who ever received
welfare—in the form of either cash, via Aid to Families with Dependent
Children (AFDC) and its replacement, TANF, or food stamps—consistently exceeded that of respondents who never received welfare benefits
(Figure 1.6). They find essentially the same pattern when they restrict
the analysis to food stamp receipt. While this result supports the hypothesis that public assistance contributes to obesity, it doesn't separate
the impact of public assistance from that of poverty.

While these three analyses produce no evidence suggesting that
childhood obesity and public assistance are related, they do find patterns

Figure 1.6. Obesity prevalence by welfare status

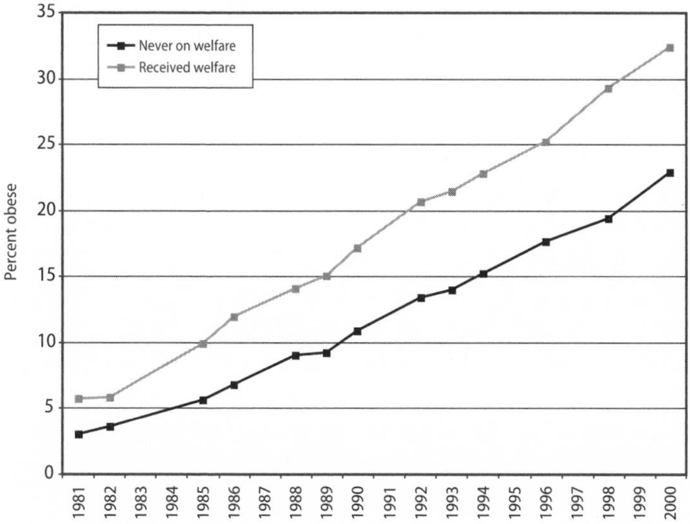

Source: Smith and Zagorsky 2006.

consistent with the notion that public assistance programs are somehow related to obesity among adult participants, especially women. Is it the receipt of public assistance that causes women to gain weight, or is there some confounding factor, such as poverty or low education, that explains the higher risk of obesity among the welfare reliant? What causes poor women, particularly those receiving welfare, to gain weight?

As a first step in addressing these questions, let's examine the trends in welfare receipt to see whether they suggest any changes that could explain poor women's elevated obesity rates. The cash assistance (AFDC/ TANF) and FSP caseloads increased from 3.7 million persons in 1962 to a peak in the early 1990s, when more than 14 million received cash benefits and more than 27 million received food stamps. After that, the caseloads began falling. In 1996 the Personal Responsibility and Work Opportunity Reconciliation Act (PRWORA) was passed, limiting the amount of time individuals could receive cash benefits, and both the cash and food stamp caseloads continued their decline. Yet despite the drop in the number of people receiving public assistance, obesity rates among the poor continued to rise during the 1990s (Figure 1.7). This pattern challenges the "Public Assistance Causes Obesity" hypothesis.

Perhaps it's not the caseload that matters so much as the composi-

Figure 1.7. Number of AFDC/TANF and FSP participants, 1962–2004

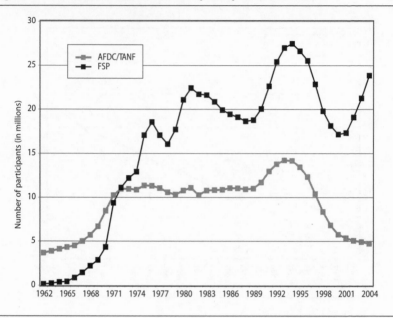

Source: Social Security Administration 2006, tables 9.G1 and 9.H1.

tion of the public assistance package. The time limits on cash benefits imposed by the 1996 welfare reform legislation shifted the focus of
federal support for the poor from monetary to food assistance. Food
stamps as a proportion of the "welfare package" had been rising in 1988
and accelerated after the 1996 welfare overhaul, exceeding 80 percent
in 2001 (Figure 1.8). The increasing importance of food stamps in the
public assistance package meant that more benefits legally had to be
used to purchase food. So although the public assistance caseload has
been falling over the past several decades, the shift from cash to food
could be forcing the remaining recipients to spend more on food than
they would otherwise, perhaps causing them to gain weight. The rise in
food stamps as a share of overall public assistance, however, could only
help explain higher obesity prevalence among participants after 1988.
Furthermore, even though food stamps' share fell between 1982 and
1988, obesity among those who ever received public assistance continued to rise.

Lastly, let's examine the simple correlations between obesity and FSP
participation rates across states (Table 1.3). If the "Public Assistance
Causes Obesity" hypothesis is correct, then higher participation rates

Figure 1.8. Food stamps as a share of welfare benefits in the NLSY

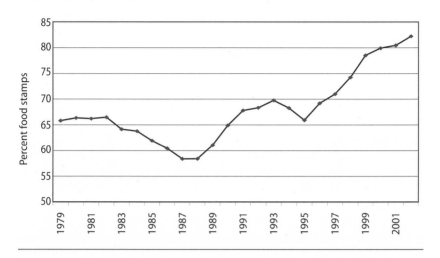

Source: Zagorsky and Smith 2006.
Note: Total benefits equal food stamps plus cash benefit from either AFDC or TANF.

Table 1.3. Simple correlations between FSP participation rates and prevalence of obesity and overweight

	FSP participation, 1999	FSP participation, 2000	FSP participation, 2001
Overweight in 2002 (25 ≤ BMI < 30)	−0.310** (p = 0.027)	−0.200 (p = 0.159)	−0.117 (p = 0.413)
Obesity in 2002 (BMI ≥ 30)	0.246* (p = 0.082)	0.139 (p = 0.330)	0.235* (p = 0.097)

Source: Obesity prevalence rates come from the Behavioral Risk Factor Surveillance System and are reported on the Centers for Disease Control and Prevention website. FSP participation rates come from Castner and Schirm 2004.
* indicates statistical significance at the 10 percent level; ** indicates statistical significance at the 5 percent level.

will be associated with higher obesity rates. FSP participation in 1999 and 2001 are positively correlated with 2002 obesity prevalence, but only at the 10 percent level of statistical significance. Curiously, FSP participation in 1999 is negatively correlated with the prevalence of overweight in 2002 at the 5 percent level of significance—that is, higher rates of FSP participation in 1999 are associated with a lower prevalence of overweight in 2002. These correlations offer little support for the "Public Assistance Causes Obesity" hypothesis.

Summary

The descriptive analysis of trends in poverty, public assistance, and excess body weight confirm that obesity prevalence is generally higher among poor women than middle- and upper-income women and among adult public assistance recipients than nonrecipients. While these results support the "Public Assistance Causes Obesity" hypothesis, we also find contradictory evidence: (1) obesity prevalence continued to rise even when public assistance caseloads fell after the 1996 reform; (2) the increase in obesity prevalence over time is greater among the rich than the poor; and (3) the simple correlations between obesity and Food Stamp Program participation are weak and not consistently positive. Thus, the descriptive evidence suggests that public assistance might contribute to obesity among poor adults, but it certainly can't be the only causal factor.

2

The "Public Assistance Causes Obesity" Hypothesis

The previous chapter documented that poor women and public assistance participants exhibit higher rates of obesity. This chapter examines the first of four possible explanations for this association, the "Public Assistance Causes Obesity" model. Public assistance is designed to help low-income families meet their fundamental needs, and the goal of the Food Stamp Program, the Special Supplemental Nutrition Program for Women, Infants and Children (WIC), and the National School Lunch Program is to assure that the poor get adequate nutrition. We should not, then, be surprised if these assistance programs increase food intake among recipients; raising the body weight of participants suffering from undernutrition is in fact a desired outcome. If recipients are not underweight, however, giving them food could lead to excess weight gain.

Public assistance could cause obesity through four causal pathways. First, benefits, whether cash or food stamps, essentially increase recipients' income, and so we would expect recipients to purchase and consume more normal goods (for example, calories) than they would otherwise. In order for the link between benefits and purchasing power to explain the higher obesity rate among the poor, however, calories must be more sensitive to income in the lower tail of the income distribution than in the upper tail; otherwise, the richest Americans would be the fattest (which is not currently the case). Furthermore, public assistance participants would have to spend their additional income on calorie-dense foods, rather than on more nutritious, lower calorie foods.

Second, the more stringent work requirements instituted in the 1996 welfare reform legislation could contribute to obesity through increased hours in the labor force. More time spent working outside the home means that public assistance participants have less time to plan and prepare healthy meals and that, consequently, they may rely more heavily on fast food or other processed foods that require little preparation. These convenience foods generally contain more calories than homemade meals and thus may contribute to weight gain (Bowman et al. 2004, French et al. 2000, Pereira et al. 2005). Increased work hours also reduce parents' time to monitor their children's food consumption and levels of physical activity. However, this pathway does little to explain the association between public assistance and obesity before 1996.

Third, the once-a-month schedule for distributing benefits may affect participants' shopping and calorie-intake patterns. Toward the end of the month they often run out of benefits and restrict their food consumption. Then, when benefits arrive at the beginning of the month, their recent deprivation may compel them to buy filling, comforting, high-calorie foods. Alternatively, when a family has little money for food at the end of the month they may focus on getting as many calories as they can afford. For example, Dietz (1995) recounts the case of a seven-year-old obese child whose family relied on public assistance. Her mother explained that when their benefits ran out she tended to serve high-fat meals in order to prevent hunger. In short, the monthly benefit-distribution schedule could encourage disordered eating, which can cause obesity (Stunkard and Allison 2003; Yanovski 2003).

Lastly, public assistance could lead to obesity by harming recipients' mental health. Participating in aid programs can be stigmatizing, and conservatives argue that it reduces self-esteem, "saps their dreams for tomorrow, and . . . takes away their hope for today" (Shaw 1996). Low self-esteem, hopelessness, and depression could cause recipients to neglect their health, eat for emotional comfort, and reduce their level of physical activity, which could result in weight gain.

Thus there are four possible reasons why public assistance participants are more likely to be obese than nonparticipants (Figure 2.1).

Research Context

Nutritionists and economists (regular and agricultural) dominate the research examining the relationship between food assistance programs, nutrient intake, and body weight. Nutritionists have produced a sizable literature on how food programs affect food purchases and nutritional intake. Economists evaluating the effectiveness of government food programs must assess the benefits and costs of such programs, including the possible unintended consequence of obesity.

Besharov and Germanis (2000) and Currie (2003) spell out the statistical problems involved in estimating the impact of food assistance programs on nutritional intake and health. Principal among these problems is how to control for nonrandom self-selection into food assistance

Figure 2.1. The "Public Assistance Causes Obesity" model

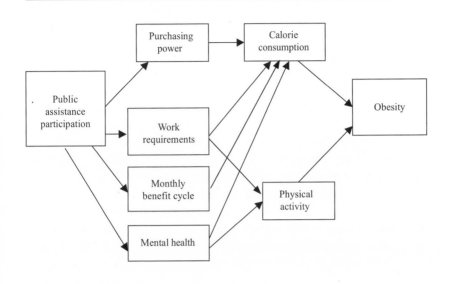

programs. Not all people who are eligible for benefits participate, and systematic differences between those who select in and those who don't could bias estimated program impacts. For example, if children with the fewest resources and poorest diets are more likely to participate in school breakfasts and lunches, program participation will be associated with poorer nutrition and health ratings and therefore could appear harmful. This review focuses on studies employing statistical techniques that attempt to control for possible selection bias. As we shall see, various approaches to the selection problem have been taken, but no one method has emerged as the best practice.

Another major barrier to empirically establishing causal pathways is the practical difficulty in designing random experiments in the context of entitlement programs. Federal law requires that all people meeting an entitlement program's criteria receive assistance. Even in the case of non-entitlement programs there may be moral resistance to the assignment of subjects to a control group receiving no aid. And although some aspects of public assistance programs do in fact lend themselves to experimental tests, they are rare. Researchers often must work with non-experimental data, preferring longitudinal data when available. Other common estimation problems include reliance on twenty-four-hour recall of dietary intake and errors in self-reported height and weight.

Empirical Evidence

If public assistance is the sole cause of obesity among the poor, then we will observe individuals gaining weight only while receiving aid. Smith and Zagorsky (2006) trace the average self-reported BMI of respondents in the National Longitudinal Survey of Youth (NLSY) who received food stamps for a single spell between 1985 and 2002. Their research shows that average BMI increases before, during, and after the food stamp spell, indicating that it can't be just public assistance that leads to weight gain among the poor (Figure 2.2). However, the amount of BMI increase per year is greater during the food stamp spell (1.57 units) than in the periods before (0.37 units) and after (0.70 units), suggesting that public assistance might accelerate weight gain.

Let's now consider the empirical evidence for each of the four possible pathways from welfare to obesity: increased purchasing power; work requirements; monthly benefit cycle; and mental health. For each pathway I review the evidence for children first and then for adults.

Increased Purchasing Power

To date, only two studies test whether cash receipt (either through AFDC or TANF) independently influences body weight. Gibson (2003, 2004) reports that in the NLSY, cash benefits are not associated with the risk of obesity among either children or adults. Consequently, this review focuses on food and nutrition assistance programs, specifically WIC, school breakfast and lunch programs, and the Food Stamp Program.

WIC

WIC aims to improve birth outcomes by improving fetal nutrition. It provides vouchers for foods that are high in protein, calcium, iron, vitamin A, and vitamin C and offers nutrition counseling and health services to low-income pregnant or postpartum women and their children up to age five (Currie 2003). Eligibility requires a household income below 185 percent of the poverty line and the presence of some nutritional risk. In 2004 approximately 2.1 million women, 2.2 million infants (under one year of age), and 4.4 million children (ages one to five) were enrolled in WIC (USDA 2006d). Hispanics constitute the biggest ethnic group among participants (39.2 percent), followed by whites (34.6 percent) and blacks (20.0 percent). In 2004 WIC program expenditures totaled $4.9 billion, with an average monthly food cost of $37.55 per person.

Figure 2.2. Average BMI in the years before and after a spell of food stamp receipt

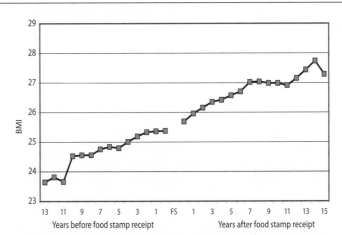

Source: Smith and Zagorsky 2006.

If WIC causes excessive weight gain in children, then obesity prevalence will be higher among WIC children than among income-eligible children not enrolled the program. The Centers for Disease Control and Prevention (1995) examined children ages two months to fifty-nine months in the third wave of the nationally representative National Health and Nutrition Examination Survey (NHANES-III), comparing weight (in relation to height) of WIC participants to that of income eligible nonparticipants. This analysis finds no statistically significant differences in average weight between the two groups among blacks and whites. Among Mexican Americans, WIC children weighed less on average than their non-WIC counterparts. Two additional studies using the same methodology replicate these results (Burstein et al. 2000; Cole and Fox 2004). These studies don't support the hypothesis that WIC leads to childhood obesity, but because they do not control for any confounding factors or possible selection bias, they provide only a descriptive analysis.

Bitler and Currie (2004) use data from the Survey of Income and Program Participation, a large, nationally representative sample, to estimate the impact of WIC participation on four year olds, adjusting for maternal selection into the program. Employing Two-Stage Least Squares to adjust for possible selection bias, they find that WIC participation has a statistically significant and negative impact on children's likelihood of being overweight (BMI above the eighty-fifth percentile). That is, WIC participation is associated with a lower probability that a four-year-old child will be overweight. This finding contradicts the hypothesis that WIC participation leads to childhood obesity.

While WIC participation doesn't appear to affect BMI in early childhood, prenatal participation might influence BMI in adulthood. Observational studies of the Dutch Famine (1944–1945) find that undernutrition in early gestation is associated with higher adult BMI and an increased risk of obesity (Painter et al. 2005; Ravelli et al. 1999; Roseboom et al. 2006). These studies support the theory of fetal programming, whereby a person's metabolism adapts to famine in utero in ways that increase fetal survival but predispose the individual to obesity and other chronic diseases later in life (Barker 1997). It would be interesting to test whether prenatal WIC benefits avert such metabolic adaptations by better preparing the fetus for life in an environment with abundant food supplies (Gluckman et al. 2007). Longitudinal data on a mother's prenatal WIC participation, a child's adult BMI, and other variables that could influence adult obesity would be required to test whether the program does indeed yield such long-term benefits.

The extensive literature on WIC's outcomes shows that the program is associated with modestly reduced chances of low birth weight and with improved child nutrition (Kowaleski-Jones and Duncan 2002; Currie 2003; Bitler and Currie 2005). In addition, Carlson and Senauer (2003) find that WIC participation in the NHANES-III is associated with a greater likelihood of a child receiving a physician rating of "excellent" health. While the empirical literature specifically examining WIC's impact on childhood weight is presently small, what evidence we do have indicates that WIC does not contribute to childhood obesity. Future studies of WIC participation and weight should continue to pursue statistical methods for controlling for selection into the program and should also investigate the impact of WIC receipt on breast-feeding practices, which may influence both child and maternal weight (Rose et al. 2006; Sherry 2005).[1]

SCHOOL BREAKFAST AND LUNCH PROGRAMS

Low-income children ages six through eighteen may receive food assistance in the School Breakfast Program (SBP) and National School Lunch Program (NSLP). The NSLP provides free lunches to schoolchildren from families with incomes at or below 130 percent of the poverty threshold and reduced-price lunches to those from families with incomes between 131 percent and 185 percent of the poverty line. The SBP provides free or reduced-price breakfasts to low-income students using similar eligibility criteria. In 2004 the SBP served 8.9 million children and cost the federal government nearly $1.8 billion, and the NSLP served 28.9 million at a cost of $6.7 billion (USDA 2006b, 2006c).

Only a few studies investigate the impact of the SBP alone. Bhattacharya et al. (2004a, 2004b) use the NHANES-III and a difference-in-difference model to estimate the SBP's impact on participating children's nutrition. Specifically, the authors compare nutritional outcomes during the school term (when the SBP is available) to the summer months (when the SBP is not available) in order to control for selection bias. Since the NHANES-III contains information on blood serum levels of nutrients, this assessment of nutrient adequacy doesn't rely on respondent recall. The authors find evidence that when the SBP is available, participants exhibit a better diet as measured by the Healthy Eating Index and improved serum levels of several nutrients. Furthermore, they find that SBP participants consume less fat. Another study directly examines the SBP's impact on children's weight. Hofferth and Curtain (2005) examine the Panel Study of Income Dynamics—Child Development Supplement (PSID-CDS) and use an instrumental-variables approach to control for selection bias. They find no evidence that participation in the SBP is associated with a greater risk of childhood excess weight.

More research examines the impact of the NSLP because of its significantly higher caseload and costs. Some evaluations examine the program's impact on food insecurity, but most focus on nutritional intake. The latter studies generally find that participation in this program improves children's lunchtime intake of several nutrients (e.g., Devaney et al. 1993). However, Gordon et al. (1995) report that children in the NSLP get a higher percentage of their food energy from saturated fat and fat in general both at lunch and during a twenty-four-hour period (at and away from school). They base their results on data from the School Nutrition Dietary Assessment Survey and adjust for possible selection bias using an instrumental-variables approach. Gleason and Suitor (2003) use the Continuing Survey of Food Intake by Individuals (CSFII), a large, nationally representative sample, and control for selection bias by using a fixed-effects model. They also find higher fat intake among program participants.

The NSLP recipients' higher fat consumption has sparked concern that the program may cause excess weight. Dunifon and Kowaleski-Jones (2004) examine the impact of the NSLP on weight using the 1998 Early Childhood Longitudinal Study—Kindergarten Cohort (ECLS-K), a nationally representative sample of about 22,000 children enrolled in kindergarten in the 1998–1999 school year. They control for selection into the NSLP using a first-difference model and find that participation in the NSLP is associated not with children's body weight but with improved reading scores for boys. Schanzenbach (2005) uses the same data set and adjusts for selection into the NSLP using a first-difference model, but also employs a regression discontinuity model as an alternative adjustment method. She concludes that by the end of first grade the probability of obesity for NSLP children is two percentage points higher than that of nonparticipants. However, this analysis focuses on higher-income white children, which might explain why her results differ from those of Dunifon and Kowaleski-Jones. Whether her results apply to poor and minority children is not clear.

Two studies consider the impact of participating in both the NSLP and the SBP. Bhattacharya and Currie (2001) use the NHANES-III to examine how these programs affect children ages twelve to sixteen, and Hofferth and Curtain (2005) use the PSID-CDS to estimate the impact on the weight of children ages six to twelve.[2] Hofferth and Curtain use instrumental variables to control for selection bias, while Bhattacharya and Currie employ a difference-in-difference model. Neither study produces evidence that school nutrition programs affect children's likelihood of being overweight, but Bhattacharya and Currie report that availability of the SBP and NSLP is associated with improved overall diet as measured by a modified version of the Healthy Eating Index (Kennedy et al. 1995).

In summary, the one study on the SBP alone finds no evidence that it contributes to excess weight. Two studies of the NSLP based on the 1998 ECLS-K produce mixed results as to whether the lunch program contributes to excess childhood weight; however, the reported significant results may not apply to poor, minority children. Two studies based on the PSID-CDS suggest that participation in both the SBP and the NSLP have no statistically significant impact on the risk of obesity among poor children ages six to twelve. The balance of the evidence indicates that school food programs do not contribute to poor children's excess weight and even suggests that they improve nutritional intake.

FOOD STAMPS

Most evaluations of the Food Stamp Program (FSP) focus on its impact on food insecurity, nutritional intake, and food spending. For example, Gundersen and Oliveira (2001) find that FSP participants are just as likely as nonparticipants to experience food insecurity; however, Kabbani and Yazbeck (2004; also Kabbani and Yazbeck-Kmeid 2005) find that the amount of food stamp benefits received is inversely related to the likelihood of food insecurity. Borjas (2004) estimates that a ten-percentage-point decrease in the share of the population receiving public assistance is followed by a five-percentage-point increase in the prevalence of food insecurity. These studies suggest that the FSP probably reduces the risk and severity of food insecurity.

Several studies of the association between FSP participation and nutrient availability and intake reviewed by Currie (2003) produce evidence of improved levels of several nutrients, while some show either no impact or reduced intake of certain nutrients. Krueger et al. (2004) report that adults who participate in the FSP exhibit a lower risk of mortality than they would if they didn't participate, suggesting that the program benefits general health. In addition, studies of the impact of food stamps on household spending consistently show that the program raises food expenditures (Fraker 1990; Currie 2003). The estimated increase in food spending caused by an additional dollar in food stamp benefits ranges from $0.17 to $0.47.

While the impact of the FSP on food access and nutrition is important, it doesn't directly address the question of whether food stamps cause obesity. In theory, food stamps could influence weight in three ways: (1) increased purchasing power enables participants to buy more calories, increasing BMI; (2) increased purchasing power enables participants to buy food higher in nutrients and lower in calories, lowering BMI; and (3) food stamps lower the price of meals at home relative to meals out, lowering BMI.

Let's begin by investigating the evidence on the FSP's impact on children's weight. A little more than half of the 23.5 million FSP participants are under age eighteen (Poikolainen 2005). Jones et al. (2003) and Hofferth and Curtain (2005) both employ PSID-CDS to investigate whether participation in the school nutrition programs and the FSP influences the risk of excess weight among school-age children.[3] Jones et al. restrict their sample to children in families with incomes below 185 percent of the poverty line, while Hofferth and Curtain examine five income groups: poor, near poor, working class, moderate income, and high income. Jones et al. find that food-insecure girls participating in the SBP, NSLP, and FSP face a lower likelihood of being overweight relative to food-insecure girls who did not participate in any of the food programs. Participation didn't affect the likelihood of being overweight for girls from food-secure households or boys from either type of household. Hofferth and Curtain find no evidence that FSP participation raises the risk of obesity among poor children.

Jones et al. (2003) don't adjust for selection bias but do control for food insecurity status, while Hofferth and Curtain (2005) control for selection bias but not for food insecurity status. Despite their differences, both studies fail to produce evidence that FSP participation raises a child's likelihood of excess weight. However, both of these studies consider only short-term effects.

Three studies estimate the impact of long-term food stamp receipt on children's BMI. Frongillo et al. (2006) use the ECLS-K to estimate the association between changes in FSP participation and changes in weight between kindergarten and third grade, a span of four years. They control for possible selection bias using a fixed-effects model. These authors find that although children whose families began participating in the FSP during this time period exhibited weight increases, the weight gain was not statistically significantly different from children whose families had stopped using food stamps.[4]

Gibson (2004, 2006) estimates the relationship between five years of FSP participation and children's risk of obesity using NLSY data from 1986 to 2000. After controlling for selection bias associated with child and family fixed effects, Gibson (2004) finds evidence that among children ages five to eleven, long-term participation in the FSP is associated with a 42.8 percent higher probability of obesity for girls and a 28.8 percent lower probability of obesity for boys. The association between weight of children ages twelve to eighteen and long-term food stamp receipt isn't statistically significant. When she repeats the analysis using long-term low income rather than long-term food stamp receipt, the associations for young children disappear. This suggests that something about FSP participation, independent of poverty status, may drive the observed association with weight in young children. However, the NLSY data don't allow Gibson to control for food insecurity status, which could affect her results; indeed, Frongillo (2003) argues that the observed associations between FSP participation and obesity result because food insecurity causes them both.

To date, the limited empirical evidence suggests that children's short-term FSP participation does not pose a risk for obesity, but long-term receipt might be associated with an elevated risk among young girls. While these studies use advanced statistical techniques, estimation problems remain. Consequently, we aren't yet in a position to confidently conclude whether food stamp receipt contributes to obesity among poor children, although it seems unlikely that there are obesity impacts in the short run.

Low-income adults receive food assistance through a variety of federal programs, but the FSP far outweighs the others in terms of caseload and expenditures.[5] In 2004 nearly twelve million adults participated in the FSP (Poikolainen 2005). Of those, 68 percent are women. The elderly constitute about 8 percent of the total caseload, working-age women 28 percent, and working-age men 13 percent. About 46 percent of FSP-participating household heads are white, 31 percent are black, and 13 percent are Hispanic.

The concern that food stamps force recipients to spend more on food than they would otherwise generally finds weak empirical support. Schanzenbach (2002) explains that theoretically only households whose food stamp benefits exceed their usual food budgets (distorted recipients) will decrease food spending upon receiving cash benefits in place of coupons. Using data from the U.S. Department of Agriculture's cash-out experiment in San Diego, she estimates that 20 to 30 percent of FSP participants are "distorted" and thus would spend less on food if given cash instead of coupons. This study uses an experimental design, which is not possible with most studies of the impacts of the FSP, but the study is not necessarily nationally representative.

Other FSP cash-out experiments also find that cash recipients reduce their average food spending (e.g., Fraker et al. 1995), suggesting that food stamps force greater food expenditure than would otherwise occur. However, two reports (Breunig et al. 2001; Breunig and Dasgupta 2005) show that generally only households with more than one adult spent less on food when given cash rather than coupons in the San Diego cash-out experiment; single-adult households exhibited no significant change in their food spending. Thus, the available literature suggests that the FSP may encourage some recipients to spend more on food than they would otherwise, but those recipients are in the minority. And if reduced food spending leads to lower calorie intake, then cashing out food stamps could lead to lower BMI among these recipients. However, if lower food spending leads to the purchase of cheaper, calorie-dense foods, then cashing out could cause their BMI to rise.

One study examines the impact of cashing out food stamps on recipients' caloric intake. Schanzenbach (2002) finds evidence that among recipients whose food stamp benefit is less than their usual food budget (inframarginal recipients), a somewhat higher proportion consumed two or more times the recommended daily allowance for calories compared to cash recipients in the San Diego experiment. This result suggests that food stamps may be encouraging weight gain among this subset of recipients. However, the estimated magnitude is modest (15 percent versus 11 percent), and Schanzenbach doesn't find the same result in Alabama, where the cash-out experiment was conducted in two counties.

She also reports that among distorted participants, those who received cash instead of stamps tended to spend less on sugary beverages, which could lead to a reduced risk of obesity. Unfortunately, none of the cash-out experiments tested impacts on BMI or the risk of obesity.

Only recently have researchers begun to directly study whether FSP participation influences adult body weight. Townsend et al. (2001) is the first to estimate the impact of food stamps on adult overweight status (BMI of greater than 27.3 for women and greater than 27.8 for men). Using the Continuing Survey of Food Intake by Individuals (CSFII), they find evidence that FSP participation among women is associated with a higher risk of overweight status in the short term. Their analysis doesn't adjust for sample selection bias; however, it does control for food insecurity status.

Three studies considering the possible short-term impact of food stamps on adult weight use statistical adjustments for possible selection bias. First, Chen et al. (2005) find evidence of increases in weight associated with short-term FSP participation among women. They use the CSFII and jointly estimate FSP participation and obesity status in order to control for selection bias. They estimate that 40 percent of obesity prevalence among low-income women is associated with FSP participation. These authors theorize that food stamps affect women's weight more than men's because the program offers the same benefit level regardless of gender, when women actually require fewer calories on average. Ethnographic studies suggest an alternative explanation: women more frequently suffer from food insecurity and disordered eating because they often reduce their own food intake to ensure that their children avoid hunger (see Chapter 4).

Other studies find less dramatic impacts. Zagorsky and Smith (2008) use the NLSY and estimate that among women, participating in the FSP is associated with having a BMI that is one to two percentage points higher than eligible nonrecipients, after controlling for family income, ethnicity, age, marital status, number of children, and county-level socioeconomic characteristics. They also find that the FSP's impact on women's BMI increases with the length of time spent in the program. They found no significant associations for men. Meyerhoefer and Pylyp-chuk (2008) use the Medical Expenditure Panel Survey and discrete factor models to adjust for selection bias. They too find no statistically significant relationship between FSP participation and the risk of obesity for men and weak evidence of an impact on women. They estimate that FSP participation is associated with a 6 to 7 percent increase in the risk of women's obesity at the 10 percent level of significance. Kaushal

(2007) uses the natural experiment created by the 1996 change in the food stamp eligibility of immigrants and the National Health Interview Survey to test the impact of FSP participation on BMI. He estimates that the BMI of foreign-born unmarried mothers with low educational attainment receiving food stamps increased only 0.3 percent. None of these studies, however, is able to control for food insecurity status.

Gibson (2003) and Jones and Frongillo (2006) focus on the impact of long-term FSP participation on adult body weight. Gibson uses the NLSY and finds evidence that long-term food stamp receipt is associated with a higher likelihood of obesity among women, but not men. Specifically, five consecutive years of food stamp receipt is associated with a 20.5 percent increase in women's risk of obesity. While Gibson's analysis controls for a wide array of socioeconomic factors and for individual fixed effects, it doesn't control for food insecurity. Jones and Frongillo investigate whether FSP participation mediates the relationship between changes in food insecurity status and changes in weight among women in the PSID between 1999 and 2001. They report that women who were food insecure over the entire observation period tended to gain less weight than women who were consistently food secure. However, FSP participation tended to offset the lower weight gain among the persistently food insecure. The authors note that this weight gain among persistently food-insecure FSP participants is relatively small and that it is not clear whether it could lead to obesity. While this analysis does account for the timing of food assistance and weight changes, it doesn't control for selection bias.

The most extensive study to consider whether food stamps cause obesity uses the NLSY and a variety of estimation techniques, including those that account for long-term receipt and possible dynamic patterns. Baum (2007) reports that current FSP participation raises women's BMI by about half a percentage point, increasing the likelihood of obesity by 2 to 5 percentage points. He also finds that duration matters, estimating that non-obese women who participate in the FSP for two years face a 10 percentage point increase in their risk of becoming obese. A drawback of this research is that it doesn't control for food insecurity status.

What do all these studies tell us? We see remarkable consistency in the evidence that FSP participation affects BMI and obesity prevalence for women and not men. However, the estimated size effects vary quite a bit. The studies that examine duration all find larger BMI effects the longer a woman participates in the program. BMI and obesity prevalence increases especially among women who stay in the program at least two years.

To what degree does the elevated BMI and obesity prevalence associated with women's FSP participation contribute to the general rise in adult obesity in the United States? Probably very little. Baum (2007) estimates that FSP participation accounts for only half a percent of the increase in adult obesity prevalence over the past thirty years. If we restrict this analysis to just poor adults, Baum's estimates imply that only 4.7 percent of the rise in the number of obese poor can be attributed to FSP participation. While FSP participation may contribute to some weight gain among women, it clearly doesn't account for much of the rise in obesity prevalence among the poor. Furthermore, Ver Ploeg et al. (2006, 2007) present evidence from the NHANES indicating that the relationship between BMI and food stamp receipt has dissipated over time. They find a BMI–food stamp relationship among women in the 1976–1980 and 1988–1994 survey waves, but not in the 1999–2000 wave.

The literature on the impact of public assistance on adult weight and obesity is nascent, with researchers still struggling with how to best control for selection bias and confounding factors such as food insecurity status. An expert panel set up by the USDA reviewed studies conducted up to 2004 and concluded that there was not solid empirical evidence that food assistance programs caused weight gain and obesity (Linz et al. 2005). The additional studies reviewed here reaffirm that WIC and school nutrition programs do not lead to excess weight in childhood.[6] The newer research on the FSP reviewed here and by Ver Ploeg and Ralston (2008) generally finds that participation is associated with small-to-modest weight gain and an increased risk of obesity among women. While these results are consistent with the "Public Assistance Causes Obesity" hypothesis, the difficulties of adjusting for selection bias and controlling for all relevant variables mean we can't yet conclude definitively that food stamps cause women's obesity, although it seems to be a possibility. Further work that better controls for selection bias and uses techniques to account for the timing of food benefit receipt and weight gain are needed to resolve the issue of causality. Richer longitudinal data including information on food purchases and consumption patterns in addition to information on FSP participation, food insecurity, and BMI would also greatly help in the effort to measure the impact of food stamps on BMI and obesity.

Work Requirements and Maternal Employment
In addition to conferring greater purchasing power, the major cash welfare program, TANF, requires most adult participants to engage in work

activity within two years of joining the rolls.[7] When mothers spend more time working in the labor market, they have less time and energy to spend preparing healthy meals and monitoring their children's dietary intake and physical activity. As one low-income caregiver explains, "You come home [from work], and it be on your mind, I'm going to cook this and that. By the time you take a shower and everything, just give me . . . a pizza" (Kelly and Patterson 2006, 348).

Indeed, Crepinsek and Burstein (2004) find evidence in their descriptive analysis of the CSFII that women who work full time spend less time grocery shopping, planning meals, and cooking than women who don't work outside the home. Employed mothers are also less likely to breast-feed their infants and more likely to place their children in the care of people outside their families, which could influence children's dietary intake. Thus, welfare's work requirements could contribute to obesity by altering mothers' time use. Concern that increased employment among mothers could lead to poorer nutrition is not new. For example, in the mid-1800s, as more women went to work in factories, the lower-class diets in England shifted heavily toward sugar (sweetened tea and jams) as a source of energy that required little preparation time: "Cheap sugar, the single most important addition to the British working-class diet during the nineteenth century, now became paramount, even, calorically. By 1900, it was contributing on average nearly one-sixth of per-capita caloric intake; if that figure could be revised to account for class, age and intrafamily differentials, the percentage for working-class women and children would be astounding" (Mintz 1985, 149).

Even before the 1996 Personal Responsibility and Work Opportunity Reconciliation Act established work requirements as a condition of benefit receipt, many states were granted waivers to initiate workfare programs. Moffitt (1999) analyzes data from the March Current Population Survey from 1977 to 1995 and finds that these waiver programs helped boost labor-force participation among less-educated women. Two studies report that labor-force participation and employment rates among single mothers continued to rise after the 1996 legislation (Corcoran et al. 2000; Burtless 2004).

Cutler et al. (2003) argue that the general rise in obesity among Americans is driven by technological advances since the 1970s that have significantly reduced the time required to prepare and clean up after meals. Lowering the time needed to acquire and prepare food increases the frequency of eating and shifts diets toward convenience foods, which tend to be more caloric. Their model predicts that groups who faced the highest time costs of food preparation in the 1960s would be most affected by these technological advances. They present evidence on changes in obesity prevalence across two waves of the NHANES and in time spent on food preparation from the Americans' Use of Time Survey Archives (1965 and 1995). Consistent with their theory, the results indicate that married women, who initially spent the most time on food preparation, exhibit the greatest increase in obesity prevalence.

This theory also predicts that women on public assistance who were not working prior to welfare reform and joined the labor force afterward will be affected by the technology-driven drop in the time cost of food more than women who worked both before and after reform. Because the rate of employment among cash assistance recipients has increased substantially since the 1996 reform (Danziger, Corcoran, and Heflin 2000), the fall in the time cost of food could exert an important influence on the caloric intake of welfare participants because prepared foods tend to be more calorie dense.

To assess the joint impact of tax and welfare reform in the 1990s on the well-being of single mothers and their families, some researchers have examined changes in food expenditures. Meyer and Sullivan (2004) find evidence in the PSID and the Interview Component of the Consumer Expenditure Survey that food spending by single mothers rose during the 1990s. DeLeire and Levy (2005) use the same data but distinguish between expenditures on food prepared at home and food consumed away from home. They report that much of the increase in food spending by single mothers results from their shift away from preparing food at home to eating out. In addition, their results indicate that this shift is driven not by changes in income but rather by a decrease in time available for home production, which is associated with increased work incentives in the revised welfare and Earned Income Tax Credit programs. Since food consumed away from home tends to be more caloric, this shift in food expenditure might contribute to weight gain among poor single mothers and their children (Guthrie et al. 2002; French et al. 2000).

Haider et al. (2003) report evidence that welfare's work requirements have modestly reduced breast-feeding rates. Reviews of observational studies report that breast-fed babies generally face a lower risk of overweight, but whether this is a causal relationship has not been firmly established (Harder et al. 2005; Owen et al. 2005; Sherry 2005). No one has directly studied the possible link between maternal employment due to welfare work requirements, breast-feeding, and child or maternal obesity.

Parents are not, however, the sole providers of food to children.

Smolensky and Gootman (2003) report that about 80 percent of children ages five years and younger with an employed mother spend an average forty hours per week in the care of someone other than their parents. Among children ages six to fourteen, 63 percent spend twenty-one hours per week on average in nonparental care. Thus, the food provided by child care institutions could have an impact on children's BMI. Unfortunately, little is known about the quality of nutrition offered in child care settings. The only published study to date using nationally representative data finds no evidence that time spent in child care centers at ages three to five predicts obesity at ages six to twelve (Lumeng et al. 2005). Indeed, the authors report that children who spent a short amount of time each week in child care centers were actually less likely to become obese.

Six studies directly examine the association between maternal employment and children's body weight. First, let's consider the two nationally representative, cross-sectional studies. Crepinsek and Burstein (2004) examine the frequency of children's vigorous exercise, hours of television and video viewing, and obesity prevalence in the CSFII by mothers' employment status. Among those with low incomes (income below 185 percent of the poverty line), only 37 percent of children whose mothers are employed full time engage in vigorous exercise, compared to 51 percent of children whose mothers don't work for pay. While children ages twelve to fourteen whose mothers work full time exhibit higher rates of overweight compared to children whose mothers don't work for pay, this difference disappears when the analysis is restricted to individuals with incomes under 185 percent of the poverty line. Delva, Johnston, and O'Malley (2007) analyze children in the eighth and tenth grades in the Monitoring the Future data. They find no evidence that maternal employment is associated with children's risk of excess weight. The cross-sectional evidence doesn't support the hypothesis that increased maternal employment leads to obesity among low-income children.

Three of the longitudinal studies of maternal employment and child weight use the NLSY. After controlling for both observable and unobservable differences across mothers, Anderson et al. (2003a; 2003b) find evidence that among higher-income women, more hours of work per week means a higher likelihood of their children being overweight. There is no evidence among poor women that hours worked affects their children's chances of excess weight.[8] Classen and Hokayem (2005) find that for a child under age eight, having a mother who works thirty-five hours or more weekly doesn't predict obesity when the child is over age eight; however, mothers' employment status is contemporaneously associated with a higher risk of obesity among children over eight years old. This study doesn't consider possible differences across maternal income.

Lastly, Fertig et al. (2006) find that in the PSID, increased employment among more-educated mothers is associated with children watching more television and having fewer meals, which lead to higher BMI. For less-educated mothers, increased employment is associated with children spending more time at school, which tends to lower BMI. While these three variables are associated with child BMI, only television watching is related to the risk of obesity among children of more-educated mothers at the 5 percent level of statistical significance.

In sum, three of the five available studies find evidence that maternal employment is associated with higher child BMI or obesity risk, and two of those indicate that the relationship holds only for women of a higher socioeconomic status (SES), who aren't likely eligible for welfare. Presently, there is little evidence that welfare's work requirements contribute to poor children's excess weight.

Do welfare's work requirements contribute to adult obesity? Kaestner and Tarlov (2006) use the Behavioral Risk Factor Surveillance System to estimate the impact of welfare reform on the health of low-SES women. They find no evidence that the work requirements adopted in 1996 are associated with single mothers' physical activity and fruit and vegetable intake. Furthermore, they find no evidence that declining caseloads following welfare reform influenced poor women's obesity rate. However, this study is limited by its cross-sectional design and its use of aggregate, rather than individual, data.

The "work requirement" pathway from public assistance to obesity is limited in that it could help explain participant obesity only after the mid-1990s, and we know obesity prevalence was rising earlier. Present evidence on the impact of maternal employment on food spending suggests an increased reliance on food eaten away from home, but no one has directly studied changes in the calorie intake and BMI of recipients since work requirements were imposed. The studies of the impact of maternal employment on child BMI generally do not support the hypothesis that welfare work requirements cause childhood obesity, and there is no evidence that increased employment leads to weight gain among the mothers themselves. The relatively small amount of research available indicates that this particular pathway probably doesn't contribute to the association between public assistance programs and obesity among the poor.

The Welfare Benefits Cycle

Dietz (1995) notes the possibility of both greater hunger and greater obesity among the poor in the United States and speculates that episodic food deprivation could have the paradoxical effect of increasing BMI by affecting eating patterns. Smith (2006, 17), however, notes that while some disciplines describe the simultaneous rise in hunger and obesity as a paradox, epidemiologists see the joint outcome "very much in accordance with the view that obesity is a natural phenomenon likely to be exacerbated by an increased risk of food shortage." Epidemiologists and anthropologists explain that the human body adapts to episodic food shortages through biochemical changes that improve its ability to store fat (Neel 1962, 1999; Barker 1997). Several experimental studies report that after a period of food deprivation, children and adults tend to over-consume previously unavailable palatable foods (e.g., Fisher and Birch 1999; Polivy 1996). That is, periods of hunger may lead to eating disorders, which in turn can encourage weight gain (Hasler et al. 2004; Yanovski 2003).

Because food stamp benefits are paid only once per month, recipients may find themselves in a cycle of food deprivation at the end of the month followed by increased intake of "comfort foods," or binge eating, when their benefits arrive. One Seattle dietician explains that upon receipt of benefits, "a lot of families tend to celebrate. They get all the things they couldn't afford, like steaks and cookies and chips. But then nothing is left in the cupboard at the end of the month. This kind of feast or famine thing . . . screws up your metabolism and makes it harder to lose weight" (Davidow 2004). Anecdotal evidence from grocery store owners suggests that food stamp recipients make most of their purchases early in the month. A grocer in the Memphis area notes, "Eighty or 90 percent of our business in the first half of the month is in food stamps" (Biggs 2004).

Frongillo et al. (1997) examine the relationships between food insecurity, disordered eating, and obesity in a small sample (*n* = 193) of women in rural New York. They find that severe food insecurity is associated with lower body weight, but that mild food insecurity is associated with higher weight. The authors conclude that while all food-insecure individuals face two opposing forces—weight gain through disordered eating and weight loss through reduced caloric intake—only among the mildly food insecure does the former exceed the latter. Wilde and Peterman (2006) find similar results in two waves of the nationally representative NHANES. Compared to women in food-secure households, women who were "marginally food insecure" or "food insecure without hunger" were more likely to be obese and to have gained at least 4.5 kilograms between 1999–2000 and 2001–2002. These two cross-sectional studies suggest that if food stamp recipients become mildly food insecure weeks after receiving benefits, then disordered eating in the first week or two following receipt could contribute to weight gain.

What do we know about food consumption patterns with respect to the timing of income receipt? An ethnographic study of poor Latino families in Brooklyn reports food abundance at the start of the month, during which adults tend to overeat and overfeed their children, followed by periods of limited food availability at the end of the month (Kaufman and Karpati 2007). Interviews with nutrition educators in New Jersey's Expanded Food and Nutrition Education program indicate that excess consumption when income is received and food becomes available is common among their clients (Kempson et al. 2002). Two quantitative studies based on small local samples also find that energy intake by children (Matheson et al. 2002) and women reporting moderate to severe food insecurity falls as time passes after the family receives their main form of income each month (Tarasuk et al. 2007).

Do large studies also find a cyclical pattern in food purchases and consumption? Stephens (2003) uses the Consumer Expenditure Survey's Diary Survey, a large sample representative of the U.S. population, to see whether the arrival of Social Security checks influences household expenditures on "instantaneous consumption," that is, the purchase of nondurables such as food. Among households that depend heavily on Social Security income, average spending on "food at home," "food away," and "fresh food" during the six days following check receipt all exceed the average expenditures during the six days prior to receipt.[9] For example, spending on "food away" rises by 21 percent, while spending on "fresh food" rises by 9 percent. Damon et al. (2006) examine ACNielsen Homescan data for 2003 and find that households in the lowest quartile of the income distribution with zero or one employed household head exhibit higher than average food spending at the beginning of the month and lower than average food spending at the end.

Two studies examine the food spending patterns of food stamp recipients in particular. Wilde and Ranney (2000) use two large, nationally representative data sets, the Consumer Expenditure Diary Survey for 1988–1992 and the CSFII for 1989–1991, to study shopping frequency and food intake among FSP participants. Their descriptive analysis shows that average food expenditure peaks in the first three days of the month (when benefits arrive) and then flattens out for the remainder of the month. Food-energy intake for individuals who shopped for groceries more than once a month ("frequent shoppers") was fairly steady over the four-week benefit cycle. For those who shopped no more than once per month ("infrequent shoppers"), food-energy intake fell significantly in the fourth week. However, the authors' regression analyses find that the value of food stamps and cash income has no statistically significant association with energy consumption over the course of a month or with the frequency of food shopping.

Shapiro (2005) uses both the CSFII and the Nationwide Food Consumption Survey 1987–1988 to examine trends in FSP participants' food expenditures and food consumption. He estimates that the amount of daily kilocalories falls by 0.32 percent over the food stamp month, while the daily value of food consumed falls by 0.73 percent. He interprets the greater decline in food value as evidence that participants are shifting expenditure to cheaper foods as the month progresses.

While there is evidence that FSP participants consume more calories at the beginning of the month than at the end and that food deprivation can trigger eating disorders, few researchers have tested whether this eating pattern affects recipients' BMI and risk of obesity. The CSFII contains self-reported height and weight information, so researchers could use these data to investigate the connection between FSP participants' food intake patterns and their BMI in a cross-sectional analysis. Superior in inferential quality, but greater in expense, would be a randomized experiment to test whether the frequency of FSP benefit distribution influences participants' BMI and obesity status. For example, the control group would receive food stamp benefits once a month as usual while the treatment group received benefits twice monthly. It is also worth investigating whether raising benefit levels and teaching recipients better food management techniques reduce the likelihood of participants running out of food toward the end of the month.

Mental Health
The fourth possible avenue from public assistance to obesity focuses on welfare's possible impact on mental health. Specifically, we must consider whether public assistance participation leads to a reduced sense of self-efficacy or self-esteem, or to increased depression, any of which could lead to changes in patterns of eating and physical activity in ways that promote weight gain.[10] For example, emotional distress may precipitate eating for comfort (Dallman et al. 2003; Epel et al. 2001; Oliver and Wardle 1999) and lethargy (Paluska and Schwenk 2000).

Studies of the impact of public assistance on children tend to focus on cognitive functioning and behavioral problems; few address the possible impact on children's mental health. One unpublished study using cross-sectional data from the National Survey of Families and Households (NSFH) reports that current welfare use is associated with lower adolescent self-esteem (Mosley 1995). However, two longitudinal studies suggest that public assistance doesn't harm children's mental health (Axinn et al. 1997; Chase-Lansdale et al. 2003).

What about public assistance and adult recipients' mental health? A substantial literature documents that women receiving welfare benefits exhibit higher rates of depression (e.g., Coiro 2001; Danziger, Corcoran, Danziger, et al. 2000; Lennon et al. 2002; Polit et al. 2001) and lower levels of self-esteem (e.g., Nichols-Casebolt 1986; Pavetti et al. 1995) than the general population. Does program participation cause adult mental health to deteriorate or are mentally distressed adults more likely to participate in public assistance programs?

First, let's consider self-efficacy. Parker (1994) reports that higher levels of self-efficacy are associated with an increased chance of exiting welfare, based on a three-year panel study of 851 welfare participants in Washington State. In the NLSY, Kunz and Kalil (1999) find that women receiving AFDC exhibit lower levels of self-efficacy before they enter the welfare system than non-AFDC mothers. These studies suggest that self-efficacy influences welfare participation rather than the reverse.

Gottschalk (2005) uses data from a Canadian wage subsidy experiment, the Self-Sufficiency Project, to test whether working more hours leads to improvements in welfare recipients' beliefs about their ability to exert control over their lives (self-efficacy). The experimental nature of the data allows him to adjust for the possible endogeneity of work hours (i.e., those with higher self-efficacy may be more likely to work, and those who work more may develop a greater sense of control). He finds evidence that increasing the number of hours worked leads to an improved sense of control among workers under age thirty, but not among older workers. The subsidies offered in this experiment are substantial—in New Brunswick, wages doubled—so it's not obvious whether the act of work itself improves beliefs regarding control or whether having a significantly higher income drives the results. The limited empirical data available suggests that self-efficacy influences the initiation and duration of welfare receipt and that exiting welfare via well-paid work increases self-efficacy.

What about welfare and self-esteem? Zill et al. (1991) examine the NLSY and report that although AFDC mothers exhibit lower self-esteem scores than nonpoor mothers, their scores don't differ significantly from those of poor mothers not in the program. This suggests that poverty rather than welfare influences self-esteem. Elliot (1996) also uses the NLSY but looks only at white women. She reports that current welfare receipt is negatively associated with self-esteem and that, in two of four model specifications, duration of welfare negatively affects self-esteem scores. Specifically, an additional year on AFDC is associated with a decline of 0.108 to 0.125 in the average self-esteem score (which has a sample mean of 33.66 and a standard deviation of 4.08). By contrast, Kunz and Kalil (1999) examine young women in the 1980 interview wave of the NLSY and compare their self-esteem scores in early adulthood with later welfare use. They find that lower self-esteem scores early in adulthood predict receipt of cash benefits later in adulthood, even after controlling for characteristics known to influence welfare use (e.g., ethnicity, mother's education level). They estimate that half a standard deviation difference in the self-esteem score leads to a 16 percent increase in the probability of later cash assistance receipt. In sum, we have evidence that lower self-esteem leads to a greater chance of later welfare participation and that longer welfare participation may lead to lower self-esteem. With the mixed evidence available, we can neither accept nor reject the notion that public assistance dampens self-esteem.

The results for depression are somewhat clearer. A panel study of African American mothers in Chicago finds that women whose families participated in public assistance during their childhood were more likely to report psychological distress as adults, and that women reporting distress in childhood were more likely to receive assistance as adults, suggesting mutual causation (Ensminger 1995). Petterson and Friel (2001) use the nationally representative NLSY and NSFH and find that long-term welfare recipients have the same levels of depression as short-term recipients. They conclude that the elevated levels of depression among welfare recipients result from material hardship rather than the stigma of receiving public assistance. Duncan, Dunifon, et al. (1998) use both the NSFH and the PSID and find little difference between the depression scores of women on welfare and those of poor, single mothers not on welfare. These results offer little support for the hypothesis that welfare participation causes depression. Knab et al. (2007), however, find evidence suggesting a link between welfare benefits and mothers' depression in certain situations. In the Fragile Families and Child Wellbeing study, which follows a cohort of children from twenty cities, they find evidence that at low levels of welfare generosity, increases in benefits are associated with improvements in maternal mental health, but that at high levels of program generosity, increases in benefits are associated with rising depression.

Two studies present evidence that participating in the Food Stamp Program improves mental health. Heflin and Ziliak (2006) use the PSID and find that FSP participation nearly eliminates emotional distress among food-insufficient households. Kim and Frongillo (2007) report evidence from the Asset and Health Dynamics among the Oldest Old that FSP participation reduces the adverse impact of food insecurity on depression among the elderly. These results contradict the hypothesis that public assistance causes depression.

The limited available evidence on the impact of public assistance on adult mental health offers mixed support for the notion that participation adversely affects self-efficacy and self-esteem and no convincing evidence that participation in public assistance causes depression. Furthermore, none of the studies of welfare's effect on mental health attempt to draw connections between mental health and BMI or obesity status. In short, the current literature offers no direct empirical evidence supporting the hypothesis that public assistance causes obesity by harming recipients' mental health.

Summary and Recommendations

I conclude that WIC doesn't contribute to childhood obesity, and thus there is no reason to curb this program out of fear that it causes excessive weight gain among children. Similarly, the balance of the evidence does not support the hypothesis that school food programs contribute to poor children's obesity, so there is no cause to curtail these programs either, although continuing to improve the nutritional content of these meals remains important.

Recent research on food stamps adds to the evidence that this program is associated with increased BMI and obesity risk among women. Although the newer studies use statistical controls for selection bias, we can't yet confidently conclude that FSP participation causes obesity, but it remains a possibility. However, even if FSP causes weight gain among some participants, it still accounts for only a small part of the rise in obesity (Baum 2007). Furthermore, even if we interpret the extant evidence as showing that FSP participation causes obesity among women, we don't have a firm grasp as to why. The additional work requirements associated with benefits after 1996 and the theorized impact of benefit receipt on mental health garner little empirical support as possible causes. If food stamps affect BMI it is most likely through increased purchasing power and the monthly payment cycle. It would be premature to make major changes to the FSP in hopes of reducing the possible impact on obesity without developing a better understanding of these two pathways. Government needs to support experimental research on the role of benefit levels and the frequency of distribution on recipients' weight. Distributing higher or more frequent benefits might reduce disordered eating patterns and the associated weight gain. Increasing the frequency of benefit payments wouldn't entail large administrative costs and likely wouldn't generate significant political opposition. Retailers in particular would probably support such a change (Associated Press 2006).

Researchers also need to experiment with disallowing certain types of foods for purchase, discounting healthy foods through the Electronic Benefit Transfer system, and expanding nutrition education. Removing certain products from the list of items that participants can purchase with food stamps might improve diets and BMI, but it would certainly generate significant opposition from food producers and would entail much debate as to which foods to exclude. Offering discounts on healthy foods, such as fresh produce and low-fat dairy products, and providing nutrition education to all public assistance participants might be more politically acceptable. Experiments in schools have found that reducing price can increase consumption of lower calorie, nutrient-dense foods (French and Wechsler 2004), and evaluations of the current federal nutrition education program, the Expanded Food and Nutrition Education Program (EFNEP), report improved nutrition knowledge and nutrient intake (e.g., Burney and Haughton 2002). However, the evidence of EFNEP's effect on obesity remains largely anecdotal. For example, one participant reports, "I'm proud to say that since cooking from the book [a recipe book distributed by EFNEP] and exercising I have lost between 30 and 35 pounds and my blood sugar has returned to normal" (Montgomery and Willis 2006, 7). Dollahite et al. (2008) offer some relevant quantitative evidence from one state. Their cost-benefit analysis of the New York State EFNEP concludes that the program is likely to reduce future health care costs and that its cost-effectiveness is comparable to other interventions designed to improve health.

The limited information from cash-out experiments suggests that replacing food stamp benefits with cash might lead to lower calorie intake among a minority of recipients. Results regarding calorie intake were not consistent across sites, however, and the experiments didn't directly assess the impact on obesity status. The preliminary evidence from a nationally representative, but nonexperimental, sample suggests that cashing out food stamps will not reduce the risk of obesity (Meyerhoefer and Pylypchuk 2008). We simply don't have sufficient evidence to recommend that food stamps be cashed out in order to reduce recipient obesity.

In general, revising public assistance programs in order to reduce the possible small contributions to obesity requires that we increase access to healthy foods and encourage physical activity among participants. Policies that address these two goals and have a decent chance of garnering political support include the following:

- Increase the frequency with which food stamp benefits are distributed to encourage consistent calorie intake over the month.
- Assure all public assistance participants access to the food management and nutrition courses offered by the EFNEP.
- Use the Electronic Benefit Transfer system to subsidize food stamp participants' purchase of fresh fruits and vegetables and low-fat dairy and meat products.
- Encourage farmers' markets to accept food stamps.
- Expand instruction on the importance of physical activity in a healthy lifestyle in existing public assistance programs.

3

The "Obesity Causes Public Assistance" Hypothesis

Whereas the previous chapter considered whether public assistance leads to obesity, this chapter considers the reverse causal flow: does obesity cause people to become poor and turn to public assistance? Obesity could influence income and eligibility for public assistance programs via two pathways (Figure 3.1). First, excess body weight can impair health, which in turn reduces prospects for educational attainment, marriage, and employment and raises the risk of poverty and participation in public assistance programs. Second, the obese face stigmatization and discrimination, which also reduce prospects for education, employment, and marriage. As Wooley et al. (1979, 18) note, "Obese people, like the physically handicapped, wear their 'problem' for all to see at all times, and yet unlike those groups are held responsible for their condition." Discrimination against obese people limits their opportunities for education, employment, and marriage, lowering their family income and raising the likelihood of poverty and welfare participation.

Research Context

Which disciplines study the possible pathways from obesity to poverty, and what methodological issues do they face? Psychiatrists and psychologists dominate the research on the presence of weight-based discrimination and its impact on marriage and employment opportunities. They develop theories of discrimination and techniques for measuring biased attitudes and study the consequences of stigmatization and discrimination. Psychological studies of discrimination often rely on modest samples from a limited geographical area and are observational in design. The need to thoroughly interview subjects and the difficulties of conducting controlled experiments necessitate this methodology. Studies of educational attainment in relation to BMI can, however, be conducted using nationally representative samples. While these studies generally find lower educational attainment among the obese, they can't tell us why this relationship occurs (e.g., Zhang and Wang 2004).

By contrast, some experiments can be conducted on the role of body weight in hiring decisions and performance evaluations, enabling researchers to test whether obesity reduces labor market opportunities. Such experiments are time consuming and consequently use modest-sized, local samples. Other approaches to testing for adverse stereotyping include surveying individuals regarding their experiences with size discrimination and testing subjects for anti-fat bias, but these also tend to rely on modest, geographically restricted samples. Descriptive analyses of the legal aspects of size discrimination in the labor market have been provided by researchers in management, communications and journalism, and, naturally, law.

Journalists also contribute to our understanding of weight-based discrimination by presenting stories about the experience of being obese. Some stories profile an obese person, and others follow a person wearing a "fat suit" and report their experiences of discrimination (e.g., ABC's "Fat Like Me," broadcast October 27, 2003, and Tyra Banks's "Undercover and Overweight," broadcast November 7, 2005). These investigations vividly portray the pervasiveness and emotional toll of the daily slights and frustrations with which the obese must contend.

The study of the health impacts of obesity on the labor market has been conducted by a mix of physicians, kinesiologists, physical educators, economists, and management experts. A few of these studies use nationally representative samples, and most are cross-sectional and observational in design, so while they are descriptive, they can't pin down causality. Most of the studies on the cost of obesity to businesses involve the examination of employees at one firm or at a group of large employers in one time period. A few have multiple years of data and can test whether changes in BMI are followed by changes in costs, which provides stronger evidence of a causal link. None can conduct random experiments because it's impossible to assign employees to obese and non-obese groups. When testing the impact of employer-provided health programs, researchers must be cautious because employees voluntarily choose whether to participate, creating the possibility of selection bias.

Studies of the impact of obesity on earnings are commonly conducted by economists using nationally representative, longitudinal data. Because longitudinal data on BMI and earnings are available, researchers can determine whether obesity at an earlier time predicts later labor market outcomes, which provides stronger evidence of causal flow than

Figure 3.1. The "Obesity Causes Public Assistance" model

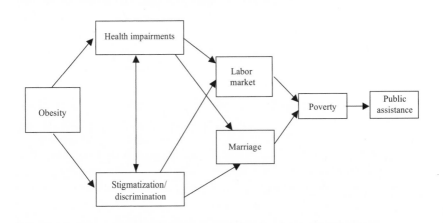

cross-sectional studies can. However, the available longitudinal data on BMI is usually self-reported rather than impartially measured.

The influence of obesity on marriage has been studied mostly by sociologists, but some economists, psychologists, and demographers have also contributed to the findings. These researchers can't conduct random experiments to test whether obesity causes reduced marriage chances, but they can analyze longitudinal data to determine whether obesity in an earlier time period predicts future marriage outcomes.

Empirical Evidence

Researchers can reliably measure differences in wages, employment rates, and marriage rates across body weight categories, but it is difficult to determine how much of the difference results from discrimination and how much stems from health problems. Nevertheless, I organize the literature by two initial pathways, health impairment and discrimination, to see whether there is empirical evidence supporting the notion that obesity leads to diminished social and employment opportunities and thus to poverty and public assistance.

Health Impairments
Obesity causes a number of serious diseases and is a risk factor for many more. Health problems in childhood can impede learning and educa-

tional attainment. For example, in a sample of 106 children referred to a hospital clinic for obesity evaluation, Schwimmer et al. (2003) find significantly higher rates of school absenteeism, and more of the children reported impaired school function on a Quality of Life survey in comparison to children of recommended weight. Swallen et al. (2005) analyze data from the nationally representative National Longitudinal Study of Adolescent Health and report evidence that obese teens are more likely than their peers of recommended weight to report poor health and functional limitations. Both studies are cross-sectional, so they don't prove that obesity causes health limitations, but they do suggest that part of the observed association between obesity and lower educational attainment may well be related to impaired childhood health.

Research on the relationship between obesity and adults' health often examines the impacts on their labor productivity. The press frequently reports on the health consequences of obesity, making them commonly known (e.g., *Time* magazine's issue on "America's Obesity Crisis," June 7, 2004, and Al Roker's Food Network documentary on childhood obesity, broadcast March 31, 2007). Thus, obesity may reduce employment opportunities because of the perception that heavy employees are more likely to have health problems and will be less productive and more expensive to insure (Burton et al. 1998; Thompson et al. 1998; Seiders and Berry 2007). Because firms' primary goal is to maximize profits, self-interest requires that they hire workers who will be more productive and less costly to insure.

Are the fears of lower productivity and higher medical costs among obese workers empirically supported? Studies of employees at individual firms generally confirm that the obese take more sick days than lower weight workers. Burton et al. (1998) analyze data on 3,066 employees at one large financial institution and observe that those who are obese take twice as many sick days and that the average number of sick days rises with BMI.[1] Tucker and Friedman (1998) examine a sample of 10,825 employees participating in a wellness screening program at various job sites around the United States. After controlling for age, gender, income, hours worked per week, and cigarette consumption, they find obese employees to be nearly twice as likely to experience moderate to high levels of absenteeism as the non-obese. In addition to greater absenteeism, excess weight may lower output on the job (Burton et al. 1999) and elevate rates of worker's compensation claims (Østbye et al. 2007).[2]

Obesity is associated not only with lower productivity measures but with higher insurance costs as well. Puhl and Brownell (2001) review seven studies and report that estimates of the rise in health care costs associated with obesity greatly vary, ranging from 8 to 44 percent. The one longitudinal study reviewed finds that the probability of health care expenditure rises in the upper tail of the BMI distribution (Black et al. 1994; n = 383). In a more recent study, Wang et al. (2004) examine a large sample of workers (n = 23,490) and again find higher health care costs among overweight and obese employees.[3]

The extant research finds that obesity, worker productivity, and firms' health care costs are associated, but they are unable to identify causal pathways. Nonetheless, the consistency of these findings across different businesses and locations is consistent with the hypothesis that obese employees are generally less productive and cost more to insure.

Another avenue of research regarding employees' body weight examines the relationship between obesity and disability. Disabilities can also reduce employee productivity and raise firms' production costs. Lakdawalla et al. (2004) analyze trends in the National Health Interview Survey and find that the obese are generally more disabled than others. Among people ages fifty to sixty-nine in the Health and Retirement Survey (HRS), a nationally representative, longitudinal sample of middle-aged individuals, Sturm et al. (2004) find that compared to people with BMIs of at least 18.5 but less than 25, those who are moderately obese (BMI of at least 30 but less than 35) are twice as likely to experience limitations related to basic activities of daily living, such as the ability to dress and bathe, while those who are severely obese (BMI of 35 or higher) are four times as likely.

Burkhauser and Cawley (2004) investigate whether obesity causes workers to move into the disability insurance program. They use two nationally representative samples, the National Longitudinal Survey of Youth (NLSY) and the Panel Study of Income Dynamics (PSID), and an instrumental-variables approach to distinguish causal flows. They find that among adults over age twenty-five, obesity raises the likelihood of receiving disability income by 1.2 to 5.6 percentage points for women and by 0.8 to 6.9 percentage points for men. Their results suggest that obesity causes health problems that reduce work capabilities, making workers eligible for disability insurance. Jung et al. (2006) report that in the longitudinal Health and Retirement Survey, BMI of more than 30 in the first wave is associated with a higher likelihood of disability (as measured by ability related to basic functioning) in the fourth wave, which again suggests that obesity causes disability.[4] However, Cawley (2000) finds no evidence that obesity causes employment disability among women ages sixteen to forty-one in the NLSY. The evidence is mixed, but it leans toward the notion that obesity can cause disability among working- and retirement-age Americans.[5]

The preponderance of the literature on obesity and labor market performance finds that excess weight is associated with reduced labor productivity and increased health care costs. These associations could discourage firms from hiring obese workers. Since many of the reviewed studies do not use nationally representative samples and are observational, the general direction of causality is difficult to establish. Consequently, we must regard these results as suggestive rather than as conclusive.

Discrimination and Stigmatization

Discrimination against the obese results from the stereotypical perception that the obese are lazy and undisciplined (Pingitore et al. 1994; Teachman et al. 2003), and it can limit opportunities in both the labor and marriage markets.[6] Psychologist Christian Crandall (1994, 1995) argues that weight-based bias results from the ideology of conservatism, which holds the individual responsible for their own condition and argues that people can and should pull themselves up by their own bootstraps. This worldview, often associated with the Protestant work ethic, frees people of "normal" weight from responsibility to take any action and confers on them a sense of moral superiority.[7]

The obese encounter stigmatization and discrimination early in life—several studies report qualitative and quantitative evidence of problems beginning in elementary school and continuing through college (Degher and Hughes 1999; Latner and Stunkard 2003; Puhl and Brownell 2001). Richardson et al.'s 1961 classic study of early friendships found that obese children rank very low in terms of being wanted as a friend. Latner and Stunkard (2003) replicate this study and find that schoolchildren's bias against obese peers not only exists today but may be even greater now. Puhl and Brownell (2001) review several additional studies that support the hypothesis that schoolchildren are often biased against their obese peers. While these studies aren't based on nationally representative samples, the long-term persistence of the evidence across different samples speaks to the likely beginnings of social discrimination against the obese in elementary school as young children begin to absorb and express cultural biases.

Studies of teasing and bullying provide additional evidence that obese children face stigmatization. Two studies based on a large sample of middle and high school students ($n = 4,746$) in Minnesota find that overweight and obese students are significantly more likely to report being teased frequently, even after the researchers control for ethnicity and parents' education (Eisenberg, Neumark-Sztainer, and Perry 2003; Eisenberg, Neumark-Sztainer, and Story 2003; Neumark-Sztainer et al. 2002). In the only available longitudinal study, Griffiths et al. (2006) estimate that boys and girls who are obese at age 7.5 are, respectively, 1.66 and 1.54 times more likely to be bullied at age 8.5 than are children of recommended weight. This study controls for parents' occupational status.

Teasing, bullying, and other forms of discrimination in school could impair the learning process by reducing attendance, concentration, and self-confidence, and could discourage pursuit of higher levels of education. For example, in Flanagan (1996, 432) an obese high school girl reports "being pushed down stairs, her hair being pulled out, being spat on, and having numerous objects thrown at her. She would find pig snouts taped to her locker." After getting no help from administrators and counselors in stopping the harassment she began skipping school and eventually dropped out. This response is not unique. In a study of nearly five thousand Midwestern school children, Eisenberg, Neumark-Sztainer, and Perry (2003) find that frequently teased students like school less. In addition to making school a place children dread rather than enjoy, weight-based teasing can also contribute to eating disorders (Haines et al. 2006; Thompson et al. 2006). Negative experiences in primary and secondary schools can dampen college aspirations. Indeed, one study using the National Longitudinal Study of Adolescent Health estimates that the psychological effects of stigmatization account for about one-third of the association between girls' obesity and their decreased likelihood of college enrollment (Crosnoe 2007).

Childhood stigmatization based on weight is not, however, limited to peers; teachers, admissions officers, and parents have also been implicated (Puhl and Brownell 2001). For example, Crandall (1991) reports that three studies of a total of 833 undergraduates all produce evidence that parents are generally less willing to finance obese children's college education and that the effect is stronger for women than for men. In a follow-up study, which controlled for income, ethnicity, family size, and the number of children in college, Crandall (1995) again finds evidence that obese undergraduate women receive less financial support for school from their parents than their lower-weight counterparts ($n = 576$). The consistency of the findings for women in these studies is suggestive, but they rely on data from only two universities. If the same trends exist among the general population, the lack of monetary support for higher education for obese women could help account for their lower educational attainment and earnings, consequently putting them at a higher risk of poverty and welfare use.

Once out of school the obese face employment barriers independent of their educational attainment. Stereotypes of the obese as lazy and lacking self-control contribute to the belief that they will be less productive employees. For example, Carr and Friedman (2005) analyze the Midlife Development in the United States Survey, a national data set of individuals ages twenty-five to seventy-four, and find that the obese are 50 to 85 percent more likely to report experiencing discrimination in the labor market than people of recommended weight. Discrimination begins at the initial stages of the employment process and persists through promotion and salary considerations. Puhl and Brownell (2001) review the literature on experimental studies of weight-based discrimination in hiring. All six studies reviewed produced evidence that heavy job applicants face adverse bias. For example, Pingitore et al. (1994) conduct a novel experiment using actors to portray job applicants; in some taped interviews the actors wear theatrical prostheses to make them appear overweight, while in others they appear as their actual, recommended-range weight. Using the same actors to portray both the normal-weight and overweight applicants controls for potentially confounding non-weight-related attributes that could influence the hiring decision (e.g., speaking style). The results indicate that body weight has a substantial negative impact on one's probability of being hired, accounting for 35 percent of the variation in the hiring decision. Furthermore, the impact was stronger for women than men: 47 percent of the variation in the hiring of women applicants could be attributed to body weight versus 29 percent for men.

The applicability of these results to the general population is limited by the fact that the experiments used undergraduate students as the persons making the hypothetical hiring decisions and they likely had little experience in personnel decision making. In a large, nationwide Gallup poll, however, roughly 20 percent of respondents said they would be less likely to hire a person if that person were heavy (Gallup Organization 2003). These studies suggest a general cultural bias against the obese that limits their access to good jobs.

Differences in the hiring process across weight groups could also arise in part because of difficulties the obese have in finding stylish clothing. As a participant in a qualitative study explains, "I can't fit into pretty clothes" (Parker and Keim 2004, 286). First impressions count when seeking good jobs, so disadvantages in access to appropriate clothing could matter. A fashion industry study reports that among young women, 56 percent of those wearing size 12 or higher have troubles finding clothing they like in their size compared to only 35 percent of those wearing smaller sizes (Cotton Incorporated 1999). Similarly, academic surveys find that women who wear size 16 and up are more dissatisfied than others with the availability, fit, and styling of clothes (Chowdhary and Beale 1988; Kind and Hathcote 2000). Recent experiments document the difficulties the obese often encounter when trying to find stylish clothing or get good service from sales personnel (King et al. 2006).[8] Poverty exacerbates the difficulties of acquiring clothing appropriate for job interviews among heavy, low-income women, possibly limiting the types of job for which they apply and their chances of being hired.

Discrimination against the obese in the labor market affects not only the hiring process but also chances for promotions and raises. Mark Roehling, a management professor, reviewed twenty-nine articles on the impact of body weight on a number of employment outcomes and concludes that weight has a significant negative impact (Roehling 1999). In an interview he commented, "I was stunned with the consistency with which weight discrimination was found in the studies. In the workplace, the magnitude of bias against fat people was far greater than for age or race or any other measure" (Smith 2001). Another review of obesity and employment finds consistent evidence that employers often hold negative stereotypes about the obese and judge them more harshly (Puhl and Brownell 2001). Such harsh judgment can translate into fewer raises and reduced chances for promotion and training (Shapiro et al. 2007). A respondent in a survey of National Association to Advance Fat Acceptance members poignantly summarizes the disadvantages obese people face in the labor market:

> I just wanted to add that on the surface of this survey I appear to be very successful—graduate education, high salary profession position. However, this was achieved with more sweat and tears than for most "normal" sized individuals. What is not shown is the two years of unemployment, living off savings and family, a job in which I wasn't paid for three months, and two instances of job discrimination in an effort to gain employment. Even my current job was taken out of desperation and not enthusiasm. Although my field does not require an "attractive" appearance, it still counts in obtaining more desirable positions. Being fat and female definitely makes it difficult to reach my goals in a tough job market. (Rothblum et al. 1990, 261–62)

Does stigmatization and discrimination lead to lower earnings for the obese? A substantial body of evidence indicates that the obese do in fact earn less than their lower-weight counterparts (e.g., Averett and Korenman 1996, 1999; Gortmaker et al. 1993; Pagán and Dávila 1997; Mitra 2001; Register and Williams 1990). I'll focus on studies that use longitudinal, rather than cross-sectional, data because they are better able to address the issue of causality. Many of these studies attempt to control for the possibility that earnings influence BMI by estimating the relationship between past BMI and current earnings (current earnings may influence current BMI but can't influence past BMI). For example, Gortmaker et al. (1993) examine NLSY respondents ages sixteen to twenty-four whose BMI lies in at least the ninety-fifth percentile and observe that in a seven-year follow-up they earn less income and exhibit higher poverty rates than their lower-weight counterparts. The annual household income of women who were initially obese falls $6,710 below the income of non-obese women on average, and they face a 10 percent higher likelihood of poverty. Averett and Korenman (1999) also analyze the NLSY and find that BMI in 1982 is negatively associated with wages in 1990. The authors report that the wage penalty is greater for whites than blacks and that about one-fifth of the wage penalty for both ethnicities is attributable to the types of occupations held.

In addition to possible reverse causality, studies of the relationship between obesity and earnings may suffer from bias because of unobserved heterogeneity—that is, unobserved factors that affect both BMI and wages (e.g., motivation). Averett and Korenman (1996) control for unobserved heterogeneity associated with family characteristics by examining sister pairs in the NLSY. Their evidence indicates that obese women earn wages 12 percent lower than those of their recommended-weight sister. They also find evidence that the effect of obesity on wages is stronger for whites than for blacks.

Baum and Ford (2004) and Cawley (2004b) also examine the NLSY, but they use alternative techniques to control for unobserved heterogeneity. Baum and Ford estimate that obese workers incur a wage penalty of 1 to 6 percent on average and that women face a larger penalty than men. Cawley concludes that greater weight causes lower wages for white, but not black, women. Specifically, a sixty-four-pound weight gain leads to a 9 percent drop in wages for white women.[9]

Conley and Glauber (2005) present the only recent findings that contradict the link between obesity and earnings for women. Using the PSID, they estimate both random-effects and sibling fixed-effects models to control for unobserved heterogeneity. They find no evidence that

BMI in 1986 has a statistically significant impact on women's earnings in 1999. They suggest that they may get these different results because their sample is generally older than the NLSY respondents, they look at a longer time period between BMI and outcomes (thirteen versus seven years), and they don't separate their analyses by ethnicity. They do, however, report that BMI in the earlier time period is associated with lower family income among women, estimating that a 1 percent increase in women's BMI is associated with a 6 percent decrease in later family income. They also find evidence that BMI in the initial period causes lower occupational prestige scores in the follow-up period. Perhaps lower-prestige occupations offer fewer hours of work, which could account for their finding that BMI influences family income but does not influence wages.

While the current literature produces compelling evidence that obese women earn less and some evidence that they are more likely to be poor, no studies directly estimate the impact of obesity on the likelihood of public assistance participation. One study does examine whether obesity lengthens welfare spells. Examining white women in the Women's Employment Study, a sample of welfare recipients in Michigan, Cawley and Danziger (2005) find that those who are morbidly obese (BMI of 40 or higher) are less likely to move from welfare to work than those who weigh less. Morbid obesity is also positively associated with the number of months on welfare among black women. These results suggest that obesity may be a barrier to leaving welfare, extending the amount of time women stay on the welfare rolls.

Overall, evidence that obese people face substantial barriers in the labor market is strong. Furthermore, the evidence that obese women, particularly white women, earn lower wages than their non-obese counterparts is compelling. This result is consistent with the feminist argument that women are generally judged more by their physical appearance than by their actual abilities (e.g., Jackson 1992; Wolf 1991). The lower wages earned by obese women could contribute to their poverty and thus could lead to public assistance participation. Gortmaker et al. (1993), in the only study to directly analyze the relationship between obesity and poverty, estimate that obesity results in a 10 percent higher chance of poverty for women. The estimated size effects for wages are generally modest, so while lower wages are a contributing factor, they probably aren't the major reason why obesity and public assistance are positively associated.

Stigmatization and discrimination in school and the labor market may adversely impact not only employment opportunities but also social opportunities that could lead to marriage. Marriage has a significant positive impact on family income, especially for women (Light 2004). If the obese are less likely to marry, their family incomes will be lower and they will be more likely to be poor and to qualify for public assistance. Sobal, Nicolopoulos, and Lee (1995) report that in a sample of 786 metropolitan secondary school students, the obese students felt stigmatized in the dating environment. Students (especially boys) also reported lower comfort with dating an overweight person. Similarly, surveys of college students confirm that they too prefer to date thinner partners (e.g., Sobal and Bursztyn 1998), and there is some evidence that physical appearance is more important in men's choice of partners than women's (e.g., Townsend and Wasserman 1997). While these studies and others (e.g., Reagan 1996) rely on local samples, the consistent findings of bias against dating heavier peers suggest that the obese, particularly women, generally face difficulty in this social arena.

Does the observed bias against dating heavier people lead to fewer dating opportunities for the obese? Several studies based on small, local samples do find an inverse association between body weight and dating activity (e.g., Harris 1990; Kallen and Doughty 1984; Sobal 1984). In one ethnographic study, a female respondent describes the social isolation she experienced in school and its long-term consequences:

> I went to very few school dances because nobody ever asked me to dance and I figured I may as well stay home. For my whole teen years I didn't go anywhere except school and home. . . . I was so envious of girls who were openly comfortable with boys. I was envious of the gangs of kids that hung out together after school. I've never been part of a group, I've always been on the outside looking in. Not surprisingly, I have very poor social skills. I just don't know how to interact with people. (Joanisse and Synnott 1999, 53)

Studies using large, nationally representative samples confirm the disadvantage of obesity in dating. Cawley (2001) uses data on children ages twelve to sixteen in the NLSY and the instrumental-variables estimation technique to test whether BMI causes dating outcomes. He estimates that being ten pounds heavier lowers the likelihood that a girl has ever dated by 10 percent, but that weight doesn't affect boys' dating activity. Cawley et al. (2006) use two nationally representative samples and find that higher body weight and obesity reduce the likelihood of initiating dating among both girls and boys. The available evidence indicates that obesity reduces dating opportunities and that the effect is more consistent for females.

Considerable evidence indicates that the dating barriers faced by the obese translate into reduced marriage rates. Fu and Goldman (1996) use the NLSY to estimate hazard models of the likelihood of first marriage among whites. They find evidence that obese individuals have lower age-specific marriage probabilities relative to individuals of recommended weight (BMI of 19 to 23) and that the impact is stronger for women than for men. Specifically, the authors report that obese women are 67 percent as likely to marry as women of recommended weight.

Three prospective analyses test whether BMI in an earlier period predicts later marital status. Gortmaker et al. (1993) examine whether obesity at ages sixteen to twenty-four is associated with marital status seven years later in the NLSY. They find that women who were initially overweight are 20 percent less likely to be married. Averett and Korenman (1996, 1999) use sister pairs in the NLSY to control for unobserved family and neighborhood factors and examine whether BMI at ages seventeen to twenty-four predicts marital status seven years later. They find that obese women, compared to their recommended-weight sister, face a 23 percent lower likelihood of marriage, and that if they do marry, their spouses earn 25 percent less. Furthermore, the effects of obesity on the marriage market appear to be more significant for white women than for black women (Averett and Korenman 1999). These authors attribute 50 to 90 percent of the family income differential between obese and recommended-weight women to the lower likelihood of marriage and lower spousal earnings.

Conley and Glauber (2005) use the PSID to determine whether BMI is related to marriage and labor market outcomes thirteen years later. The average age in their sample is higher than in the previous studies, and they employ both random-effects and sibling fixed-effects models to address possible reverse causality. They report evidence that obesity among unmarried women in the initial time period is associated with a 0.349 lower probability of marriage in the final period. Like the previous studies, they also find that higher initial BMI among women is associated with having a spouse with lower occupational prestige and lower earnings in the later period. By contrast, a higher initial BMI among men is associated with higher spousal earnings.

While marriage tends to increase family income, divorce has the opposite effect for women (Duncan and Hoffman 1985; Holden and Smock 1991). Researchers using both the NLSY and the PSID estimate that women's economic status falls roughly 30 percent during the year following divorce (Hoffman and Duncan 1988). If obese women are more likely to divorce, this would elevate their risk of poverty. Sobal, Rauschenbach, and Frongillo (1995) report mostly statistically insignificant correlations between body weight and marital happiness among married persons in the National Survey of Personal Health Practices and Consequences. Fu and Goldman (2000) estimate hazard models of divorce for whites in the NLSY and conclude that obesity is not associated with the risk of divorce for white women. However, Conley and Glauber (2005) find evidence in the PSID that BMI in 1986 is associated with a higher probability of divorce by 2001 among women, especially women over age thirty-five. Unfortunately, the available research doesn't allow us to draw a firm conclusion as to obesity's impact on divorce.

Summary and Recommendations

The literature produces considerable evidence that obesity poses a barrier to education and leads to health problems that reduce worker productivity and raise firms' health care costs. These effects contribute to reduced earnings among obese women, although the impact appears to be modest. Discrimination also reduces obese women's marriage prospects, which lowers their family income substantially. Consequently, there is good reason to think that obesity increases the risk of poverty, with the evidence being strongest for white women. It seems logical that a greater risk of poverty among obese women would lead to their increased participation in public assistance programs, but no one has directly tested whether BMI affects the probability of beginning a spell of public assistance. One study does find, however, that morbid obesity (BMI of 40 or higher) lengthens the duration of welfare spells (Cawley and Danziger 2005). So while the "Obesity Causes Public Assistance" model appears possible, it has not been empirically established.

Two general policy strategies follow from the "Obesity Causes Public Assistance" model: to reduce obesity, and to reduce the impoverishing effects of obesity. Policies often proposed to reduce obesity include the following:[10]

- Provide free or low-cost facilities for physical activity, such as safe bike paths and public parks.
- Encourage new communities to use designs that facilitate walking and bicycling and reduce the need to use cars.

- Improve physical and health education in public schools.
- Improve the nutritional quality of foods offered in public schools and use marketing techniques to encourage students to consume high-nutrient, low-calorie foods.
- Subsidize consumption of fresh fruits and vegetables and low-fat dairy products.
- Reduce production subsidies for high-calorie, low-nutrient foods (e.g., sweeteners and saturated fats).
- Expand education about healthy lifestyles (focusing on such aspects as nutrition, physical activity, and reduced television viewing) in schools and other public settings.
- Improve nutritional labeling for grocery items and require large chain restaurants to provide nutritional information for their meals.
- Limit advertising of high-calorie, low-nutrient foods to young children and incorporate media literacy curricula in public schools.

Because increasing the expenditure of calories can help reduce body fat (Sherry 2005), policy makers need to develop strategies to encourage physical activity. A prospective study of the Centers for Disease Control and Prevention's VERB campaign, a mass media effort to encourage children's physical activity, indicates that the program succeeded in raising awareness and encouraging physical activity (Huhman et al. 2005). Ecological models of physical activity predict that features of the built environment, such as parks, bike and walking paths, neighborhood density, and land use patterns, influence levels of physical activity. The available evidence consistently indicates that the built environment shapes our choices about leisure activities and transportation methods (Heath et al. 2006). The Safe Routes to School program, which is sponsored by the Department of Transportation, offers one strategy for increasing physical activity among children: encourage them to walk or ride their bicycles to school. Two evaluations of Safe Routes to School initiatives implemented in California offer preliminary evidence that government efforts to encourage active transportation to school can increase the frequency of walking and biking to school (Boarnet et al. 2005; Staunton et al. 2003). However, most studies are observational and cross-sectional. The few studies examining physical activity before and after an environmental intervention find some evidence of small to modest improvements in physical activity (Sallis et al. 1998). Changing our neighborhoods and cities in ways that facilitate physical activity may not only improve health but could also increase social connections and reduce air pollution. More research is needed to rigorously test the effectiveness of such interventions.

Some states have enacted laws aimed at increasing children's physical activity during the school day (National Conference of State Legislatures 2007). For example, in 2006, Tennessee enacted a bill requiring schools to provide a minimum of ninety minutes of physical activity per week during school. The available studies on the effectiveness of increased physical education (PE) courses produce mixed evidence. For example, Datar and Sturm (2004) find that in the nationally representative Early Childhood Longitudinal Study, increasing PE time between kindergarten and first grade is associated with lower BMI among initially heavy girls but is not associated with BMI among lighter girls or boys in general. They estimate that requiring at least five hours of PE per week for all kindergartners would lead to a 43 percent drop in first grade girls' overweight prevalence. However, two other large studies report no BMI reduction resulting from greater PE time. Cawley et al. (2007) examine a nationally representative sample of high school students and report that increasing PE time leads to greater physical activity among girls but not to reductions in their BMI. Kahn and the Task Force on Community Preventive Services (2002) review thirteen studies of PE's impact, ten of which focus on BMI as an outcome. They find no consistent evidence that PE time lowers BMI or the percentage of body fat, but they do find improvements in physical fitness.

The mixed evidence on PE courses in general and the findings that some specific programs can reduce BMI (Datar and Sturm 2004) suggest that schools should review their PE programs and explore possible improvements. In particular, raising PE requirements won't lead to greater physical activity unless enforcement is improved (Institute of Medicine 2006) and the amount of time actually spent being active in PE courses is substantial. Better enforcement of current requirements and increases in the amount of active time in PE classes could yield positive results. However, if students reduce their out-of-school physical activity when their in-school physical activity increases, their BMIs won't improve (Cawley et al. 2007).

Can policy change the way we eat? Schools can exert considerable influence over children's diets by determining what foods are available during the school day (Nestle 2002). In 2006 states enacted seventeen laws directed at school nutrition standards (National Conference of State Legislatures 2007). Wansink (2006) proposes that the marketing techniques used by food companies to encourage consumption of burgers and soda pop can also be used in school and other public institutions to promote the consumption of healthier foods. Historian Laura Lovett (2005) provides an example of how cartoon characters could help in this cause, describing how Popeye's popularity in the 1930s helped make spinach children's third favorite food. Public health researchers designing policies to improve nutritional intake should test the effectiveness of various food marketing strategies on nutritional intake.

Among the general population, lowering the relative price of low-calorie, nutrient-dense foods could help alter eating patterns in ways that reduce weight gain. French (2003) reviews evidence that lowering the price of healthy foods can increase their consumption in school settings and some studies suggest that giving coupons for farmers' markets to low-income adults encourages the purchase of fresh fruits and vegetables (Anderson et al. 2001; Kunkel et al. 2003). Whether these price interventions lower obesity prevalence has yet to be formally tested.

The last three highlighted recommendations involve consumer access to information. Accurate information is vital to the functioning of competitive markets, but it tends to be underprovided by the private sector (Cawley 2004a; Seiders and Petty 2004). Government can address this shortcoming. First, expanded offerings of nutrition education programs can help consumers make more informed nutrition choices. Several studies indicate that nutrition education programs can positively influence dietary practices, but again the impact on obesity has not been tested (Beaudoin et al. 2007; Burney and Haughton 2002; Leibtag and Mancino 2005; Montgomery and Willis 2006; Townsend et al. 2006). Expanded nutrition education in schools could help children develop healthy lifelong dietary patterns. Currently, only eleven states have adopted laws regarding nutrition education in their public schools (National Conference of State Legislatures 2007).

Second, government can increase the availability of nutrition information through food labeling requirements (Hayne et al. 2004). The evidence on the impact of current nutrition labeling laws is mixed. Two studies report that the Nutrition Labeling and Education Act (1990) improved only motivated consumers' ability to obtain and understand nutrition information (Balasubramanian and Cole 2002; Moorman 1996). Wansink (2006) argues that most consumers are too busy to bother with current nutrition labels and can't effectively appreciate what the calories listed mean for their weight. He suggests that labels may be more effective if they provide concrete information as to how a serving of the product would contribute to weight or how much physical activity would be needed to expend the calories in a serving (Wansink and

Huckabee 2005). Researchers should test this suggested label revision to determine the benefits and costs of such a change. An alternate explanation for the apparent low impact of current labeling laws is that consumers are exposed to billions of dollars of ads promoting high-calorie foods as delicious, convenient, and fun (Institute of Medicine 2005, 2006). The persuasive content of ads may overwhelm the nutrition information on food labels. In addition, the proportion of meals eaten out has been increasing (Guthrie et al. 2002; Stewart et al. 2004), and restaurants are not required to provide nutrition information for their meals.

Finally, government can regulate food information conveyed in commercial advertising that targets children, who are unable to make informed, rational decisions for themselves (Linn 2004; Linn and Novosat 2008; Schor 2004). Major review studies in the United States and Britain report evidence that television advertising influences children's food preferences, food requests, and consumption in favor of high-calorie, low-nutrient products (Coon and Tucker 2002; Hastings et al. 2003; McGinnis et al. 2006; Story and French 2004). In addition, several studies find moderate to strong evidence that viewing television ads is positively associated with children's consumption of frequently advertised foods as well as with their caloric intake (e.g., Coon and Tucker 2002; Wiecha et al. 2006) and their BMI (e.g., Boone et al. 2007; Jordan and Robinson 2008; Hu et al. 2003; World Health Organization/Food and Agricultural Organization of the United Nations 2003). Lastly, some studies suggest that television ads may confuse children as to which foods are good for them (e.g., Harrison 2005). While one review of studies on the relationship between television viewing, a proxy for ad exposure, and child adiposity concludes that the association is small (Marshall et al. 2004), others estimate that banning television promotions for fast food could reduce the number of obese children by 10 to 12 percent (Chou et al. 2005). We know little about the impact of other forms of advertising, especially Internet-based promotions and stealth marketing, despite children's increasing exposure to them (Dunnewind 2004; Linn and Novosat 2008; Ruskin 2005; Story and French 2004). In short, children see and hear a large number of promotional messages in a variety of formats that generally influence preferences and consumption in ways that encourage weight gain.

Whereas adults have the cognitive skills to recognize ads as persuasive and biased, children eight and younger do not. Furthermore, children under six years old cannot distinguish ads from program content. Consequently, the American Psychological Association's Task Force on

Advertising and Children concludes that "advertising targeting children below the ages of 7–8 years is inherently unfair because it capitalizes on younger children's inability to attribute persuasive intent to advertising" (APA 2004, 7). Similarly, the American Academy of Pediatrics (2006) concludes that advertising to young children is deceptive and exploitive. It strikes me as unethical to allow firms to take advantage of children's cognitive underdevelopment in general, and particularly in this case because children's health may well be compromised.

Yet restricting ads for high-calorie, low-nutrient foods raises First Amendment concerns. Courts have supported regulations on the "time, place, and manner" of commercial speech and seem more accepting when restrictions seek to protect children (Glantz 1997; Mello et al. 2006). Stringent restrictions on advertising tobacco products to children have been accepted; however, tobacco, unlike food, is an illegal product for minors. Restrictions on advertising legal products to children have occasionally been accepted—for example, the ban on advertising 1-900 numbers to children under twelve years old (Acs and Lyles 2007). An early attempt by the Federal Trade Commission to regulate advertising of high-sugar foods to children, the 1978 Children's Advertising Rulemaking (nicknamed KidVid), met with overwhelming protest from both the food industry and the public. Recent surveys suggest, however, that the public has grown more concerned about childhood obesity, and increasingly the support for restrictions on ads for high-calorie, low-nutrient foods is substantial (Evans et al. 2005; Harris Interactive 2007).

A Federal Trade Commission report (Holt et al. 2007) raises an important question: if we ban ads for high-calorie, low-nutrient foods, what ads will take their place? If we prohibit the advertising of foods high in sugar and fat to young children, and the promotion of sedentary leisure pursuits increases to fill the gap, children's weight may not improve. The federal government should reconsider the current free reign given to advertisers of high-calorie, low-nutrient foods and sedentary entertainment. Evaluations of current restrictions on advertising to children in other countries could help identify the most effective interventions (Caraher et al. 2006).

Because government is responsible for children's well-being while they attend public school, restrictions of advertisements on school property for products that contribute to an unhealthy lifestyle seem most urgent and acceptable. While not the major source of advertising exposure, commercial promotion in public schools has increased in the past decade (GAO 2000; Molnar 2003). Ads at school for high-calorie, low-nutrient foods and sedentary entertainments not only take advantage of compulsory attendance but may benefit from the appearance of approval by public authorities (APA 2004). Consequently the American Psychological Association's Task Force on Advertising to Children recommends "that advertising in all forms be restricted in school environments serving children 8 years and younger." Similarly, the American Public Health Association (2003) encourages government "to designate schools as food advertising–free zones, where children and adolescents can pursue learning free of commercial influences and pressures." Eliminating advertising will reduce school revenues, so government will need to compensate by raising funding levels. In addition, media literacy curricula in public schools should be explored as a means to improve children's ability to critically evaluate advertising (APA 2004).

Independent of the efforts to reduce obesity, what can be done to reduce its impoverishing effects? Policy options to consider include the following:

- Develop effective public service campaigns to regularly remind the public that discrimination on the basis of body weight is harmful and unacceptable.
- Strengthen anti-bullying and anti-teasing rules and enforcement in public schools and provide effective counseling for both victims and perpetrators.
- Establish nationwide laws prohibiting employment discrimination on the basis of body weight.

Psychological studies investigating strategies to reduce bias against the obese, such as education about the causes of obesity and the suffering that weight discrimination causes, produce mixed results (Teachman et al. 2003). The generally unflattering image of the overweight portrayed on television may contribute to general bias against heavy people (Greenberg et al. 2003), but any government proposals to change such portrayals would certainly face stiff opposition on the basis of free speech.

Could anti-discrimination laws improve labor market results for the obese? Roehling (1999) concludes that under the Rehabilitation Act of 1973 and the Americans with Disabilities Act of 1990, much of the discrimination against the obese in the labor market is legal. However, Carpenter (2006) compares the employment rates of obese and non-obese people ages eighteen to forty-five years old before and after 1993, when a federal appeals court first ruled that obesity can, in certain circumstances, be considered a disability under the 1973 and 1990 acts, and that firms cannot discriminate against people "perceived" to be obese (*Cook v. Rhode Island*, 1993). Carpenter finds that the employment rate of the obese, particularly women, rose soon after this ruling. At the state level, only Michigan specifically prohibits discrimination in employment on the basis of body weight (Roehling 1999; Carpenter 2006). Although no published studies investigate whether the obese fare better in Michigan's labor market than in other states as a result, one is in progress.

While the current evidence on the impact of anti-size discrimination laws on employment and earnings is sparse, studies of laws against discrimination on the basis of ethnicity and gender generally find that they have improved employment and earnings opportunities for blacks and women (e.g., Altonji and Blank 1999; Blau et al. 2006; Neumark and Stock 2001). Even if laws against weight-based discrimination don't produce large income gains, they might increase fairness and help diminish stigmatization of the obese in the long run.

It's unlikely, however, that policy can play a large role in improving the social acceptance of obese people, which will require a major cultural shift in attitudes and perceptions. Until then, obese people, particularly women, will continue to experience decreased family income via reduced marriage and employment opportunities, factors that could account for an important portion of the public assistance–obesity relationship.

4

The "Poverty Causes Both Public Assistance and Obesity" Hypothesis

This chapter examines the third model of the obesity–public assistance association: poverty simultaneously causes both obesity and public assistance participation. The pathway from poverty to public assistance is mechanical: to qualify a person must have sufficiently low income. For example, eligibility in the Food Stamps Program requires income (minus certain deductions) to be less than 130 percent of the poverty line. The causal flow from poverty to obesity is more complicated, with several possible routes. Furthermore, both past and current poverty may shape the risk of current obesity.

There are several pathways through which poverty could cause obesity (Figure 4.1). First, childhood poverty influences the quantity and quality of education, which in turn affects health, including body weight. Education directly affects health and BMI by determining exposure to and ability to process health information, and by providing skills to cope with problems and adapt to environmental changes. Education indirectly affects body weight by influencing job opportunities and access to material and social resources. Adults' education not only affects their own health but their children's health as well, which can then carry over into their adulthood.

Second, poverty could also cause obesity through its impact on food purchasing patterns. Calorie-dense foods tend to be cheaper and less perishable, so economizing on food purchases may lead the poor to choose more fats and sugars and fewer fresh fruits and vegetables. The price of food may vary by neighborhood economic status as well as by food type. Stores in lower-income areas may charge higher prices, because they are generally smaller and therefore don't enjoy economies of scale and because they often face less competition. Poverty may also limit physical access to healthy foods—that is, the grocery stores in poor neighborhoods may simply not offer many healthy foods for sale.

Third, poverty leads to food insecurity, which may encourage poor families to buy cheaper, calorie-dense foods. It might also alter food

Figure 4.1. The "Poverty Causes Both Public Assistance and Obesity" model

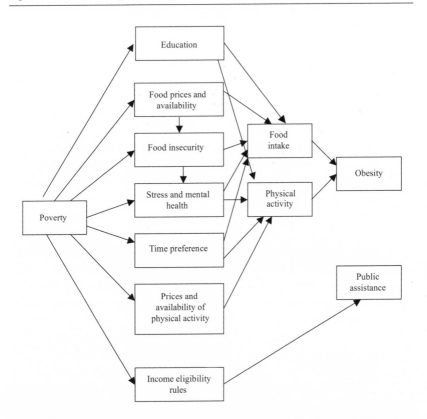

consumption patterns through both physiological and psychological processes. After experiencing food deprivation, people tend to consume large amounts of palatable foods, so episodes of food shortages can lead to eating patterns that encourage weight gain.

Fourth, poverty increases exposure to stressors, which can affect both health and eating patterns. Stress among the poor results from food insecurity and from the inability to acquire other basic necessities, such as adequate housing and medical care. Poverty may also prevent individuals from fully participating in their communities, creating a sense of isolation. Stress, especially when prolonged, can lead to depression and other mental illnesses, which in turn can affect food consumption and physical activity in ways that encourage weight gain. Stress can also alter the body's biochemistry in ways that promote the accumulation of fat.

A fifth possible pathway from poverty to obesity lies in the concept of time preference. Time preference refers to a person's willingness to delay current happiness in order to promote future happiness. Simply put, time preference refers to patience or the ability to delay gratification. Economist Irving Fisher argues that poverty "increases the want for immediate income even more than it increases the want for future income" (1961, 72). That is, poverty tends to increase the preference for current consumption over future consumption. If this hypothesis is correct, then poverty would encourage individuals to engage in behaviors that provide immediate satisfaction, such as consuming highly palatable, calorie-dense foods, rather than deny themselves such pleasures in the hopes of enjoying better health in the future.

Finally, poverty may limit access to physical activity. People with low incomes cannot afford to join health clubs or buy exercise equipment. Having a low income can also limit people to living in neighborhoods with few public parks and bike or walking paths. Such neighborhoods may also have greater safety concerns. The lack of opportunities for physical activity could encourage sedentary leisure pursuits, such as watching television. Television offers cheap entertainment in the safety of one's home, but requires little energy expenditure and promotes calorie consumption.

Research Context

The "Poverty Causes Both Public Assistance and Obesity" model is the most complex of the four models and involves the greatest number of disciplines. Economists, psychologists, and sociologists dominate the research on how poverty affects educational attainment, while epidemiologists focus on how poverty and educational attainment influence the risk of obesity. Economists, epidemiologists, and public health experts lead the work on how food prices vary by type and neighborhood socioeconomic status (SES). Nutritionists have produced the most work on the relationship between poverty, food insecurity, and BMI, while psychologists, psychiatrists, physicians, and physiologists lead the research on links between poverty, stress, mental health, and obesity. The small literature on poverty's connection to time preference and health comes largely from economists and psychologists, while exercise and sports physiologists and epidemiologists contribute heavily to the more extensive literature on the pathway from poverty and physical activity. A host of additional disciplines—including anthropology, criminology, environmental studies, geography, history, management, marketing, and urban studies—make contributions throughout.

A common problem in studying the connections between poverty and obesity involves disentangling the impacts of individual characteristics from those of neighborhood characteristics: to what extent does a person's own poverty influence BMI independent of the deprivation of the neighborhood in which they live? Another problem for those investigating the impact of neighborhood characteristics on residents' BMI is potential self-selection. Perhaps people living in neighborhoods with parks are more physically active because of their proximity to facilities for physical activity, or perhaps they chose to live in a neighborhood with such facilities because they are interested in being physically active. While a valid concern, I suspect this issue is less significant when it comes to low-income Americans. Their lack of resources restricts their choice of neighborhoods, so even if a poor person is interested in being physically active or having easy access to a supermarket, she may not be able to afford to live in neighborhoods with those amenities.

Researchers from all disciplines also struggle with measurement issues. How do we measure time preference or define a neighborhood? How can we collect reliable data on the prices and availability of food items and facilities for physical activity across large geographical areas? Can we afford to measure body weight and physical activity directly, or must we rely on self-reports, which no doubt contain errors?

In addition to measurement problems, researchers often can't conduct random experiments to determine causal flows. For example, we can't randomly assign persons into poverty and then observe their educational and BMI outcomes. Sometimes, however, researchers can vary certain parameters of income support programs to see whether doing so influences education and health. While we can't randomly assign individuals into high- versus low-stress lifestyles to see how their BMI changes, we can put individuals in temporarily stressful situations, such as public speaking, and then observe their subsequent food choices immediately afterward. More often than not, studying how poverty influences food intake, physical activity, and obesity status necessarily relies on observational studies rather than random experiments.

Empirical Evidence

Many cross-sectional studies report higher obesity prevalence among the poor (e.g., Wardle et al. 2002), and several longitudinal studies find that low childhood SES predicts higher BMI and a greater risk of obesity later in life (Oliver and Hayes 2008; Poulton et al. 2002; Power et al. 2003). Furthermore, Baltrus et al. (2005) find in a thirty-four-year panel study that the association between adult weight gain and ethnicity is largely accounted for by chronic poverty. The task now is to explore why poverty and BMI are linked by examining each of the six possible pathways from poverty to obesity.

Poverty's Impact on Education

An extensive literature covering developmental psychology, sociology, education, and economics produces consistent evidence that childhood poverty correlates with lower education attainment (e.g., Brooks-Gunn and Duncan 1997; Knitzer 2007). Greater family income enables parents to acquire things that are important to the production of cognitive development, such as nutritious foods, books, and good schools, and improves family interactions and psychological functioning by reducing the stress associated with material hardship. Evans (2004) reviews the literature on the many disadvantages poor children face in terms of their psychosocial and physical environments, noting that they generally enjoy less social support, attend lower-quality schools, and endure more dangerous environments.

Reviews of longitudinal studies present a consensus that low parental income, especially in early childhood, is related to children's reduced cognitive development and educational achievement (Duncan 2005; Duncan and Brooks-Gunn 1997). These studies include controls for parental education and other family characteristics, but they may not adequately control for parental characteristics that influence both income and educational attainment (e.g., motivation). Duncan, Yeung, et al. (1998) adjust for parental and family characteristics by examining children within a single family, exploiting variation in family income over time to see how income levels affect different children at the same age. They again find that lower family income adversely influences schooling, strengthening the case that income is causal.

Duncan (2005) reviews studies based on natural and random experiments to evaluate income policies and concludes that childhood poverty harms children's educational performance, with the greatest impacts occurring in early childhood when children's brains are still being "wired." Two likely avenues through which poverty influences educational outcomes are poor nutrition and elevated stress, both of which can impair cognitive, emotional, and social development (Jyoti et al. 2005; Knitzer 2007; Murphy et al. 1998; National Research Council and Institute of Medicine 2000; Winicki and Jemison 2003).

The evidence that childhood poverty leads to lower educational attainment is strong, and less education is associated with more obesity, especially in women. When we look at obesity prevalence by gender and education level in the National Health and Nutrition Examination Survey (NHANES) for 1992–2000, we see that among women, the rate of obesity consistently falls with each successive increase in educational attainment (Figure 4.2). McDonough et al. (1997) find that this educational gradient in obesity persists even when they control for income. However, the education gradient in obesity is more consistent among white than black women (Zhang and Wang 2004).

We also observe educational gradients in levels of physical activity (Macera et al. 2005), the consumption of fruits and vegetables (Guthrie et al. 2005), and the consumption of saturated fats (Variyam 2003) that are consistent with the variation in obesity across education levels. Leonetti et al. (1995) produce an exception to the generally observed inverse relationship between education and BMI. They examine Japanese-American men (mean age of sixty-one) and find that BMI is not negatively associated with their educational attainment, although the amount of abdominal fat is.

Not only is a person's education level associated with BMI, but parental education matters as well. Three longitudinal studies examine whether parents' educational attainment predicts a child's future obesity status. Goodman et al. (2003) examine the nationally representative National Longitudinal Study of Adolescent Health and find that parental

Figure 4.2. Obesity prevalence by gender and education, 1999–2000

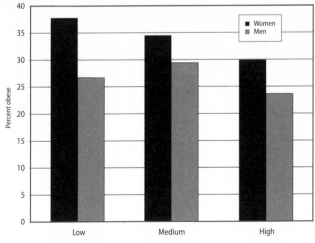

Source: Zhang and Wang 2004.

education has a greater association with the probability of teen obesity than does income. However, their analysis doesn't adjust for possible confounders. Classen and Hokayem (2005) use the National Longitudinal Survey of Youth (NLSY) and report that having a mother with at least some college education at age eight or younger predicts a lower probability of obesity when the child exceeds eight years in age. Greenlund et al. (1996) report that in the Coronary Artery Risk Development in Young Adults (CARDIA) data, a longitudinal sample of individuals ages eighteen to thirty at baseline from four large U.S. cities, fathers' education predicts the seven-year change in BMI among white women, but not among black women or men of either ethnicity. Overall, the literature suggests that parents' educational attainment is inversely associated with obesity, especially among white children.

Why would education and the risk of obesity be inversely related? Education could affect obesity directly by influencing an individual's ability to cope with stressors and to process health information. In economists' lingo, more education increases human capital and improves the efficiency of health production. Sociologists John Mirowsky and Catherine E. Ross (2003) refer to the increased coping skills conferred by education as "learned effectiveness." Grzywacz et al. (2004) analyze the National Study of Daily Experience ($n = 1,031$) to estimate the associations between daily stress and general health. They report that while the less educated experience fewer daily hassles, the stressors they experience tend to be more severe and the health effects associated with stressors are greater. Two studies of the impact of employment status on mental health find that those with higher education report fewer symptoms of depression (Gyamfi et al. 2001; Rodriguez et al. 2001). These results are consistent with the notion that education improves the ability to cope with problems, reducing the adverse health impacts of stress.

Researchers also find that education influences health knowledge and responses to health information. For example, Wardle et al. (2000) find that part of the impact of SES (measured by education and occupation) on nutritional intake arises from variation in nutritional knowledge. Specifically, people with better nutritional knowledge tend to eat more fruits and vegetables and are more likely to be higher in the socioeconomic distribution. However, Nayga (2001) reports that in the 1994 Diet and Health Knowledge Survey, educational attainment is significantly and negatively associated with the likelihood of adult obesity even when the analysis controls for health knowledge. This suggests that education's impact is not limited to the current stock of health knowledge. Researchers have also found evidence that more-educated people respond to health information campaigns more rapidly (e.g., Wardle et al. 2001) and exhibit greater compliance to complex, long-term medical regimes than do the less educated (Goldman and Smith 2002). These studies suggest that poverty affects access to, and the ability to process and act on, health information.

Education could indirectly affect BMI by influencing access to material and social resources and reducing exposure to risk factors at home and on the job (Ross and Wu 1995). It is also possible, however, that factors such as the ability the delay gratification, or time preference, influence both the level of education acquired and health behaviors (Farrell and Fuchs 1982).

In summary, many studies support the notion that both individual and parental education influences general health (e.g., Marmot 2000; Lleras-Muney 2005), and the available longitudinal analyses of education and obesity support the hypothesis that greater educational attainment protects against obesity. Lower levels of education observed among the poor likely contribute to their greater prevalence of obesity. This association means there may well be a health bonus generated by policies that improve access to education and encourage the completion of high school and the pursuit of college.

Poverty's Impact on Food Prices and Availability

Price is a critical factor in the decision to buy any product, and food is no exception. In a nationally representative sample of nearly three thousand adults, Glanz et al. (1998) find that cost is the second most important factor in food choice (taste is first). Thus, variations in price across food types will likely influence what people eat and, consequently, their nutrition intake and BMI.

Do food price trends help explain the rise in American obesity, especially among the poor? Putnam et al. (2002) report that while the Consumer Price Index (CPI) for fresh fruits and vegetables rose by 118 percent from 1985 to 2000, the CPI for "fats and oils" and "sugars and sweets" rose by only 35 percent and 46 percent, respectively, making these calorie-dense foods relatively cheaper. A growing body of literature finds that cheaper foods do indeed contain more calories on average (Bradbard et al. 1997; Darmon et al. 2004; Drewnowski 2004; Drewnowski and Darmon 2005; Drewnowski, Darmon, and Briend 2004; Maillot et al. 2007). For example, Drewnowski and Spector (2004) report that cookies and potato chips provide 1,200 kilocalories per dollar, whereas fresh carrots provide only 250 kilocalories per dollar. In addition, two studies created "healthy food baskets" containing whole-grain, low-fat, and low-sodium substitutes for some of the foods included in the USDA's Thrifty Food Plan, the national standard set of food products that meets certain dietary requirements at low cost, and found that the healthy food baskets cost 18 to 23 percent more (Jetter and Cassady 2006; Neault et al. 2005).

Microeconomic theory predicts that when relative prices change, consumers will substitute away from relatively more expensive goods toward relatively cheaper goods, so we would expect greater consumption of calorie-dense foods in response to these price trends. Indeed, Putnam et al. (2002) find that per capita consumption of added fats rose by 38 percent from 1970 to 2000 and the consumption of added sugars increased by 20 percent. Since the poor spend a greater share of their income on food (Rogers and Gray 1994; Tan 2000), they may be more sensitive to food prices—that is, the shift in relative prices might influence their food-buying behavior more than that of middle- and upper-income individuals. Some evidence supports this hypothesis; for example, Glanz et al. (1998) report that the impact of cost on food decisions is greater among those with low incomes than it is among the more affluent.

In ethnographic studies the poor often report that it is more expensive to eat diets recommended by health professionals. A public housing resident in the Memphis area explains, "You eat the cheapest thing there is. You eat rice, you eat potatoes, you eat filling stuff" (Biggs 2004). The primary concern among the poor is often not nutrition; it is avoiding the physical and psychological discomforts of hunger (Basiotis et al. 1998). Even when the poor are well aware of what constitutes a healthy diet, they often simply cannot afford to eat nutritious meals on a regular basis. A diabetic resident of a poor Detroit neighborhood states, "The diet itself requires you to spend more money than you would normally because it is easier to buy beans and rice but we can't; we need to buy vegetables" (Kieffer et al. 2004, S1-31).

Participants in the Food Stamp Challenge, a program in which affluent individuals, often policy makers, pledge to eat for one week on the Food Stamp Program's average benefit of three dollars a day, report similar experiences. Oregon food critic Ken Hoyt thought he was gaining weight "because of the high carbs."[1] Representative Barbara Lee (D-Oakland) reported, "I was struck by how hard it is to eat in a healthy manner on a tight budget. I had to put the apples back because they were too expensive. Whole wheat tortillas were twice as expensive as flour" (2007). I too recently encountered the influence of food prices, but not in a poverty setting. During a stay in a well-respected, financially successful hospital, I ordered a fresh fruit plate for lunch and was told it was no longer offered, but I could have a cup of canned fruit. When I inquired what motivated the change, the hospital food worker immediately responded that fresh fruit was too expensive.

Quantitative studies of food intake by income level generally confirm that as we move down the income distribution, consumption of fruits and vegetables, especially the non-starchy kinds, declines (e.g., Edmonds et al. 2001; Lin 2005; Subar et al. 1992). Krebs-Smith et al. (1995) find this pattern in the Continuing Survey of Food Intake by Individuals (CSFII), and Lutz et al. (1993) in the USDA's Nationwide Food Consumption Surveys (NFCS), both large, nationally representative samples.

Studies of purchasing patterns among low-income Americans also produce evidence consistent with the hypothesized association between income and the types of foods consumed. Studies generally find that low-income households save money by buying fewer fruits, vegetables, and dairy products and instead buying more low-quality cuts of meat and calorie-dense carbohydrates (Adelaja and Nayga 1997; Curtis and McClellan 1995; Leibtag and Kaufman 2003). Budget simulations also indicate that lower income exerts pressure to eat cheaper, calorie-dense, low-nutrient foods. For example, three studies (Darmon, Ferguson, and Briend 2002, 2003; Darmon, Briend, and Drewnowski 2004) use survey data from Paris and linear programming simulations to explore the impact of declining income on food choices, constraining choices to be similar to local norms and to meet palatability standards. They find that as the budget constraint grows tighter, the proportion of calories that comes from cereals and added fats increases and the proportion from fruits and vegetables decreases.

Overall, the literature presents a consensus that economic constraints are an important determinant of diet, with the poor rationally responding by consuming more calorie-dense foods. Poverty appears to significantly influence food options in ways that encourage weight gain by constraining food budgets. It's not surprising then that in the CSFII, lower-income individuals and people who report that price is very important to food-purchasing decisions also tend to exhibit lower scores on the Healthy Eating Index (Huston and Finke 2003). The impact of price on poor people's food choices may be exacerbated by its impact on housing options. As writer Barbara Ehrenreich (2001) experienced in her investigation of low-wage workers, the housing that poor people can afford often lacks adequate cooking facilities—for example, they might have hot plates instead of stoves.

While many researchers have studied the relationship between food prices and quality and between income and food choices, few have investigated whether the resulting consumption patterns actually affect obesity. Sturm and Datar (2005) match anthropometric data on young children from three years of the Early Childhood Longitudinal Study with metropolitan-level data on food prices. They find that higher prices for fruits and vegetables are associated with greater BMI gain from kindergarten to third grade. Controlling for family income, ethnicity, maternal education, and birth weight, each unit increase in the fruit and vegetable price index corresponds to a rise in BMI of 0.11 units, on average. While this study is unique in estimating a link between food prices and childhood BMI, it does not incorporate actual food consumption data, so we can't draw firm conclusions about causal patterns, but this result is suggestive.

Food prices can vary by geographic location as well as by food type. Early research on whether food prices are higher in poor neighborhoods initially produced mixed results (e.g., Alcaly and Klevorick 1971; Kunreuther 1973). More recent research generally finds that food prices are higher in lower-income neighborhoods. For example, three studies using small, local samples report higher mean food prices in low-income areas (Alwitt and Donley 1997; Chung and Myers 1999; Jetter and Cassady 2006). Finke et al. (1997), using the 1987–1988 NFCS, report that in urban areas the poor face higher average food prices than middle- and high-income consumers. In suburban areas, however, food prices paid by high- and low-income consumers are about the same.

Several studies present evidence that the poor tend to pay more for groceries because they are concentrated in urban and rural areas, where food prices are generally higher (Frankel and Gould 2001; Kaufman et al. 1997; Troutt 1993). Prices tend to be higher in these areas because they are served by smaller stores rather than supermarkets and bulk discounters, which concentrate in the suburbs (Eisenhauer 2001; Moore and Diez Roux 2006; Sloane et al. 2003). In a survey of 132 different products across more than three thousand grocery stores, Fellowes (2006) finds that 67 percent of the items cost more in stores of less than ten thousand square feet than they do in larger facilities. MacDonald and Nelson (1991) report that in a survey of 322 supermarkets in ten large U.S. cities, a defined market basket of groceries cost 4 percent less in suburban areas than in central city stores. Similarly, Kaufman et al. (1997), using the nationwide Census of Retail Trade, estimate that supermarkets offer food prices 10 percent lower than other types of stores. Small grocers may charge more on average because they don't enjoy economies of scale in purchasing and distribution and often face fewer competitive pressures. Morland, Wing, Diez Roux, and Poole (2002) note that households in poorer areas and areas with a higher proportion of blacks have significantly reduced access to private transportation, limiting their ability to shop around. Higher prices in neighborhood markets could exacerbate the pressure that the poor feel to cut food costs by consuming cheaper, calorie-dense foods.

Not all studies conclude that the poor pay higher prices for food. Hayes (2000) examines food prices in New York City and doesn't find any statistically significant differences across neighborhood SES. He does, however, observe that in low-income areas refrigeration standards are less frequently met and that the prices of half of the nonperishable items he surveyed were higher in poorer areas. Ohls et al. (1999) conclude from their analysis of the National Food Stamp Program Survey that most low-income citizens have good access to food, noting that 61 percent of participants and 66 percent of eligible nonparticipants shop in neighborhood stores. However, 38 percent of participants and 35 percent of eligible nonparticipants don't shop in their own neighborhoods, and one of the top three reasons given is "high prices." Overall, the evidence suggests that in many low-income areas, residents must contend with higher grocery prices.

Price isn't the only factor that influences what food people buy. Anthropologists explain that eating is more than just consuming sufficient calories to maintain our existence; it has cultural and psychological meanings as well. Fitchen (1988) notes that the cost pressure that leads the poor to consume calorie-dense foods is reinforced by cultural pressures to eat the socially dominant type of food, which is increasingly food that is high in sugar and fats. She argues that "low-income people express their membership [in mainstream America] in the same food choices that characterize the rest of the population" (323). Thus, she warns against attributing the consumption of calorie-dense foods among the poor to a lack of nutritional understanding or bad judgment: they prefer the same foods as the rest of society but face additional cost pressures to buy these foods.

In addition to often facing higher food prices, the poor frequently have less physical access to nutritious food. For example, one participant in a Detroit focus group explains that "you've got to go out to the suburbs now to get some decent food. And therefore, it's not available to us in this community. By the time you get to that store and get some fresh fruits and vegetables, you're going to pass about 30 fast food joints and about 100 liquor stores" (Kieffer et al. 2004, S1-31). My personal vantage point living between affluent Ann Arbor to the west and the poorer city of Ypsilanti to the east also suggests that healthy foods are less accessible in lower income areas. A 2005 study of the food environment of Ypsilanti found only six grocery stores among the thirty-seven food stores in the city, and of those six, only two were centrally located (Bacolor et al. 2007). The one supermarket was located on the southeast corner of the city, across the interstate highway from where the vast majority of residents live. Seventy-three percent of the city's food stores were convenience stores selling mostly snacks and alcohol. By contrast, within just three miles west of my house in Ann Arbor, there are six large chain supermarkets stores and an array of specialty grocers.

Quantitative research on the availability of healthy food products by neighborhood income status frequently confirms the pattern suggested by qualitative analyses. Studies using city-level data report that residents of low socioeconomic areas face reduced access to grocery stores (e.g., Gallagher 2006), low-fat dairy products (Gordon et al. 2007; New York Department of Health and Hygiene 2006; Sloane et al. 2003; Wechsler et al. 1995), fresh produce (Bacolor et al. 2007; Gordon et al. 2007; Horowitz et al. 2004; Latham and Moffat 2007; New York Department of Health and Hygiene 2006; Sloane et al. 2003), and healthy choices at restaurants (Lewis et al. 2005). Two studies using data from multiple states also find that poor neighborhoods have less access to healthy foods (Moore and Diez Roux 2006; Morland, Wing, Diez Roux, and Poole 2002). National Food Stamp Program Survey respondents who did not grocery shop in their own neighborhoods frequently cited limited food selection as the reason why (Ohls et al. 1999). The term "food desert" has been used to describe poor neighborhoods lacking regular access to healthy foods (Furey et al. 2001).

Why do stores in poor neighborhoods tend to carry fewer healthy foods? Like price differentials by neighborhood SES, food availability is related to the spatial distribution of store types, small independent grocers versus chain supermarkets. Fellowes (2006) reports that grocery stores in low-income areas have significantly less square footage than those in wealthier areas, which may increase reliance on processed, non-perishable products rather than fresh produce. Are smaller stores less able to properly handle fresh produce, or are they merely responding to their customers' preferences, stocking the items their patrons buy most frequently? Researchers have not yet answered this question.

While small neighborhood stores may charge higher prices and offer fewer healthy foods, they are convenient. These stores are located close by so they don't require owning a car or taking a cab or bus, all of which increase the cost of shopping. And unlike chain supermarkets, local grocery store owners are often willing to extend credit based on social connections and familiarity, which is vital toward the end of the month when financial resources are often low (Kaufman and Karpati 2007).

The literature reviewed suggests that poor people often have less physical access to healthy foods, but what about their access to less-nutritious foods? Gaming scholar Ian Bogost (2005) notes that the perception that restaurants in low-income areas offer predominantly calorie-dense fast foods is so pervasive that the designers of the popular game *Grand Theft Auto: San Andreas* programmed in only restaurants based on actual fast food outlets. Five studies examining the distribution of fast food restaurants by neighborhood SES at the city level support this perception. Reidpath et al. (2002) find that the density of fast food establishments rises as SES falls in Melbourne, Australia. Block et al. (2004) report that New Orleans neighborhoods with larger black populations have more than twice the number of fast food restaurants found in mostly white areas. Kipke et al. (2007) study East Los Angeles and find that nearly half of all restaurants offer fast food, and that the majority of those are within walking distance of a school. By contrast, only four grocery stores offering fruits and vegetables were located close to schools. Similarly, Lewis et al. (2005) find that in South Los Angeles poorer neighborhoods have more fast food outlets than wealthier areas. Finally, Powell, Auld, et al. (2007) analyze nationwide data on restaurant availability by ZIP code. They report that in urban areas, the proportion of restaurants that serve fast food is higher where SES is lower. A study in Glasgow, Scotland, presents an exception to the general finding that fast food is more available in lower-income neighborhoods (Macintyre et al. 2005). Overall, however, the evidence suggests that living in a poor neighborhood in the United States increases exposure to fast foods, which tend to be high in calories.

The availability of both healthy and less-nutritious foods offered in public schools may also vary by neighborhood SES. Schools in low-income areas generally have fewer resources and may face greater financial pressures to enter contracts with soft drink bottlers and fast food chains. Research finds that greater consumption of non-diet soft drinks and fast food contribute to weight gain (Malik et al. 2006; Pereira et al. 2005; Vartanian et al. 2007). Two studies based on the nationally representative Monitoring the Future and Youth, Education, and Society surveys examine whether the availability of low-calorie, high-nutrient foods varies by school SES, as measured by average parental educational attainment. Delva et al. (2007) report that in general, "less-healthy" foods are more available than "more-healthy" foods in our public schools. Furthermore, they find evidence that healthier snacks are more available in schools with a higher SES. Johnston et al. (2007) report an inverse relationship between high school SES and the proportion of students whose school and school district have contracted with a soft drink company. While they find no evidence that access to soft drinks in vending machines throughout the school day varies by school SES, the results show that students in wealthier schools do have greater access to diet sodas and 100 percent vegetable and fruit juices in cafeterias at lunchtime. Lastly, this study finds that in middle schools, administrators are more likely to report initiatives to promote healthy diets in schools with a higher SES. These studies support the hypothesis that students attending schools in disadvantaged areas may experience more food promotions and have less access to high-nutrient, low-calorie foods on campus.

In sum, the evidence points to reduced access to high-nutrient, low-calorie foods and greater exposure to high-calorie, low-nutrient foods in low-income neighborhoods. This finding is consistent with historian Sidney Mintz's hypothesis (1985) that sugar and other "drug foods" offer a cheap method for maintaining an economy's low-skilled workforce.

The differences in food prices and availability by area SES could affect nutritional intake and BMI of the poor, and of public assistance participants in particular, because a larger proportion reside in central cities than in the suburbs (Danziger 2002; Fisher and Weber 2002). A study of black women in Detroit reports that those with lower incomes are less likely to shop at supermarkets and consume fewer fruits and vegetables than those with higher incomes (Zenk et al. 2005). A study of pregnant lower- and middle-class women in North Carolina reports that living more than four miles from a supermarket is associated with poorer nutritional intake (Laraia et al. 2004). Cheadle et al. (1991) analyze diets in twelve cities, and Morland, Wing, and Diez Roux (2002) use the Atherosclerosis Risk in Communities (ARIC) data, which covers four states, and both groups find evidence that the availability of supermarkets and healthy foods is positively associated with the intake of fruits and vegetables. The latter study estimates that each additional supermarket in a census tract is associated with a 32 percent increase in fruit and vegetable consumption among blacks. Diez Roux et al. (1999), also using ARIC data, report that the intake of fruits, vegetables, and fish is lower in low-income neighborhoods, but the association between nutrient consumption and area SES evaporates when the analysis controls for individual income. In sum, three of the five studies find an inverse association between neighborhood SES and the consumption of fresh produce, while the other two indicate that individual poverty, rather than area poverty, diminishes consumption of healthy foods.

Do the differences in food price, availability, and intake by neighborhood income level contribute to higher obesity rates among the poor? Few studies address this important question. Burdette and Whitaker (2004) examine distance to fast food outlets in a sample of 7,020 low-income five year olds in Cincinnati. After controlling for household income, ethnicity, and gender, they find no evidence that fast food proximity is associated with the likelihood of a child being overweight. However, O'Malley et al. (2007) find that among middle and high school students in the nationally representative Monitoring the Future (MTF) sample that lower SES schools exhibit higher average self-reported BMI and greater overweight prevalence. This suggests that school characteristics, such as food advertising and availability, exert some influence on adolescent BMI. Powell, Chaloupka, and Bao (2007) also analyze the MTF sample and find that the more chain supermarkets and the fewer convenience stores there are in a ZIP code, the lower adolescent BMI and risk of obesity are. The estimated impact of the number of convenience stores on teen BMI drops considerably when the analysis controls for area income, suggesting that these food outlets are more concentrated in lower-income neighborhoods. The evidence on the association between area food availability and children's BMI is somewhat mixed, but the studies based on nationally representative data support the hypothesis that among adolescents, food availability by area SES can influence the risk of excess weight.

Is adult BMI influenced by neighborhood food accessibility? Two studies shed some light on this question. Adults living in the Chicago neighborhoods with the worst access to grocery stores, but good access to fast food, exhibit higher BMIs and a greater prevalence of diabetes (Gallagher 2006). Furthermore, Morland et al. (2006) find that in the ARIC, the number of supermarkets is inversely associated with adult obesity while the number of convenience stores is positively associated. These findings suggest that availability of food types by area SES can influence the risk of obesity among adults.

The extant literature suggests that living in poor neighborhoods in the United States generally means having less access to healthy foods and greater exposure to high-calorie foods. This supports the idea of "deprivation amplification": neighborhood characteristics amplify individual risk factors for obesity (Cummins and Macintyre 2005). There is some evidence that this differential access helps explain part of the association between poverty and obesity. However, this literature is relatively new and faces some methodological constraints. It is hard to separate individual from neighborhood characteristics that could influence obesity, and the available data are cross-sectional, limiting inference about causality.

Overall, there is good reason to think that people living in poorer areas face somewhat higher grocery prices and have less physical access to healthy foods and greater access to fast foods. The migration of supermarkets to the suburbs and the development of suburban discount outlets have left central cities and rural areas with fewer and smaller grocery stores. These stores tend to charge higher prices and have fewer healthy foods available. The agricultural trend from raising a variety of produce to growing a single commodity crop, like corn, further reduces rural access to fresh fruits and vegetables (Pollan 2006). Reduced consumption of such foods in favor of cheaper, high-calorie, easily accessible foods may be contributing to obesity among the urban and rural poor.

Poverty's Impact on Food Insecurity

Food insecurity is commonly defined as "limited or uncertain availability of nutritionally adequate and safe food or uncertain ability to acquire acceptable foods in socially acceptable ways," while hunger is characterized by "the uneasy or painful sensation caused by lack of food" (Jones 2004, 83). Researchers measure these concepts using a food security questionnaire, such as the USDA Household Food Security Scale. Nord et al. (2006) report that based on the nationally representative Current Population Survey, the prevalence of food insecurity decreases as the poverty-income ratio (that is, the ratio of family income to the official poverty line) increases (Figure 4.3). Furthermore, Rose et al. (1998) analyze the CSFII and the 1992 Survey of Income and Program Participation and find that controlling for basic demographic factors, the poor are nearly four times more likely to be food insufficient than the nonpoor.[2] While not all poor people report food insecurity, there is no doubt that poverty can cause food insecurity (FRAC 2005; Rose 1999).

Researchers offer two basic reasons why food insecurity could lead to obesity (Center on Hunger and Poverty 2002; FRAC 2005). First, episodic food deprivation is theorized to lead to disordered eating, which encourages weight gain. The idea is that food-insecure individuals experience periods of food deprivation followed by periods of bingeing when food becomes available. Several studies find this pattern in food consumption (e.g., Fisher and Birch 1999; Polivy 1996). Such "feasting" following periods of "famine" may result from both psychological and biological pressures. Second, food-insecure families may sub-

Figure 4.3. Food insecurity prevalence by poverty-income ratio, 2005

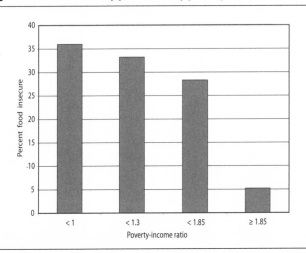

Source: Nord et al. 2006.

Note: In this data, a ratio of <1 indicates official poverty, <1.3 indicates eligibility for the Food Stamp Program, and <1.85 indicates being "near poor."

stitute cheaper, high-calorie, low-nutrient foods to prevent hunger as their money dwindles (Drewnowski and Spector 2004; Darmon et al. 2004).

How does food insecurity affect eating patterns? In qualitative studies, poor mothers often report skipping meals to make sure their children have enough to eat, sometimes followed by bingeing when food becomes available (McIntyre et al. 2003; Olson 2005). For example, one study participant in rural New York explained, "Cause I normally don't eat, I let the kids eat, and then I go for two days without eating and then when I do eat it's big meals that I eat" (Bove and Olson 2006, 67). Two quantitative studies of a small sample of rural white women in New York examine whether food insecurity is associated with eating disorders. Kendall et al. (1996) report increasing scores on a disordered eating scale as food insecurity grows more severe, while Frongillo et al. (1997) present evidence that part of the impact of food insecurity on BMI is mediated by eating disorders. Replicating these results using a larger, nationally representative sample would tell us whether the observed association between food insecurity and disturbed eating patterns holds in general.

While the evidence on food insecurity and eating disorders is presently sparse, more studies examine the association between food insecurity and nutritional intake. Several large cross-sectional studies find that food-insecure children and adults consume less of certain important nutrients than those in food-secure households (Bhattacharya et al. 2004c; Cristofar and Basiotis 1992; Dixon et al. 2001; Rose 1999; Skalicky et al. 2006). However, Bhattacharya et al. (2004c) find no association in the NHANES-III between children's food insecurity and nutrition; instead, they find that poverty predicts poor nutrition in preschool children. Among adults the evidence suggests that food insecurity is associated with reduced consumption of fruits and vegetables; however, there is no evidence that food-insecure adults consume significantly more fat and sugar (Basiotis 2002; Townsend et al. 2001). In short, food insecurity is associated with adults' poorer nutrition and perhaps with children's, but given the absence of relevant longitudinal data we can't confirm whether the relationship is causal.

Could a relationship between food insecurity, nutritional intake, and eating patterns affect the likelihood of obesity? Jones (2004) reviews the literature on food insecurity and obesity among both children and adults. The four childhood studies reviewed using nationally representative data produce mixed results. Alaimo et al. (2001), using the NHANES-III, and Casey et al. (2001), using the CSFII, both report evidence that some food-insecure or food-insufficient children face a higher risk of being overweight. By contrast, Bhattacharya and Currie (2004) find little association between food security status and child weight status in the NHANES-III, and Jones et al. (2003) report that in the Panel Study of Income Dynamics (PSID) the likelihood of overweight is actually lower among low-income, food-insecure children.

Five other studies in addition to those reviewed by Jones use nationally representative data from the United States to examine the relationship between food insecurity and childhood weight, and a sixth study uses data from Canada. Winicki and Jemison (2003) use data from one wave of the Early Childhood Longitudinal Study—Kindergarten Cohort (ECLS-K) and find no relationship between food insecurity and children's BMI. Bhattacharya et al. (2004c) use the NHANES-III (1988–1994) to examine three age groups. Controlling for poverty and other sociodemographic variables, they find no evidence that food insecurity is associated with obesity among children ages two to five and twelve to seventeen. Among children ages six to eleven, they report that those who are food insecure are less likely to carry excess weight. Casey et al. (2006) examines the relationship between food insecurity and the weight status of children ages three to seventeen years in a more recent wave of the NHANES (1999–2000). They find that food insecurity is positively associated with the probability of being overweight among children ages twelve to seventeen, girls, whites, those living in households below the poverty line, and those in households with income four times the poverty line.

Three longitudinal studies offer stronger evidence regarding whether food insecurity causes obesity. Rose and Bodor (2006) use two waves of the ECLS-K and a large set of control variables in their logistic regressions. They find that food insecurity in 1999 predicts a lower probability of overweight one year later. Furthermore, food-insecure children in 1999 were less likely to experience large weight gains by 2000 than food-secure children. Jyoti et al. (2005) examine a longer time span, comparing measures from kindergarten (1999) with those from third grade (2002), and test three types of model specifications: lagged, dynamic, and difference. The lagged model indicates that food insecurity in kindergarten is positively associated with girls' later BMI, with coefficients ranging from 0.38 to 0.50 BMI units. The dynamic model finds that persistently food-insecure girls exhibit third grade BMIs that are, on average, half a unit higher than persistently food-secure girls. In the difference model, becoming food insecure is associated with greater BMI gains among boys, but not girls. Dubois et al. (2006) offer evidence from the Longitudinal Study of Child Development in Québec, which examines children from age 1.5 to 4.5. Controlling for an array of socioeconomic factors they find that food insecurity raises the chance of obesity at age 4.5 by two to three times.

At the moment it is not clear whether food insecurity causes childhood obesity. Three of the seven cross-sectional studies find positive associations between food insecurity and obesity for some groups of children. Two of the three longitudinal studies report that food insecurity predicts higher BMI in early childhood. The study reporting contrary results used a shorter panel, suggesting that the impact of food insecurity on the BMI of young children may accumulate over years.

Jones (2004) reviews six papers on food insecurity and adult obesity, two of which analyze nationally representative data. The first presents a descriptive analysis finding that the prevalence of overweight (BMI of 25 or higher) is 11 percentage points higher among women in food-insufficient households than it is among food-sufficient women (Basiotis and Lino 2002). The second paper uses logistic regression analysis and reports that among women, moderate and severe food insecurity aren't associated with the likelihood of being overweight, but mild food insecurity is, even after controlling for income and various socioeconomic factors (Townsend et al. 2001). The authors estimate that mildly food-insecure women are 30 percent more likely than food-secure women to be overweight, but men's weight is not related to their food security status.

More recently, Bhattacharya et al. (2004c) use the NHANES-III to investigate the associations between food insecurity and adult obesity, controlling for poverty status and other sociodemographic factors. Among individuals ages eighteen to sixty-four, those who report skipping meals are more likely to be obese, but meal skippers older than sixty-four are less likely to be obese. However, their measures of food insecurity in addition to "meal skipping" did not prove significantly associated with adult obesity. Hanson et al. (2007) use the NHANES (1999–2002) and report that women with low food security are more likely to be obese than fully food-secure women. Among men, the marginally food secure exhibited a higher mean BMI, and those with low food security were less likely to be overweight. Wilde and Peterman (2006) also use data from the NHANES and control for ethnicity, income, education, and health status. They estimate that women who are marginally food secure and those who are food insecure without hunger are 1.58 and 1.76 times, respectively, more likely to be obese than food-secure women. Marginally food-insecure men are 1.43 times more likely to be obese than food-secure men. Furthermore, marginally food-insecure women are more likely to have gained at least five pounds between the 1999–2000 and 2001–2002 data waves. More severely food-insecure women are not more likely to be obese or gain weight, and men's weight gain doesn't appear to be associated with food security status.

Kim and Frongillo (2007) investigate the relationship between food insecurity and BMI among the elderly using two nationally representative longitudinal data sets: the Health and Retirement Study (HRS) and the Asset and Health Dynamics among the Oldest Old (AHEAD). The mean age of the first waves of these samples is sixty-one years for HRS and eighty for AHEAD. In the HRS sample there is no evidence that food insecurity is associated with BMI, but in the older AHEAD sample, past food insecurity weakly predicts higher BMI ($p = 0.092$). Furthermore, there is evidence that becoming food insecure predicts a rise in BMI ($p = 0.025$).

While the results for adults are generally consistent with the hypothesis that moderate food insecurity leads to greater weight, especially for women, we can't be sure of the direction of causality given the cross-sectional nature of most of the available studies. Food insecurity could cause BMI, or BMI could cause food insecurity through its impact on family income (Chapter 3), or both. More longitudinal data are needed to examine the association between food insecurity and adult BMI in order to more reliably infer the causal flow. While there are more longitudinal studies of children's food insecurity and BMI, the current results are somewhat mixed, so additional studies are needed. At this point, we can neither accept nor reject with confidence the hypothesis that food insecurity causes obesity.

Poverty's Impact on Stress and Mental Health

There is good reason for the expression "grinding poverty"—being poor is stressful and can wear a person down. The "life stress hypothesis," offered by sociologists and social epidemiologists, posits that differences in exposure and vulnerability to stressors help account for the social gradient in health, both physical and mental (e.g., Ensel and Lin 1991). In surveys, poor people generally report a greater frequency of stressful events than higher-income individuals (Turner et al. 1995; Turner and Lloyd 1999; Brady and Matthews 2002; Evans and English 2002) and smaller social networks to call upon to help them cope (Turner and Lloyd 1999; Marmot 2004). Biomedical research supports these survey results; cross-sectional studies of physiological markers of stress, such as cortisol and neuroendocrine levels, find evidence of greater stress at the lower end of the socioeconomic distribution (Evans and English 2002; Kunz-Ebrecht et al. 2004; Lupien et al. 2000). A longitudinal study of 207 white children supports the hypothesis that childhood poverty increases stress and harms long-term health (Evans and Kim 2007). The authors find that the more time a child spends in poverty, the higher their cortisol levels are and the lower their cardiovascular response to an acute stressor. They interpret these results as suggesting that the greater the proportion of early childhood spent in poverty, the higher the children's exposure to chronic stressors. This exposure, in turn, damages their biological mechanisms for managing stress, which could then lead to poorer health in adulthood.

The stress caused by poverty could affect BMI through two channels. First, stress may adversely influence mental health (Adler et al. 1994; Mirowsky and Ross 1986; Kunz and Kalil 1999), which in turn shapes food intake and physical activity. Second, stress can alter metabolic processes that encourage fat accumulation and increase the risk of chronic disease (Dallman et al. 2004; Rosmond and Björntorp 2000).

Let's consider how the stress associated with poverty may affect mental well-being and how, in turn, mental health influences the risk of obesity. The literature suggests several theoretical reasons why poverty could cause stress and depression: material deprivation (Ennis et al. 2000; Siefert et al. 2000); financial strain (Gyamfi et al. 2001; Zimmerman and Katon 2005); inability to adequately fulfill important social roles (e.g., Edin and Lein 1997); reduced ability to control one's life (Siegrist and Marmot 2004); increased exposure to social disorder (Latkin and Curry 2003; Ross 2000); reduced sleep (e.g., Moore et al. 2002; Spilsbury et al. 2006); and discrimination (Bullock et al. 2001; Cozzarelli et al. 2001; Lott 2002). Belle and Doucet (2003) liken the emotional distress of the poor in America's highly unequal society to that of an enlisted seaman whose boat was sunk in battle; his greatest trauma was not from the enemy attack, physical pain, or fear of death but from seeing officers already in lifeboats being rescued before the enlisted men in the water, some of whom drowned while waiting. Being regarded by one's own community as "expendable" is stressful and depressing.

Persistent stress is strongly associated with the onset and duration of depression (e.g., Brown and Harris 1978; Brown and Moran 1997). Reviews of the literature on SES and depression report that in both animal experiments and observational studies of humans, individuals lower in the social hierarchy exhibit greater stress and depressive symptoms (e.g., Adler et al. 1994; Marmot 2004). The link from poverty to stress to depression underlies the social causation theory, which posits that poverty causes depression. In contrast, the social selection theory holds that depression causes people to become poor. Consistent with both these theories, the literature reveals a consensus that the prevalence of depression is significantly higher among the poor than the nonpoor (Everson et al. 2002; Hobfoll et al. 1995; Kahn et al. 2000; Ritchey et al. 1990). When we look at the prevalence of major depressive disorder in the NHANES-III by poverty status, we see that nearly 13 percent of the officially poor are depressed compared to 9 percent of the nonpoor, a difference that is statistically significant at the 1 percent level (Figure 4.4). Depression is also common among welfare recipients (Coiro 2001; Danziger 2002; Jayakody et al. 2000; Lennon 2001; Siefert et al. 2001). In their review of the literature, Lennon et al. (2002) find that approximately 44 percent of welfare recipients report depressive symptoms and 22 percent suffer from major depression.

Is there evidence that poverty among children can lead to depression? A qualitative study of Canadian children documents the teasing that poor children face ("Ha, ha, you're in the breakfast program, you're a bum") and their struggles with feelings of inferiority and not belonging (Robinson et al. 2005). Such feelings could lead to depression. Lupien et al. (2000) document higher levels of salivary cortisol, a stress

Figure 4.4. Depression prevalence by poverty status in the NHANES-III, 1988–1994

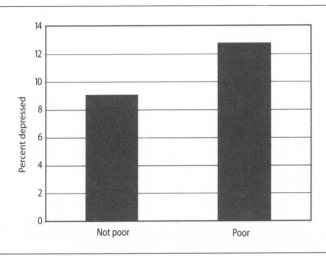

Source: Riolo et al. 2005.

indicator, among poor children in a cross-sectional sample from Québec (n = 217), suggesting that poor children endure more stressful lives.

Longitudinal studies of the impact of poverty on children's depression focus on the role of neighborhood characteristics. A large two-year panel study of Chicagoans finds that the family income-to-needs ratio loses significance in estimates of children's anxiety and depression when census tract disadvantage (high rates of poverty, female family heads, welfare participation, and minority residents) is included in the analysis (Xue et al. 2005). Children ages five to eleven living in disadvantaged neighborhoods exhibit higher scores on measures of depression and anxiety. Another longitudinal study supports these findings and has the advantage of using an experimental design. The Moving to Opportunity (MTO) program randomly assigned public-housing residents in five large cities to a group receiving housing vouchers applicable only in low-poverty neighborhoods, a group receiving Section 8 vouchers, and a control group receiving no housing vouchers. Leventhal and Brooks-Gunn (2003) report that in the New York site (n = 550), boys in families who moved to low-poverty areas exhibited fewer symptoms of anxiety and depression at the two-year follow-up than boys who remained in public housing. Evaluations of all five MTO sites also find that children who moved experienced improvements in their levels of psychological distress and depression (Kling et al. 2007; Orr et al. 2003). These findings support the social causation model of depression in the case of children.

While there is evidence that living in poverty, and especially living in a poor neighborhood, can lead to depression in children, the same may not be true for adolescents. Miech et al. (1999) follow a group of New Zealanders from age fifteen to twenty-one. They find no evidence that parental poverty predicts depression at age fifteen. They do report, however, that parental poverty predicts attention deficit disorder at age fifteen, which supports the social causation model, and that adolescents with conduct disorders are more likely to select out of the educational system by age twenty-one, supporting the social selection model.

Does poverty lead to depression among adults? Longitudinal studies generally find that it does. For example, in their prospective analysis using the New Haven Epidemiologic Catchment Area study, Bruce et al. (1991) find that poor adults are twice as likely as nonpoor adults to experience a new episode of major depression. Lynch et al. (1997) report that in California, respondents in the Alameda County Study whose income fell below 200 percent of the poverty line in all three survey waves were two and half times more likely to be depressed than those who were never low-income by this standard, and four times more likely to exhibit a high degree of cynicism and pessimism. Furthermore, these authors report little evidence that illness predicts later low-income status as posited by the social selection model. Finally, using the NLSY, Zimmerman and Katon (2005) find that when they control for time-invariant, unobservable individual characteristics using fixed effects models, income isn't associated with adult depression, but unemployment and financial strain (debt-to-asset ratio) are. These results support the social causation theory that low socioeconomic status can cause depression.

Longitudinal studies also suggest that living in a poor neighborhood can cause adult depression. In a nine-month-long panel study of poor Baltimore residents, Latkin and Curry (2003) find that participants who initially reported greater perceived neighborhood disorder (crime, litter, vacant housing) exhibited higher depression scores at follow-up. In the MTO's New York site, parents who moved from low-income to higher-income neighborhoods reported fewer depressive symptoms two years after their relocation (Leventhal and Brooks-Gunn 2003). Evaluations of all five MTO sites also indicate that adults who moved enjoyed declines in depression and improvements in "feelings of calm and peacefulness" (Kling et al. 2007; Orr et al. 2003). These four studies support the notion that poverty causes adult depression by limiting people to poor neighborhoods that contain more stressors. By contrast, the quasi-experimental Yonkers Project produces no evidence that moving from a high- to low-poverty neighborhood reduced depression among the sample of 315 minority participants two years after relocation (Fauth et al. 2004). In sum, the majority of panel studies suggest that living in poor neighborhoods can raise adults' risk of depression.

So far, the literature indicates that poverty may lead to children's depression by restricting them to disadvantaged neighborhoods. Among adults, there is also some evidence that poverty may contribute to depression through neighborhood effects and financial strain. Additional studies suggest that poverty affects the mental health of both children and adults through a particular form of material deprivation: food insecurity.

A growing body of research links food insecurity status with the mental health of children (Alaimo et al. 2002; Whitaker at al. 2006) and adults (Siefert et al. 2001; Siefert et al. 2004; Heflin et al. 2005). Both undernutrition and the stress associated with a lack of food could adversely affect psychological well-being. The studies showing an association between food insecurity and children's mental health are all cross-sectional, but four adult studies use longitudinal data. Siefert et al. (2004) use the 1997 and 1998 waves of the Women's Employment Study (WES), a panel of welfare mothers in an urban area of Michigan. Controlling for standard sociodemographic variables and measures of life stress (e.g., homelessness), domestic violence, and discrimination, they find that food insufficiency in both waves is associated with lower self-mastery scores and a greater likelihood of major depression in 1998. Heflin et al. (2005) find evidence, even when they control for time-invariant, unobservable differences among women in three waves of the WES, that an increase in food insufficiency significantly predicts an increase in major depression. Heflin and Ziliak (2006) find evidence in the 1999 and 2001 waves of the PSID that food insufficiency is associated with a higher risk of emotional distress. Finally, Kim and Frongillo (2007) investigate the relationship between food insecurity and depression among the elderly using the HRS and the AHEAD. The analysis of the HRS sample produces strong evidence that past food insecurity predicts depression. In the AHEAD sample, current food insecurity is positively associated with depression.

While the reviewed studies for children are unable to definitively establish causal patterns, they do suggest that food insecurity may lead to mental health problems. The longitudinal evidence for adults provides stronger evidence that food insecurity can cause depression. Overall, the literature generally supports the social causation model: poverty can contribute to depression in part by causing food insecurity. However, we cannot rule out the possibility that poor mental health sometimes leads to food insecurity by reducing earnings capacity.

Finally, four cross-sectional studies suggest that having a low income and living in poor neighborhoods are associated with reduced sleep time and quality, which can contribute to stress and depression. Hardesty and Krakow (2000) report that in a small sample ($n = 22$) of welfare-to-work program participants in New Mexico, 59 percent exhibited at least one type of sleep disorder. In the larger Study of Women's Health across the Nation, Hall et al. (1999) report that financial stress can impair sleep, and in the Detroit Area Study results indicate that sleep mediated the impact of income on psychological distress in both women and men (Moore et al. 2002). Spilsbury et al. (2006) present an analysis by area SES. They examine children ages eight to eleven in Cleveland ($n = 843$) and find that living in a disadvantaged neighborhood triples the odds of sleep apnea. Experimental evidence suggests that sleep deprivation reduces glucose tolerance, increases physiological markers of stress (Van Cauter and Spiegel 1999), and increases hunger (Spiegel et al. 2004). The cross-sectional design of most poverty-sleep studies means that the results are suggestive but do not prove that poverty causes sleep deprivation. Further study would be useful, particularly in light of recent longitudinal evidence that reduced sleep duration among children predicts an elevated risk of obesity (Lumeng et al. 2007; Taveras et al. 2008).

While the literature paints a fairly clear picture of an association between depression and poverty, our understanding of the causal mechanism is still clouded. The social causation theory posits that poverty causes depression, while the social selection theory holds that depression causes people to become poor. Both theories garner some evidence. While my review finds empirical support for the social causation model in studies of adults and children, that doesn't preclude the possibility that causality also runs from depression to poverty and from other variables, such as childhood trauma, to both depression and poverty.

How does the apparent link between poverty and depression relate to the association between poverty and obesity? Depression could cause obesity by reducing physical activity (Paluska and Schwenk 2000) and altering eating patterns (Measelle et al. 2006). In a qualitative study of a small sample ($n = 28$) of poor, rural women conducted by nutritionists, the majority reported "emotional eating," defined as consuming larger than usual quantities when feeling stressed, sad, lonely, or bored (Bove and Olson 2006). Sociologist Sharon Hayes (2003) interviewed a depressed low-income woman who so feared separating from her infant that she rarely left her home: "We'd just eat and sleep and eat and sleep. That's when I put on all the weight [over one hundred pounds]" (156). In another qualitative study, a participant explained, "You get down and you just don't want to do nothing. It's hard to get out of the house and get motivated and then you eat, you eat when you're under stress. Eating fills the void, I mean you're thinking about food, you're tasting it, it makes you feel better" (Parker and Keim 2004, 285). In a study of eating disorders among poor women, Thompson (2004) notes that several participants report that eating was a cheaper method of anesthetizing themselves from life's troubles than alcohol and drugs and didn't involve hangovers or illegal behavior.

Quantitative evidence also supports the hypothesis that depression can adversely affect eating patterns. Two studies find that higher-stressed adolescents consume less-healthy diets (Fulkerson et al. 2004; Cartwright et al. 2003). Fulkerson et al. present only differences in means across stress groups without any controls, but Cartwright's team controls for gender, weight, ethnicity, and area deprivation. They find that teens reporting higher stress levels are more likely to eat fatty foods, snack often, and skip meals. Stressed teens are also less likely to eat five or more servings of fruits and vegetables daily. Due to the cross-sectional design of these studies, the results can be interpreted only as suggestive rather than as evidence that stress causes poor dietary practices and binge eating. However, two longitudinal studies of young women find evidence that depression predicts later eating disorders, strengthening the evidence that depression can alter eating patterns (Cooley et al. 2007; Measelle et al. 2006).

In addition to affecting eating patterns, stress and depression could also lead to obesity because weight gain is a side effect of several antidepressants (Devlin et al. 2000; McElroy et al. 2004; Schwartz et al. 2004; Stunkard et al. 2003; Zimmermann et al. 2003). The poor can access antidepressants through the Medicaid program, and usage is growing. A review of antidepressant use among Medicaid participants finds that between 1995 and 1998 prescriptions increased by more than 40 percent, from 13.7 to 19.3 million (Lewin Group 2000). Of the specific medications discussed by this report, two are associated with moderate weight gain: Paroxetine and Mirtazapine. Could trends in the use of these antidepressants play a role in the elevated prevalence of obesity among the poor? Medicaid prescriptions for Paroxetine increased by 142 percent from 1995 to 1998, from 1.2 to 2.9 million. By 1998 this drug accounted for 15 percent of Medicaid's antidepressant prescriptions. Medicaid prescriptions for Mirtazapine also increased, though less dramatically, and accounted for about 3 percent of the program's antidepressant prescriptions. If each Medicaid prescription reflects an individual, then the number of poor persons who may have experienced weight gain pharmacologically in 1998 totals at least three million, roughly 9 percent of the poverty population. While it seems possible that some obesity among the poor may be related to the use of certain antidepressants, probably only a small proportion is affected.

So far I have considered indirect evidence linking stress, depression, and obesity. Is there direct quantitative evidence that depression causes obesity? A variety of studies document a higher prevalence of depression and other psychiatric disorders among obese individuals seeking treatment than among the general population (e.g., Black et al. 1992; Britz et al. 2000; Prather and Williamson 1988). However, cross-sectional studies of the relationship between the obese in general (not just those seeking treatment) and mood disorders fail to produce consistent evidence that depression and obesity are associated (Faith and Allison 1997; Friedman and Brownell 1995).

Since longitudinal studies are better suited for testing whether depression causes obesity, my review focuses on studies using this design. First, let's consider studies based on local panels. Stice et al. (2005) follow a sample of nearly five hundred southwestern girls ages eleven to fifteen at baseline for four years. They report that baseline depression is not associated with later obesity, but that voluntary dietary restriction and perceived parental obesity are. Pine et al. (2001) study 177 children in New York City and find that those depressed at baseline had BMIs that were, on average, two units higher ten to fifteen years later. This modest increment would push only those on the higher side of the overweight range into obesity.

Barefoot et al. (1998) study a sample of 4,726 college students, predominantly white and male, from North Carolina and check on their outcomes twenty years later. They report that depression in adolescence predicts greater weight gain among those initially in the highest BMI quintile and lower weight gain among those initially in the lower BMI quintiles, suggesting that depression may exaggerate pre-existing weight propensities. Anderson et al. (2006) analyze data from the Children in the Community Study, a longitudinal study of children in upstate New York running from 1983 to 2003. They find that depression among females, but not males, is associated with higher mean BMIs, with larger BMI increases observed the earlier the onset of depression. They estimate that a thirty-year-old woman of average height whose depression began at age fourteen will be about ten to sixteen pounds heavier than a similar woman never afflicted with the disorder. Richardson et al. (2003) report that in a panel of adolescents from New Zealand, depression during ages eighteen to twenty-one doubles the risk of obesity at age twenty-six among females, but not males. Similarly, Hasler et al. (2005) estimate that depressive symptoms before age seventeen has a large positive impact on the probability of adult obesity among Swiss women. In contrast to the studies beginning in childhood, Roberts et al. (2003) find no evidence that depression among adults fifty years or older at baseline predicts obesity five years later. These local studies suggest that childhood and adolescent depression encourages long-term weight gain and raises the risk of adult obesity.

Longitudinal studies using nationally representative samples provide the best available evidence on the obesity-depression link. Classen and Hokayem (2005) use the NLSY and report that depressive symptoms before age nine predict obesity approximately eight to nine years later. Goodman and Whitaker (2002) use the National Longitudinal Study of Adolescent Health and estimate that depression in 1995 doubles the risk of obesity one year later among adolescents, controlling for baseline BMI, age, race, parental obesity, and additional factors. DiPietro et al. (1992) examine adults from the NHANES 1971–1975 wave who also participated in the National Health Epidemiologic Follow-Up Study in 1982–1984. They report that men who were under age fifty-five and depressed at baseline (1971–1975) gained about three kilograms more than similarly aged men who were not initially depressed, but that women who were initially under age fifty-five and depressed gained less weight than their nondepressed counterparts. Collectively, these results indicate that depression can contribute to the development of obesity, but the effect varies by gender and age. Childhood depression increases the risk of later obesity, but among adults depression appears to lead to modest weight gain among men only.[3]

In summary, the literature on the relationships between poverty, mental health, and obesity indicates that poverty can lead to depression and that adolescent depression can lead to adult obesity, especially among women. These results support the hypothesis that poverty can lead to obesity via its impact on mental health. Because childhood depression appears to influence later obesity, expanding mental health screening and treatment for children and adolescents may prove useful in reducing the prevalence of obesity in the long run.

In addition to harming mental health, stress can alter our biochemistry in ways that encourage weight gain. Stress activates the sympathetic nervous system, specifically the hypothalamic-pituitary-adrenal

(HPA) axis, and the immune system. These systems respond to acute stress in ways that enable individuals to successfully cope with an immediate threat (e.g., flee from danger). If individuals face chronic stress, however, the prolonged activation of these physiological systems can harm the body (National Scientific Council on the Developing Child 2005). These biological adaptations are called allostasis (Sterling and Eyer 1988), and "allostatic load" refers to "the price the body pays over long periods of time for adapting to challenges" (McEwen 2001, 44).

How does allostatic load relate to obesity among the poor? Several studies find that chronic stress can alter metabolic function via impacts on the HPA axis in ways that tend to increase body weight, especially in the abdomen (Björntorp 2001; Chrousos 2000; Dallman et al. 2004, 2005; Drapeau et al. 2003; Rosmond and Björntorp 1998). Daniel et al. (2006) report that in an observational study of a small sample of blue-collar, southern women (n = 129), changes in cortisol levels over the course of a day indicate that greater stress is associated with higher BMI. Epel et al. (2001) conduct an experiment using fifty-nine premenopausal women to see how stress affects snacking amounts and preferences. They observe that women with high salivary cortisol levels following snacking after a stressful experience tend to consume more calories than those with low cortisol levels and that they prefer sweeter foods. This suggests that those with greater physiological stress responses are likely to consume more calories, possibly leading to weight gain.

In addition to the effects of long-term activation of the HPA axis on eating, researchers have recently found that stress also stimulates release of a neurotransmitter (NPY) and receptor (Y2R), which promotes the development of abdominal fat in mice who eat a diet high in fat and sugar (Kuo et al. 2007; Warne and Dallman 2007). This suggests that chronic stress coupled with a "Western" diet, which contains large amounts of fats and sweeteners, can cause obesity. Whether the NPY pathway from stress to obesity exists in humans is under analysis, but like rats we do have the NPY peptide and receptors in our fat tissue.

Since the poor are more likely to endure chronic stress than those with greater income, they probably suffer a greater allostatic load. Szanton et al. (2005) review the four available studies on allostatic load and SES. While there isn't a standard measure for the allostatic load, the studies all produce evidence that lower SES people exhibit higher allostatic loads, suggesting that it may play a role in explaining the inverse relationship between SES and general health (Baum et al. 1999) and the specific relationship between SES and obesity. Investigation of allostatic load as a possible link between poverty and obesity is an important avenue for future research.

The literature reviewed shows strong evidence that the poor face more severe and longer-term stress than do people with higher incomes. There is also compelling evidence that such stress can impair mental well-being, causing depression in particular. The hypothesis that depression can lead to weight gain garners moderate evidence. In addition to the link via mental health, there is growing evidence that stress can also influence biological function in ways that encourage fat accumulation and raise the chance of chronic disease. In sum, the link from poverty to stress and poor mental health and then to obesity appears possible, but it's not yet firmly empirically established.

Poverty's Impact on Time Preference
Time preference refers to a person's willingness to trade present happiness or satisfaction for future happiness—in other words, patience. Psychologists often refer to this as the ability to delay gratification. Impatient people are present-oriented and greatly discount future outcomes; they have a high rate of time preference. By contrast, patient people value future outcomes and don't discount them as highly; they have lower time preference.

The poor may have higher time preference because they more frequently face acute crises. For example, if your heat is about to be shut off and there is no food in the house, you have more immediate concerns than the possible future adverse health consequences of some French fries a friend offers. Sociologist Mark Rank (1994) explains:

> Families in poverty are forced to deal with the here and now; it is simply unrealistic for them to make long-range plans. This is reflected in the philosophy of Ruth Miller, a long-term welfare recipient, "I take one day at a time. One day at a time that's what I'm doing. 'Cause every time I make a plan, or do something, you know, it always turns—always something a little different. One of the kids will get sick or somebody real close to me will get sick or something, something happens." (93)

Psychologists report evidence from a variety of experiments that self-control, or willpower, is a depletable resource; if a person must draw on it frequently, less is left and there is pressure to conserve it (Baumeister and Vohs 2003). That is, people who must exercise self-control more often are more likely to give into impulses. Psychologists also find that emotional distress reduces the ability to self-regulate. Poverty certainly leads to emotional distress and necessitates more acts of self-regulation, and thus could raise time preference.

Becker and Mulligan (1997) develop a formal economic theory that predicts that time preference falls (i.e., patience rises) as wealth increases. The main difficulty in testing this theory is how to measure time preference. Researchers have taken two general approaches: experimental and field studies (Frederick et al. 2002). Experimental studies ask subjects to make hypothetical trades between current and future values, report willingness to pay to get something in varying time periods, or rate the attractiveness of a situation according to when it occurs (sooner or later). Problems with the experimental approach include the impact of how the experiment is structured and how questions are worded on the responses, and the possible difference between behaviors in an artificial setting compared to actual decision-making situations. Field studies use data from actual choices to compute a discount rate consistent with the observed behavior. For example, researchers have inferred time preference from observed consumption and savings behavior and from workers' choices between wages and job risk. Problems with the field approach include variation in response depending on the particular choice observed.

Harrison et al. (2002) take the experimental approach and report that the poor exhibit higher average rates of time preference than the rich. Four studies using the field approach produce mixed results. Evans and English (2002), Lawrance (1991), and Samwick (1998) find evidence supporting the hypothesized relationship between income and time preference, while Trostel and Taylor (2001) find no such evidence with respect to permanent income.

Fuchs (1986, 1991) discusses the likely relationship between time preference and health. Preserving health into the future requires us to forgo some current pleasures. For example, giving up high-fat foods and reducing television viewing in favor of physical activity lowers the chance of disease in the future. Few studies, however, test the hypothesized connection between time preference and health. Huston and Finke (2003), using adults in the CSFII, examine whether time preference influences nutrition. They find that those with higher time preference exhibit poorer nutrition, measured by the Healthy Eating Index (HEI). Furthermore, the time preference variables explain a greater proportion of the variation in HEI than do sociocultural and market condition variables. The strength of their results relies on the quality of their five time-preference proxies: educational attainment, smoking, exercise, use of nutritional labels, and degree of nutrition knowledge.

Is there any evidence linking time preference and obesity? Komlos et al. (2004) use aggregate data from developed countries and proxy time preference with national savings rates. They find patterns in savings and average BMI that are consistent with the notion that higher time preference leads to increased body weight. Some studies using individual data have found evidence of the predicted relationship. Friedman et al. (1995) find no relationship between childhood "conscientiousness," a concept related to time preference, and adult BMI in a sample of gifted California children, but Borghans and Golsteyn (2006) find evidence of the predicted association between adult BMI and some time-preference proxies in a survey of Dutch adults. Smith et al. (2005) use the NLSY and report evidence that time preference, as measured by savings behavior, is positively correlated with BMI among minorities. Lastly, Zhang and Rashad (2008) report that in the Behavioral Risk Factor Surveillance System their proxy for "lack of willpower" is associated with a higher probability of obesity. Thus, there is some empirical evidence supporting the hypothesis that high time preference (greater impatience) contributes to greater BMI, but it isn't yet strong. One critique of this proposed pathway from poverty to obesity is that high time preference reduces investment in education and other forms of human capital formation, increasing the risk of poverty. So poverty could lead to high time preference and subsequent obesity, or high time preference could lead to poverty and obesity. We presently don't have enough empirical evidence to sort out the flow of causality between poverty, time preference, and obesity.

If we did conclude that high time preference causes obesity among the poor, how might policy makers respond? Chapman (2003) argues that time preference is too variable across situations to be useful to policy makers. However, there is some evidence that impatience can be reduced through training (e.g., Baumeister and Vohs 2003). Our general ignorance about time preference impairs our ability to devise policies to reduce it, although school curricula designed to promote social and emotional learning shows promise (Greenberg, Weissberg, et al. 2003; Zins et al. 2004). Developmental psychologists who study the ability to delay gratification urge that we offer training designed to help children develop more long-term thinking and self-control: "Unless children are able to sustain delay for desired goals when they want to do so, their freedom to make that choice risks becoming illusory" (Shoda et al. 1990, 985).

If education increases future-orientation and the ability to delay gratification, then programs to keep children in school could improve health and reduce obesity. Perhaps programs teaching children the benefits of monetary savings would increase their general ability to delay gratification. Community gardening projects might encourage long-term thinking as well as increase access to fresh produce. At the moment we can only speculate. While time preference is a difficult area of research, learning more about its determinants and malleability might prove fruitful to health-related policy development.

Poverty's Impact on Physical Activity

The previous pathways focused on calories consumed, but physical activity also plays an important role in determining body weight (CDC 1996; Must and Tybor 2005). Does poverty influence an individual's level of physical activity? A study by the Centers for Disease Control and Prevention (2003) shows that while the level of leisure-time physical activity is only modestly greater among the highest-income children than among the lowest-income children, wealthier children exhibit twice the prevalence of organized physical activity (Figure 4.5). Among adults, levels of leisure-time physical activity rise as income rises (Figure 4.6). Furthermore, the share of adults reporting no leisure-time physical activity is twice as high among the poorest group as it is among wealthiest (53.4 percent versus 23.4 percent). Marshall et al. (2007) report that the income–physical inactivity gradient holds within ethnic categories, suggesting that ethnicity doesn't account for this relationship.

When we break down the prevalence of adult inactivity by gender in addition to poverty status, we see that both women and men exhibit an income gradient (Figure 4.7). With each step up in income, a smaller fraction of adults report physical inactivity, suggesting that gender doesn't account for this relationship. While women are more likely to be physically inactive than men at each income level, the size of the gender difference varies according to whether physical activity includes household chores (Eyler et al. 1998).

The relationship between income and physical inactivity observed in these cross-sectional studies also appears in the longitudinal Alameda County Study. While all respondents in this study exhibited a decrease in physical activity from 1965 to 1974, those living in high-poverty areas experienced the greatest decline, even when the analysis controls for an array of individual demographic characteristics (Yen and Kaplan 1998).

Why would the poor be less physically active? Results from a nation-

Figure 4.5. Prevalence of organized and free-time physical activity among children ages nine to thirteen, by parental income, 2002

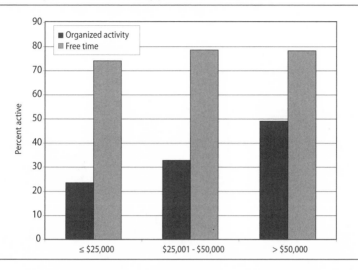

Source: CDC 2003, table 1.

Figure 4.6. Percentage of adults who engage in regular leisure-time physical activity, by poverty-income ratio, 1997–1998

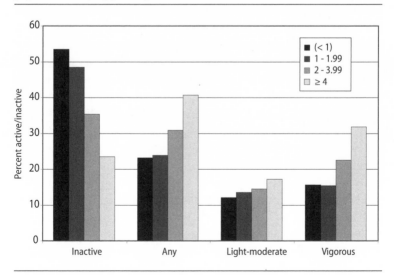

Source: National Center for Health Statistics 2002, tables 1 and 4.

Note: In this study, a ratio of <1 indicates official poverty, and 1–1.99 indicates being "near poor."

Figure 4.7. Percentage of adults who are physically inactive, by gender and poverty-income ratio, 1997–1998

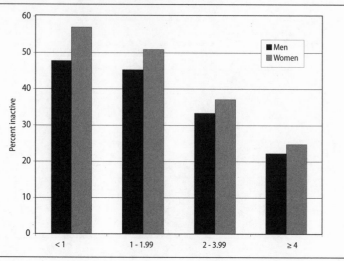

Source: National Center for Health Statistics 2002, table 1.

Note: In this study, a ratio of <1 indicates official poverty, and 1–1.99 indicates being "near poor."

ally representative survey of children indicate that the poor face more barriers to physical activity than the affluent (CDC 2003). According to this survey, expense presents the most common barrier to physical activity for lower-income children (Figure 4.8). Data on participation in sports from the National Sporting Goods Association also suggest that cost is a significant barrier; participation is highest among those with household incomes of $75,000 or more and lowest among those with less than $25,000 (U.S. Census Bureau 2007, table 1233). The same income gradient generally holds for sporting goods purchases. Poverty makes it harder for children and adults to afford the fees associated with organized athletic leagues and clubs and the equipment required to play many sports. A participant in a focus group of minority women sums it up: "At ten dollars a class [exercise] who can afford that?" (Eyler et al. 1998, 648).

Transportation problems and lack of opportunities also pose significant barriers to physical activity. Lower-income children are three times more likely than the wealthiest children to report transportation problems, lack of opportunities in their area, and lack of neighborhood safety as factors restricting their levels of physical activity. Why would the poor face reduced access to nearby facilities for physical activity? In-

Figure 4.8. Percentage of children ages nine to thirteen who report barriers to physical activity, by parental income, 2002

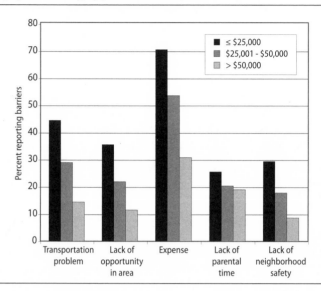

Source: CDC 2003, table 2.

come greatly influences where a person can afford to live, so poor people often live in disadvantaged neighborhoods. These neighborhoods may not offer the same number or quality of facilities for physical activity as wealthier areas, and proximity to such facilities is linked to greater physical activity (e.g., Duncan et al. 2002; Sallis et al. 1990). Local area studies generally find that people in lower-income neighborhoods perceive facilities for physical activity to be less available (Duncan et al. 2002; Wilson et al. 2004).

Studies that count the number of recreational facilities by neighborhood tend to confirm the perception of limited access. For example, Estabrook et al. (2003) examine the availability of physical activity resources (parks, fitness centers, and sports facilities) across neighborhoods of varying socioeconomic status in a midwestern city. They find that low and medium SES census tracts have about the same number of pay-for-use facilities as wealthier tracts, but significantly fewer free facilities. Two studies in the Southeast suggest that poorer neighborhoods have fewer trails for walking and biking than their wealthier counterparts (Huston et al. 2003; Wilson et al. 2004). Studies using nationwide data also report that poor neighborhoods offer fewer public and commercial recreational facilities (Gordon-Larsen et al. 2006; Powell et al.

2004, 2006). In sum, the literature supports the hypothesis that living in a poor neighborhood results in limited access to places to be physically active. All of these studies are cross-sectional, however, so they can't determine whether the relationship between availability of recreational facilities and area SES is causal.

Is there evidence that physical activity and BMI vary by the availability of facilities for physical activity? Sallis et al. (2000) reviews studies of the correlates of children's physical activity published between 1970 and 1998, most of which are based on cross-sectional data. They find that among children ages three to twelve, access to facilities and programs for physical activity are positively associated with levels of physical activity in three of the four available studies. These three studies also report that more time spent outdoors is associated with greater physical activity among children. More recently, Roemmich et al. (2006) report that in a small sample of New York children, living near a park is associated with greater physical activity as measured by accelerometers. Two recent reviews of the correlates of adult physical activity report that the majority of studies produce evidence that accessibility of recreational facilities is positively associated with adults' physical activity (Humpel et al. 2002; Trost 2002). However, evaluations of the Women's Cardiovascular Health Network Project find no evidence that the number of places to exercise affects the likelihood of physical activity (Eyler et al. 2003).

Two recent nationally representative studies find that the greater the number of places to be physically active, the higher the levels of physical activity among adolescents (Gordon-Larsen et al. 2006) and adults (Parks et al. 2003). Gordon-Larsen et al. also examine the relationship between recreational facilities and BMI and report that having more facilities is associated with lower odds of obesity among adolescents.

In addition to the lack of facilities, neighborhood safety may prevent the poor from engaging in physical activity, particularly outdoors (CDC 1999; Patterson 1991; Steptoe and Feldman 2001). For example, a middle-aged resident of a poor Chicago neighborhood, upon being encouraged by his doctor to walk to help him recover from a stroke, responded, "I do not want to be no prey" (Abraham 1993, 140).

Let's first consider the evidence on neighborhood safety and disorder on children's physical activity. Fear for children's safety could be a significant barrier to outdoor physical activity. When asked what could be done to increase neighborhood physical activity, a participant in a focus group of poor women answered, "Maybe they will give the parks a cleanup so that families can go walk . . . instead of . . . easy women and drunks, so families can feel like going" (Kieffer et al. 2002, 551). Sallis et al. (2000) review the studies of correlates of children's physical activity published in the 1990s and find no evidence that reported safety is statistically significant. By contrast, two more recent cross-sectional analyses find evidence that neighborhood safety is positively associated with children's increased physical activity. Molnar et al. (2004) investigate a sample of 1,378 children ages eleven to sixteen in Chicago and control for both individual and neighborhood characteristics. They find that perceived lack of safety and greater social disorder are negatively related to physical activity. Gordon-Larsen et al. (2000) present the only nationally representative study of the relationship between children's physical activity level and their environment. Using the National Longitudinal Study of Adolescent Health, these authors find that teens living in counties with greater reported crime are less likely to engage in moderate to vigorous physical activity.

The latest evidence indicates that safety concerns can reduce children's physical activity, but does reduced neighborhood safety affect children's obesity status? Burdette and Whitaker (2004) find no evidence that reported crime and preschoolers' obesity status are associated in Cincinnati. However, Hillier et al. (2007) report that children living in Philadelphia census block groups with more narcotics arrests are more likely to be overweight (BMI between the eighty-fifth and ninety-fifth percentiles), although this measure of neighborhood crime doesn't affect the likelihood of obesity (BMI above the ninety-fifth percentile). In a multisite sample of children, Lumeng et al. (2006) report that parents' perception of neighborhood safety is inversely associated with the likelihood of a first grader being obese when the analysis controls for gender, but not when BMI at age 4.5 is included as a covariate. The literature on neighborhood safety and children's BMI is presently limited and offers mixed results; we can neither reject nor accept the hypothesis that neighborhood safety influences children's weight.

The literature on neighborhood safety and adult physical activity and BMI is also rather scant. Three bivariate analyses produce evidence that perceived neighborhood safety is positively correlated with adults' physical activity (Eyler et al. 2003; Wilbur et al. 2003; Wilson et al. 2004). Burdette et al. (2006) use data from the Fragile Families and Child Wellbeing Study and adjust for an array of individual sociodemographic characteristics. They find that the greater the perception of neighborhood safety, the lower the obesity prevalence among mothers of young children. In contrast, King et al. (2000) find that perceived safety and crime don't affect the physical activity of women over forty years old. These results suggest that safety may be an important factor in the obesity of younger, but not older, women.

Ross and Mirowsky (2001) challenge the idea that area poverty reduces health by reducing physical activity. They use multilevel statistical modelling to account for both individual and census tract characteristics in a sample of 2,482 adults in Illinois to examine the relationship between neighborhood disadvantage, disorder, walking (their only measure of physical activity), and general health.[4] Consistent with prior studies, they report that greater neighborhood disadvantage is associated with more reported disorder and that both neighborhood disadvantage and disorder are positively correlated with residents' reported fear. However, the results indicate that while disorder and fear mediate the relationship between neighborhood disadvantage and health, walking doesn't. Ross and Mirowsky find that residents of disadvantaged and disordered neighborhoods walk as much as individuals living in better neighborhoods, perhaps out of necessity. The authors conclude that it is not reduced walking but stress due to social disorder and fear that links poor health to neighborhood disadvantage. However, they don't specifically examine associations with BMI or obesity.

In addition to availability of recreational facilities and neighborhood safety, air quality could help explain reduced physical activity among the poor. The environmental justice movement has produced strong evidence that exposure to air pollution is greater in poorer neighborhoods (e.g., Bullard 2005; Gwynn and Thurston 2001; Institute of Medicine 1999; Jerrett et al. 2001). Poor air quality could discourage outdoor activity, and it is also linked to elevated respiratory problems, which could further impede physical activity (American Lung Association 2001). For example, Corburn et al. (2006) analyze pollution and asthma-related hospital admissions data in New York City using the Geographic Information System and report that living in a low-income area and substandard housing predicts asthma hospitalizations. Furthermore, reducing air pollution from transportation is associated with a drop in asthma-related emergencies, indicating that pollution can cause asthma (Friedman et al. 2001).

Respiratory problems associated with elevated pollution exposure could contribute to obesity by reducing physical activity and raising inflammation levels. Indeed, analyses of the NHANES-III indicate that childhood BMI and asthma are positively correlated (Epstein et al. 2000; von Mutius et al. 2001), and Jones et al. (2006) find that having asthma raises the likelihood of excess weight among high school students in the Youth Risk Behavior Survey. Thus, it is possible that poverty contributes to obesity by causing respiratory problems induced by increased pollution exposure. It is also possible, however, that the environments and lifestyles that produce obesity also cause asthma or that obesity contributes to asthma risk (Tantisira and Weiss 2001; Mamun et al. 2007).

The lack of recreational facilities and concerns about safety and air quality may reduce the physical activity of residents of poor neighborhoods, driving them to more sedentary, indoor leisure-time activities. Television provides cheap entertainment in the safety of one's home and is positively associated with the risk of excess weight (Boone et al. 2007; Delva et al. 2007; Hu et al. 2003). Four controlled experiments report that decreasing TV time leads to declines in children's BMI, suggesting that TV viewing is causal (Jordan and Robinson 2008). In their review of the literature on children and TV, Gorely et al. (2004) find that parental income and education are consistently inversely related with children's TV viewing time, while minority status and having only one parent in the house are positively associated with it. Similarly, low-income adults and children spend more time watching TV than their wealthier counterparts (Kumanyika and Grier 2006; Shalla and Schellenberg 1998). These results suggest that people at higher risk of public assistance participation generally spend more time watching TV. In addition, Rose and Bodor (2006) find in a longitudinal analysis that the prevalence of watching two or more hours of TV daily is significantly higher among food-insecure children than food-secure children (54 percent versus 40 percent). TV requires little energy expenditure, encourages snacking, and is consistently associated with BMI among children and women (Gore et al. 2003, Gorely et al. 2004; Jeffery and French 1998; Sherry 2005), although the size effects often are not large (Boone et al. 2007; Marshall et al. 2004). The small size effects may result from errors in measuring TV viewing time, which are generally self-reported rather than directly measured (Must and Tybor 2005).

Thus far, my review of poverty's impact on physical activity produces solid evidence that the poor are less physically active because of their limited budgets and the reduced number of recreational facilities in their neighborhoods. Increased pollution may also contribute to the problem, although present research is not extensive enough to draw a firm conclusion. Evidence suggests that elevated safety concerns limit their physical activity, but few of the available studies are longitudinal and none are experimental. Evaluations of the Moving to Opportunity (MTO) study, in which a random selection of families living in public housing received vouchers enabling them to move to better areas, fill this empirical gap (Kling et al. 2004; Orr et al. 2003). At follow-up, adults who moved exhibited lower obesity prevalence than those in the control group, who remained in public housing (Kling et al. 2007; Orr et al. 2003). These findings provide compelling evidence that neighborhood effects play an important role in adult obesity. Unfortunately, specific aspects of the neighborhoods weren't collected, so we can't tell what features of the new neighborhood contributed to this decline in obesity—was it reduced crime and pollution, improved access to facilities, or some combination of factors?

Summary and Recommendations

Poverty, both on the individual and community levels, influences food intake and physical activity and thus obesity status. Poverty reduces educational attainment, access to healthy foods, opportunities for physical activity, and mental health while it increases food insecurity and stress. Poverty may also increase time preference, focusing attention on the present rather than the long run. Social epidemiologist George Kaplan (2007) characterizes the various adverse health impacts of poverty as the result of "compound disinterest." Economists estimate that childhood poverty costs the nation $500 billion annually in reduced productivity and increased crime and health care costs (Holzer et al. 2007). Thus, policies that succeed in reducing childhood poverty may not only slow the obesity epidemic but also contribute to increased national economic growth.

What can government do to diminish the obesity consequences of poverty? Public schools offer an important opportunity for policy makers to improve the daily environments of most children. School changes that policy makers should consider include the following:

- Increase funding to schools in low socioeconomic areas. Disadvantaged schools need additional help in offering effective health education and greater opportunities for physical activity, and in retaining students through high school graduation and encouraging college attendance.
- Increase mental health screenings and treatment available in low-income schools.
- Consider incorporating social and emotional learning curricula to help students better manage their emotions and develop the

skills needed for long-term thinking and the ability to delay
gratification.

- Make sure children have safe walkways and bike paths to school.
  This may require providing or repairing sidewalks, street lighting,
  and bike paths.

In terms of preventing obesity among all low-income Americans, not
just school children, the government can:

- Develop new programs (and support existing ones) to attract
  supermarkets and farmers' markets to low socioeconomic areas. In
  Pennsylvania the Fresh Food Financing Initiative has successfully
  encouraged the opening of supermarkets in low-income areas and
  could serve as a model for other states.[5]
- Support community gardening projects in low-income areas.
- Expand nutrition and food management education offered
  through the Expanded Food and Nutrition Education Program.
- Test the BMI consequences of distributing food stamp benefits
  more than once a month.
- Test the BMI consequences of using the Electronic Benefit
  Transfer system to discount purchases of fresh fruits and vegetables
  and low-fat meats and dairy products.
- Expand public safety efforts in poor areas to increase the likelihood
  of outdoor physical activity and reduce stress.
- Review environmental and zoning regulations, looking for
  opportunities to reduce exposure to pollution in low-income areas.
- Increase mental health screening and treatment among public
  assistance recipients and other low-income citizens.
- Review guidelines for Medicaid and Medicare coverage of
  antidepressants to determine whether drugs with weight-gain side
  effects are somehow encouraged by program parameters.
- Alter agricultural subsidies and price supports so that policy
  doesn't encourage the consumption of high-calorie foods
  (e.g., corn sweeteners and whole milk) and instead encourages
  consumption of low-calorie foods (fresh produce and low-fat milk)
  by lowering their relative price.

Some evidence suggests that promotion of farmers' markets in low-
income areas increases fruit and vegetable consumption (Kunkel et al.
2003), but more rigorous testing is needed to confirm this result and to

see whether these programs reduce BMI. Community gardening projects may increase both physical activity and the availability of fresh produce (Armstrong 2000; Wakefield et al. 2007) and may increase fruit and vegetable intake (Alaimo et al. 2008), but their impact on BMI remains untested. Nutrition education and school efforts to promote produce consumption show promise in improving diets and merit further exploration (Burney and Haughton 2002; Perry et al. 2004). One study indicates that providing coupons to farmers' markets increases fruit and vegetable consumption (Anderson et al. 2001), and several studies find that lowering the price of fresh fruits and vegetables in schools raises their consumption (French 2003; French and Wechsler 2004; Hannan et al. 2002). These results suggest that policies that reduce the price of healthy foods will encourage their consumption. Whether such policies also reduce BMI needs to be directly investigated.

5

The "Factor X Causes Both Public Assistance and Obesity" Hypothesis

Factors in addition to poverty may cause both obesity and public assistance participation. Disabling physical disorders and mental illness limit the ability to earn income and can pose barriers to physical activity and a nutritious diet. Abuse in either childhood or adulthood may lead to both physiological and psychological responses that raise the risk of poverty, public assistance receipt, and obesity. Low intelligence and high time preference could impede the ability to consider the future consequences of current actions and thus lead to both poverty and obesity. This chapter reviews these five possible variables, which I generically refer to as "Factor X," that could contribute to the association between public assistance and obesity (Figure 5.1).

Research Context

Given that mental illness, low intelligence, and abuse are potential pathways in this model, it's not surprising that psychologists, psychiatrists, and other physicians dominate the research relevant to this chapter. They develop tools for assessing intelligence and mental health, and study the causes and consequences of these conditions. Researchers from these disciplines have also done much of the work on the impact of abuse, along with sociologists, social workers, and legal scholars. Epidemiologists, psychologists, and sociologists lead the research on examining connections between intelligence and health. Finally, economists join the psychologists and psychiatrists in studying humans' ability to delay gratification, or time preference, and how it might influence obesity status.

Measuring mental health, intelligence, and time preference present substantial technical problems that require a trade-off between accuracy and generalizability. Studies using multiple measures and in-depth interviews offer greater accuracy, but they also require considerable time and money, and thus are usually used only in studies of smaller, geographically limited samples. Larger, more representative studies rely on fewer measures, offering greater generalizability at the price of reduced accuracy.

Researchers studying time preference and domestic violence prevention can conduct some random experiments; those studying the impact of mental illness, disability, and intelligence on health and poverty status cannot. Consequently, many of the available studies on possible X factors rely on cross-sectional data, which don't allow tests for causality. Some longitudinal studies are available, and they offer the best insight into whether mental illness, disability, and intelligence cause both poverty and obesity.

Empirical Evidence: Possible X Factors

Physical and Intellectual Disabilities

Physical and intellectual disabilities can be inherited or may result from disease and injury. According to a report by the Centers for Disease Control and Prevention (2002), obesity is much more prevalent among the disabled than the non-disabled (Figure 5.2). This pattern could arise because obesity causes disability (as discussed in Chapter 3), or because disability causes obesity, or both. Why might disability lead to obesity? First, the biological foundations for some disabilities may predispose individuals to obesity. For example, two genetic disorders that impair mental abilities, Down syndrome and Prader-Willi syndrome, are also associated with obesity. Second, the disabled are less likely than those without disabilities to engage in regular physical activity, probably because is it harder for them to do so (CDC, n.d.). Third, the disabled may consume a less nutritious diet than the non-disabled because they face greater barriers to acquiring and preparing food on their own and frequently rely on meals provided by caregivers. Unfortunately, little research has examined the diets of the disabled in either institutional or community settings. Draheim et al. (2007) analyze the food intake of 325 mentally retarded adults and find that in community living arrangements they consume less than the recommended amount of fruits and vegetables, and that the proportion who eat an adequate amount of these foods falls below that of the general population.[1] Residents also consume more than the recommended amount of fat, but the prevalence of high fat diets is similar to that of the general population. Longitudinal studies on the timing of disability and obesity onset, which would suggest the direction of causality, have not yet been published. So while we know that the disabled are more likely to be obese, and we

Figure 5.1. The "Factor X Causes Both Public Assistance and Obesity" model

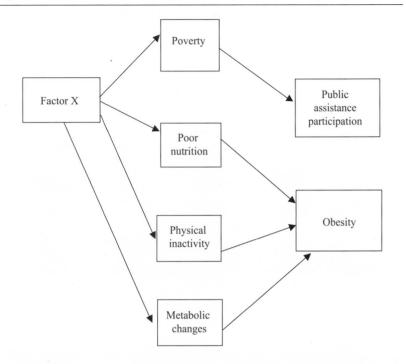

have theoretical reasons why disability may lead to obesity, we don't have enough evidence to conclude that disability causes obesity.

Can disability lead to poverty and public assistance participation? It seems logical that people with physical or mental impairments would enjoy less success in labor markets, given the link between wages and productivity. Two studies employing nationally representative, longitudinal data find evidence that disability leads to significantly lower earnings and greater participation in public assistance programs. In the Survey of Income and Program Participation, McNeil (2000) finds that those with a non-severe disability earn on average $27,091 annually, compared to the $31,407 earned by the non-disabled. Those with a severe disability fare even worse, earning only $18,886 on average. More important, the percentage of people with any earned income drops dramatically with disability status. Only 2.9 percent and 6.3 percent of those with severe and non-severe disabilities, respectively, report earnings, compared to 90.9 percent of the non-disabled. In a logistic regression estimating the probability that a single woman with children will receive cash welfare

Figure 5.2. Obesity prevalence by disability status, 1998–1999

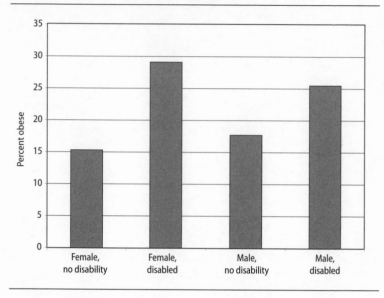

Source: CDC 2002.

benefits, both non-severe and severe disability status exert a statistically significant positive impact.

In the Panel Study of Income Dynamics (PSID), Meyer and Mok (2006) also find that earnings drop significantly following the onset of disability. For example, ten years after the onset of a chronic, severe disability, the earnings of male household heads decline by 61 percent on average.[2] The poverty rate also rises, from about 9 percent before the disability to about 12 percent in the year after onset and 16 percent six years after onset. About 20 percent of those who experience a chronic, severe disability persistently live below the poverty line. By contrast, those with a temporary disability experience a rise in poverty during the first two years after onset, which falls thereafter as earnings rebound. The authors observe a corresponding pattern in public assistance: the temporarily disabled experience a rise in the receipt of benefits following onset, which then declines, while the chronic, severely disabled experience a rise in public assistance that persists over the long run. These authors estimate that chronic severe disability raises the likelihood of Food Stamp Program participation by 6 percent the year of onset, 8 percent the year after, and 11 percent ten years after.

The hypothesis that disability can cause obesity appears theoretically plausible, and the evidence that disability can cause poverty and public assistance participation is strong. Thus, disability may account for some of the observed associations between obesity, poverty, and public assistance.

Mental Illness

To the extent that mental illness is caused by factors other than obesity and poverty, it constitutes a possible independent pathway to both obesity and public assistance. Three mental problems seem particularly associated with obesity: depression, bipolar disorder, and anxiety disorder. In the National Comorbidity Survey Replication the prevalence of these mental illnesses is higher among the obese than the non-obese, with 22 percent of the obese suffering from either depression or bipolar disorder and 12 percent from anxiety disorder (Simon et al. 2006). Not only are these mental illnesses associated with obesity, but they also impair the ability to earn income. According to the World Health Organization (2004) neuropsychiatric conditions are the leading source of Disability Adjusted Life Years (DALYs) in the United States.[3] The three mental disorders most associated with obesity together constitute the third leading cause of DALYs.

Greater prevalence of these illnesses among the obese may result because obesity causes mental disorders (Chapter 3), mental disorders cause obesity (Chapter 4), or some underlying factor causes them both. An important potential underlying causal factor lies in our biology, specifically our brain structure and chemistry (National Institute for Mental Health 2007). Psychiatrists and psychologists explain that depression, bipolar disorder, and anxiety disorder result from the interaction of multiple causes rather than from a lone cause. Three causal agents common to these disorders are genetics, biology, and life stress (Hersen and Thomas 2006; Hersen and Turner 2003). It is possible that without a genetic or biological vulnerability, many individuals who experience high levels of stress wouldn't suffer as much mental illness. To the extent that this is the case, mental illness constitutes a pathway, albeit not a completely independent one, to both obesity and public assistance.

Depression is fairly prevalent in the United States. Between 16 and 17 percent of adults have suffered from depression at some point in their lives, with women facing nearly twice the risk as men (Kessler et al. 2003; Kessler, Berglund, et al. 2005; Kessler, Chiu, et al. 2005). This mental disorder can impair one's ability to earn income in the labor market (Kessler et al. 1999, 2001; Goldberg and Steury 2001; Stewart et al. 2003), raising the risk of poverty and participation in public assistance programs. Bipolar and anxiety disorders are less prevalent than depression, afflicting 1 to 4 percent of adults in a given year (Holmes and Newman 2006; Kessler, Berglund, 2005; Newman 2006), but also pose barriers to labor market performance (Kessler et al. 2001), reducing the ability to earn adequate income.

To the extent that depression, bipolar disorder, and anxiety disorder have a physiological basis, these mental illnesses could contribute to the correlation between obesity and public assistance. Strong evidence supports the hypothesis that these mental illnesses impair earnings and increase the risk of poverty. Whether they contribute to obesity has been less firmly established, however. Evidence reviewed in Chapters 3 and 4 show a clear link between depression and obesity, but some studies suggest that depression causes obesity while others indicate the reverse.

Physical and Sexual Abuse
Physical abuse of children and women is, unfortunately, fairly common in the United States. In the 2001–2002 wave of the National Longitudinal Study of Adolescent Health, 28 percent of respondents reported experiencing physical assault and 12 percent reported physical neglect (Hussey et al. 2006). Sexual abuse is less prevalent at 4.5 percent. Among adults, about 25 percent of women, compared to 8 percent of men, report experiencing domestic abuse in their lifetime (Tjaden and Thoenes 2000). In a prospective study of teen mothers, who face an elevated risk of welfare eligibility, 21 percent reported experiencing domestic abuse in the three months after giving birth (Harrykissoon et al. 2002). In general, both current and lifetime rates of abuse among women on welfare exceed that of the general population, with lifetime prevalence estimated at 50 to 70 percent (Polit et al. 2001; Tolman and Raphael 2000). If abuse causes both obesity and welfare participation, it would contribute to the positive association between obesity and public assistance.

First, let's consider the relationship between abuse and public assistance participation. Childhood abuse can contribute to physical and mental health problems that persist into adulthood, which could subsequently create barriers in the labor market (Felitti et al. 1998; Gustafson and Sarwer 2004; Weiss et al. 1999). Adult victims of domestic violence also suffer substantial physical and psychological trauma (Anderson and Saunders 2007). Difficulties in acquiring or maintaining employment because of impaired physical and mental health can increase the need for public assistance. In addition, intimate partner abuse often includes specific efforts to block women from improving their educations and working (Coulter 2004; Raphael 1996). For example, one welfare recipient describes her boyfriend's behavior before an important exam: "He wouldn't watch the children, he wouldn't feed them, he wouldn't let me study, he would take my books from me. I never got a chance to either sleep or study" (Raphael 2000, 43). Other tactics abusers use to prevent women from going to school or work include hiding clothing, causing scenes at the job site, and picking fights before interviews. Studies of welfare-to-work programs suggest that 40 to 45 percent of female participants face such interference (Raphael 2000). One woman in Raphael's ethnographic study reported that her partner encouraged her to eat and liked that she was morbidly obese because it prevented her from working.

Does the elevated prevalence of domestic violence among welfare participants result because abuse causes women to leave the labor market and join the public assistance rolls? Two review articles report that while cross-sectional studies generally find no association between domestic violence and employment, some longitudinal studies find that abuse is associated with greater employment instability (Riger and Staggs 2004; Tolman and Raphael 2000). Two recent publications produce further evidence that domestic violence impedes a woman's labor market success and can lead to welfare participation. First, Yoshihama et al. (2006) use the Life Course Calendar method to collect retrospective social and economic data on forty low-income, midwestern black women for every year since their first relationship, generating a sample of 722 person-years. They find evidence that cumulative domestic abuse, but not cumulative welfare receipt, is associated with a greater likelihood of current welfare participation, suggesting that prolonged partner abuse can cause women to join the public assistance rolls. Yoshihama's study, however, relies on the accuracy of participants' memory and doesn't control for respondents' educational attainment or area characteristics that could influence employment.

The second study, Riger et al. (2004), analyzes three waves of the Illinois Families Study, which was designed to evaluate the effectiveness of the state's welfare reforms and includes both white and black women. They find that recent intimate partner violence is associated with fewer months worked, even when the analysis controls for an array of human capital, mental health, and parenting responsibility variables. Overall, the qualitative and quantitative evidence produces a fairly consistent picture of domestic abuse thwarting women's efforts to earn income, increasing the likelihood that they will join public assistance programs or stay in them longer than they would otherwise.

In sum, there is consistent evidence that abuse in either childhood or adulthood harms physical and mental health, which can impede success in the labor market. There is growing evidence that intimate partner abuse increases women's employment instability and raises the risk of public assistance participation. The hypothesis that family violence can lead to public assistance garners moderate support.

Next, we consider the link between abuse and obesity. Several studies suggest that childhood abuse is associated with eating disorders, including bingeing (Johnson et al. 2002; Logio 2003; Selway 2006; Smolak and Murnen 2002); the study by Moyer et al. (1997) is the exception. Of the articles that directly examine the relationship between childhood abuse and obesity, only two employ longitudinal data. Lissau and Sorenson (1994) analyze data on respondents initially at ages nine and ten in Copenhagen and at a ten-year follow-up. They find that children initially identified by their teacher as having low family support are seven times more likely to be obese at follow-up, and that the risk of obesity for children identified as "dirty and neglected" rises tenfold. They control for family structure, number of siblings, and parental socioeconomic status (SES), but whether teacher reports of family support and hygiene reflect actual abuse is not clear. Johnson et al. (2002) use a longitudinal sample from upstate New York that follows predominantly white respondents from childhood (1975) to young adulthood (1991–1993). They find that, after controlling for age, gender, parental psychiatric problems, childhood temperament, and childhood eating disorders, physical neglect quintuples and sexual abuse triples the odds of eating disorders and excess weight in adulthood.

Selway (2006) reviews ten retrospective studies of the association between childhood abuse and obesity and concludes that the "current evidence lends moderate support to the associations between self-reported child maltreatment and adult obesity" (273). The most convincing of the retrospective studies uses the Adverse Childhood Experiences data, a large sample of HMO participants in San Diego. Studies using these data find that increased exposure to adverse experiences (which include, but are not limited to, physical and sexual abuse) is associated with higher odds of obesity, suggesting a "dose-response relationship"—more doses of maltreatment produce bigger responses in weight (Felitti et al. 1998; Williamson et al. 2002). The latter study estimates that childhood adversity explains 8 percent of obesity and 17 percent of extreme obesity (BMI at or above 40) in adulthood. Since Selway's review was published an analysis of the California Women's Health Survey has produced similar results. Alvarez et al. (2007) also find that childhood abuse raises the chance of adult obesity, but they estimate a smaller impact of 4.5 percent.

Researchers offer both psychological and neurobiological explanations for the connection between abuse and obesity. Psychologists and psychiatrists note that abuse erodes self-esteem and body image, which can lead to self-destructive behaviors such as unhealthy eating patterns (Gustafson and Sarwer 2004; Logio 2003). Obesity may serve an "adaptive function," helping the abused cope with their trauma (Gustafson and Sarwer 2004; Wiederman et al. 1999). For example, victims may use obesity to reduce the risk of sexual advances or, if they are in an intimate relationship, of their partner becoming jealous. For example, a young woman who gained 105 pounds the year after she was raped explained to a researcher, "Overweight is overlooked, and that's the way I need to be" (Stevens 2005).

Neurologists and endocrinologists note that stress, which abuse certainly causes, affects metabolism in ways that encourage weight gain (Chapter 4). Furthermore, Teicher (2002) reports evidence that "child abuse can cause permanent damage to the neural structure and function of the developing brain itself" (70). Specifically, abuse is associated with changes in brain structures associated with stress, depression, irritability, and language (e.g., the hippocampus). These neurological changes could predispose abused children to both excess weight and difficulties in the labor market.

Overall the evidence indicates that abuse harms physical and mental health in ways that can create barriers to earning sufficient income in the labor market and can encourage weight gain. While abuse doesn't account for the majority of obesity prevalence among the poor, it probably is a contributing factor to the elevated prevalence of obesity among low-income women. What can be done to reduce childhood and partner abuse and its harmful consequences? Domestic violence experts note that abuse of girls and women is more prevalent in societies in which women have less power than men (Fedler and Tanzer 2000). Policies that strengthen gender equality in general and promote the social unacceptability of domestic violence may help reduce abuse and its attendant problems, including obesity. Evidence indicates that arresting abusers generally reduces the likelihood of renewed violence somewhat (Maxwell 2005), and that the provision of emergency shelters, longer-term affordable housing, and comprehensive support services for women help them escape further abuse (Mears 2003; Menard 2001; Sullivan and Bybee 1999). Certain provisions of protective orders—for example, ex-

panding coverage to women not living with their abuser—are associated
with a lower probability of domestic violence (Dugan 2003). Finally,
some therapy programs appear to help victims cope with their trauma,
which may reduce the destructive impact of abuse (Farrington and
Welsh 2005; Chadwick Center on Children and Families 2004).

Low Intelligence

Low intelligence may be biologically based or may result from growing
up in an impoverished environment (Chapter 4). Several longitudinal
studies find a health gradient by cognitive ability as measured by IQ;
those with progressively lower IQs experience increasingly poorer health
and greater mortality (Hart et al. 2003; Whalley and Deary 2001).
Researchers theorize that this gradient arises because higher cognitive
ability increases the capacity to make good health decisions and increases access to education and income earning opportunities. Because
low intelligence poses a barrier to education and reduces labor market
success, it may also increase the chance of poverty and public assistance
participation.

To assess the plausibility of a pathway from low intelligence to both
obesity and public assistance, we'll first consider the relationship between intelligence and obesity. Prospective studies show not only an inverse gradient between IQ and general health but also one between IQ
and obesity in particular. In the Aberdeen Children of the 1950s study,
a data set of over 12,000 children born in Aberdeen, Scotland, between
1950 and 1956, Lawlor et al. (2006) find that a standard-deviation
lower intelligence score at age seven is associated with a 0.35 unit rise
in adult BMI on average. A three-standard-deviation lower intelligence
score predicts a 1 unit increase in BMI, which would not push many
people into the obesity category or cause a marked decline in health.
Furthermore, the significance of this association disappears when the
analysis controls for educational attainment. These authors also find no
relationship between intelligence and BMI when they restrict the analysis to pairs of siblings close in age, suggesting that the influence of common biological and environmental factors matters more to adult BMI
than to childhood intelligence scores.

Similar findings for intelligence, BMI, and education are reported by
Halkjær et al. (2003), using men appearing before Danish draft boards,
and by Chandola et al. (2006), using the National Child Development
(1958) Survey in Great Britain. Together, these results suggest that education mediates the relationship between IQ and BMI; those with lower
IQs achieve lower educational attainment, which in turn is associated

with higher body weight. However, Batty et al. (2007) report that in the Aberdeen Children of the 1950s study, childhood IQ at age eleven remains significantly related to adult obesity even when the analysis controls for educational attainment, although at a reduced magnitude. In general, the evidence that low intelligence directly influences adult BMI and obesity is weak.

Examination of the possible link between intelligence and public assistance participation is hampered by the fact that nationally representative samples generally don't include good measures of both intelligence and public assistance usage. Herrnstein and Murray (1994) and Cao (1996) use the National Longitudinal Survey of Youth (NLSY) and find that lower scores on the Armed Forces Qualification Test (AFQT) are associated with an increased risk of a first spell of cash welfare receipt. However, most scholars view the AFQT as a measure of ability and education rather than as a measure of innate intelligence (e.g., Heckman 1995). Furthermore, when Fischer et al. (1996) reanalyze these data incorporating measures of social context, they find that family SES, school characteristics, educational attainment, and gender are better predictors of who becomes poor than AFQT scores. Without good measures of intelligence in large, nationally representative samples, we aren't able to confirm or refute the possible pathway from intelligence to public assistance participation. The available evidence suggests that intelligence as measured by AFQT plays a small role in influencing the likelihood of adult poverty and welfare receipt, but that characteristics of a person's childhood environment play a bigger role.

Overall, there is little evidence that intelligence directly contributes to either public assistance participation or obesity. Until better data become available we remain unable to adequately test the hypothesis that intelligence contributes to both welfare participation and obesity.

High Time Preference

To the extent that time preference is determined independent of income and the environment, it could constitute an exogenous pathway to both obesity and public assistance. High time preference would, in theory, reduce the ability to follow nutritional guidelines and stick to an exercise program (Fuchs 1991; Laibson 1997), leading to weight gain. Testing this theory is complicated by the fact that measuring time preference is difficult. Chapter 4 presented evidence that higher time preference is associated with poorer nutrition (Huston and Finke 2003) and greater BMI (Smith et al. 2005). The strength of this evidence depends on how well the proxy variables actually measure time preference. Only one study to date has directly tested the relationship between time preference and BMI. Zhang and Rashad (2008) use data on attitudes about weight loss from the 2004 Roper Center Obesity Survey and the desire to lose weight compared to reported weight change in the Behavioral Risk Factor Surveillance System (2003 and 2004) to create variables measuring willpower, which are their proxies for time preference. They find a positive association between the willpower variables and the likelihood of obesity, supporting the hypothesis that high time preference could be one factor contributing to obesity trends.

No studies have directly investigated the possible link between time preference and the likelihood of public assistance participation. Psychological research finds that children who were more impulsive at age four are less able to cope with challenges and frustration and to have lower academic achievement when they reach adolescence (Goleman 1995). This suggests that high time preference may influence educational attainment and the ability to cope with stress, which could in turn influence the likelihood of poverty and public assistance. Further investigation of this possible link would be helpful.

Even if we had convincing evidence that time preference causes both obesity and public assistance participation, we really don't know what determines time preference. Psychiatrists Vaughan and Oldham (1997) report that there is some evidence that a biochemical irregularity in the brain is associated with impulse control problems. Pignatti et al. (2006) test the ability to make favorable long-term decisions in twenty obese and twenty non-obese adults. They report that the obese subjects made more poor choices and seemed less able to learn how to make good long-term choices in their experiment. They note that such impaired learning and judgment is consistent with a brain defect impairing executive decision making. Such a physiological basis would suggest that time preference is an independent causal factor and thus a possible Factor X in our model.

Psychologists find variation in impulsivity among four year olds, which is consistent with a biological predisposition but could also be explained by the quality of the early childhood environment (e.g., Shoda et al. 1990). Several studies produce evidence that educational programs can increase a person's ability to delay gratification, so time preference probably is not immutable (Commission on Positive Youth Development 2005; Goleman 1995; Zins et al. 2004). This suggests that well-designed programs in social and emotional learning could, in theory, improve children's weight in addition to their academic achievement. However, if time preference is determined by childhood environment rather than by physiology, it is not an independent causal factor—that is, it is not a Factor X.

Summary and Recommendations

While the literature strongly indicates that disability and mental illness reduce earnings and increase the likelihood of eligibility for public assistance programs, it is less clear that they also cause obesity. The hypothesis that these two variables contribute to the link between public assistance and obesity appears plausible but is not empirically established. The literature produces little evidence that low intelligence is linked to obesity or that it increases the risk of public assistance usage, so it is not a viable Factor X. Evidence that time preference and obesity are linked is presently weak. The extent to which time preference is innate versus environmentally determined is not clear, so it would be premature to claim this variable as a likely Factor X.

Of the five possible Factor X variables identified, only one garners substantial empirical support as a cause of both obesity and public assistance participation. The evidence that physical and sexual abuse impair health is strong, and there is consistent evidence that such health impairments negatively affect earnings. Furthermore, moderate evidence supports the hypothesis that abuse can lead to physiological and psychological changes that increase the chance of obesity. Thus, abuse probably contributes to the association between public assistance and obesity.

Providing nutrition information or altering the Food Stamp Program probably will not help abuse victims maintain a healthy body weight. Instead, government needs to take a variety of actions to reduce family violence and lessen its detrimental health impacts:

- Support the design and implementation of public education efforts to help widely establish nonviolent norms for social relationships.
- Support social and emotional learning curricula in school to help students better manage their emotions, think through consequences, and learn nonviolent means of dealing with conflict.
- Adequately fund both emergency shelters and long-term affordable housing for victims of domestic violence.
- Support comprehensive programs to help women leave abusive relationships and establish independent households.
- Support therapy programs for abusers which are shown to be effective in reducing additional offenses.

6

Common Threads and Conclusions

Does public assistance cause participants to gain weight and lead to higher obesity prevalence among the poor? While the literature suggests that long-term food stamp receipt may contribute somewhat to women's weight, a much more complex picture of obesity among the poor emerges from this investigation. Obesity contributes to lower earnings and reduced marriage opportunities, increasing a woman's risk of qualifying for public assistance. In addition, poverty can affect body weight through a variety of pathways, suggesting that it can simultaneously cause both obesity and public assistance use. Finally, abuse as either a child or adult can lead to both impoverishment and obesity. To argue that there is one factor linking obesity to socioeconomic status is overly reductive, and, consequently, a single policy cannot adequately address this problem.

Many disciplines contribute to our understanding of the complex association between obesity and public assistance, and three themes emerge from their literatures: individual versus social responsibility for obesity; the obesity effects of non-obesity policy; and the types of evidence that are possible and available to test the models of the obesity–public assistance relationship.

Who Is Responsible for Obesity?

The debate about whether government should undertake policy interventions in order to stem the rise in obesity and which policies to employ hinges largely on the degree to which obesity is a matter of free, personal choice. If obesity arises strictly from an individual's decisions about what and how much to eat and how physically active to be, then obesity is arguably a matter of personal, not social, responsibility. Political conservatives and libertarians generally emphasize personal responsibility for obesity and argue against most government action on the grounds that interventions to influence our diets and physical activity intrude on our personal freedom (Guttman and Ressler 2001). At the extreme, they issue ominous warnings about the "nanny state" and the "food police" (Harsanyi 2007).

America was founded on the principle of individual liberty (at least for the dominant group), and personal freedom remains a top cultural value, so it's not surprising that we tend to hold individuals responsible for their health in general and their body weight in particular (Leichter 2003). Indeed, communications researchers' content analysis of newspaper articles and television broadcasts finds that the majority of media stories frame obesity as the consequence of personal choice, with the individual being responsible for solving the problem (Kim and Willis 2007). Obese people who publicly lose large amounts of weight—for example, on the show "The Biggest Loser"—reap considerable social approval.

However, those who believe that obesity results largely from personal choices often do support government efforts to provide nutrition and health education, because complete information enables people to make better decisions regarding their diet and physical activity (Brownell 2005; Knowles 1977; Wang and Brownell 2005). This support for educational interventions dovetails with economists' argument that free markets often fail to provide adequate information to consumers and that government can potentially improve market functioning by providing such information (Cawley 2004a). Several epidemiological studies provide support for informational policies, finding that modifiable lifestyle factors are strongly associated with morbidity and mortality (e.g., McGinnis and Foege 1993) and that efforts to change individual behavior through education can improve health (e.g., Puska et al. 1995).

In addition to appeals to personal freedom and epidemiological evidence, proponents of the personal responsibility model of obesity argue that telling people that their weight is not under their control but is instead due to genes or the environment leads to fatalism and diminishes their sense of self-efficacy (Klein 2000). They worry that educational programs emphasizing situational causes of population obesity may remove the incentive for individuals to work to avoid excess weight. Indeed, British policy advisors David Halpern and Clive Bates (2004) assert that effective government intervention on behalf of public health needs to convince people that "they can change their behavior and that it will make a difference" (39).

Critics of the personal responsibility argument note several limitations of this view of obesity. For example, physician John H. Knowles (1977) observes that "one man's freedom in health is another man's shackle in taxes and insurance premiums" (59). Some question the degree to which people are truly free to choose their diets and levels of physical activity. For example, are the poor really free to choose healthy diets? Nutrition education can improve individuals' understanding of and appreciation for the health benefits of nutritious diets, but if fresh fruits and vegetables and low-fat dairy products aren't available in local markets or are prohibitively expensive, people's dietary behavior can't change, despite their willingness to change it. To what degree are any of us completely free to choose our diets in the face of our genetic predisposition toward fats and sugars, and the growing pervasiveness of external cues that activate unconscious responses to eat (Cohen and Farley 2008; Wansink 2006)?

Trends in obesity prevalence raise further questions about the personal responsibility argument. For example, does the greater increase in obesity prevalence among the middle and upper socioeconomic strata documented in Chapter 1 mean that those classes have recently become more irresponsible than the poor? In short, placing responsibility for obesity solely on the individual has many limits (Minkler 1999).

Despite the shortcomings of the personal responsibility model, it still has considerable traction in our society. The concept of "fundamental attribution error," familiar to psychologists and sociologists, may explain why (Guttman and Ressler 2001; Wang and Brownell 2005). By incorrectly attributing responsibility for obesity mostly to individual characteristics rather than to the environment or context, the non-obese can view themselves as morally superior, and policy makers are excused from the work and expense of developing and implementing effective government interventions.

Rather than continue the debate about the responsibility for obesity as an "either/or" problem, we would be better served to recognize that individuals, families, communities, organizations, and governments all share responsibility and have the capacity to make changes leading to lower obesity prevalence and better health. Epidemiologists have long explained the spread of disease with the triad of host, vector, and environment and note that to be successful, interventions must address all three components (Swinburn and Egger 2002). In the case of obesity, recommendations designed to change individual behavior will affect only the host, leaving two sides of the triad unfettered in their contribution to population weight gain. Furthermore, the impact of individual interventions tends to be shorter-lived than that of environmental changes (Sallis and Glanz 2006). We will make greater progress in slow-ing the obesity epidemic if we complement actions designed to influence individuals with interventions designed to influence vectors (e.g., the relative price and availability of low-nutrient, high-calorie foods) and the environment. As international public health expert Derek Yach explains, "Individual responsibility can have its full effect only in a society where governments, private interests and other sectors work together to support individuals making healthy choices" (Gorman 2006, 38).

Obesity Effects of Non-obesity Policy

Many policies not directed at influencing obesity prevalence do in fact impact population BMI.[1] For example, some aspects of the Food Stamp Program, which was intended to reduce undernutrition among low-income Americans, may contribute to obesity among women participants (Chapter 2). Educational policies designed to improve student assessment scores can adversely influence body weight because increased emphasis on standardized test scores can reduce the time and resources that schools allocate to physical activity and health education. School funding decisions affect the financial appeal of permitting the advertising and sale of high-calorie, low-nutrient foods and beverages at public schools (Chapter 4).

In addition to education and food assistance, urban design that focuses on roads and favors cars can reduce levels of physical activity, as can inadequate crime prevention efforts, and the location of supermarkets and restaurants affects food choices. Zoning ordinances, housing policy, and environmental regulations help determine exposure to pollutants, which can reduce physical activity and increase stress. Non-obesity programs can also help improve body weight. For example, programs providing mental health screenings and services may reduce the weight consequences of depression and other mental illnesses. Similarly, efforts to reduce the abuse of children and intimate partners and assist victims of domestic violence could also dampen the psychological and biological responses that contribute to weight gain (Chapter 5).

In sum, reducing obesity prevalence and its attendant costs relies not just on employing a variety of anti-obesity policies but also on recognizing and working to avert the possible contributions of non-obesity policies to population weight gain. When policy makers assess the costs and benefits of a program or proposal, they should consider whether there will be unintended health consequences.

Summary of the Evidence

Few of the studies this book discusses employ the ideal research design for determining causality: controlled, random experiments. Running such tests with respect to many aspects of obesity is physically impossible or unethical. This limits researchers' ability to produce incontrovertible evidence regarding whether public assistance programs cause obesity or whether any of the other three models of elevated obesity among the poor hold. Another common limitation of obesity studies is that to collect a large, nationally representative longitudinal sample, researchers often must rely on self-reported height and weight to construct BMI as a measure of body fatness. We know that such data contain reporting errors and that BMI is a limited measure of adiposity, but the expense of accurately collecting an array of anthropometric measures that better assess body fat distribution on a large number of individuals longitudinally is quite expensive.

Given the limits of the data, we will probably never know with certainty which causal pathways truly exist. Yet arguing against taking action to reduce obesity because of lack of absolute proof is a weak justification for doing nothing. While we can't know with certainty which factors cause which, we can make informed decisions based on the accumulation of different types of evidence from varying sources and move forward in terms of an obesity research agenda and policy design.

What does the available evidence tell us about obesity among low-income Americans? Table 6.1 summarizes the strength of the findings. The evidence doesn't support the hypothesis that WIC and school nutrition programs contribute to childhood obesity. Likewise, I found no empirical basis for the notion that cash benefits increase the risk of obesity for either children or adults. Evaluations of the Food Stamp Program (FSP) produce some evidence that participation increases the likelihood of becoming obese, but these results are consistent only among women who participate for an extended period of time. Long-term participants constitute only a small portion of all FSP participants; two-thirds of all new program entrants leave within one year (Cody et al. 2005). They constitute an even smaller portion of poor citizens. While we have no hard evidence on what accounts for the link between women's FSP participation and their BMI, the literature suggests that increased purchasing power and the monthly benefit distribution cycle may play a role. This literature is relatively new and is growing in both volume and methodological sophistication. Perhaps improved statistical methods and better data will enable us to gain a better understanding of what drives the elevated BMIs of women who participate in the FSP for years.

A larger, more established body of research examines whether obesity reduces the ability to earn income and the likelihood of marriage. There is no doubt that obese people face pervasive stigmatization and that obesity can impair health, both of which reduce opportunities for employment and marriage. Strong evidence indicates that obesity moderately lowers women's earnings and significantly reduces their likelihood of finding a mate with whom to pool economic resources. The few studies that examine the impact of obesity on poverty suggest that excessive BMI raises the likelihood of poverty, so it seems possible that obesity could increase the likelihood of participating in public assistance. While no one has directly tested whether obesity impacts the likelihood of public assistance participation, one study reports that morbid obesity (BMI at or above 40) slows the transition from welfare to work (Cawley and Danziger 2005).

The overall picture provided by the review of the "Public Assistance Causes Obesity" and the "Obesity Causes Public Assistance" models suggests that the elevated prevalence of obesity among FSP participants may be due to both the program's impact on obesity and obesity's impacts on family income—that is, there is mutual causation. We are not talking, however, about a simple feedback loop between the FSP and

Table 6.1. Summary of evidence on causal pathways between public assistance and obesity

Public assistance causes obesity	Possible in the case of women's long-term food stamp receipt
Obesity causes public assistance	Probable in the case of women
Poverty causes both public assistance and obesity	Probable
Childhood abuse and intimate partner violence cause both public assistance and obesity	Probable
Disability and mental illness (not caused by obesity) cause both public assistance and obesity	Possible

obesity. Poverty casts a large shadow, constraining the food and physical activity choices available. Specifically, the literature offers strong evidence that poverty limits educational attainment and increases stress and food insecurity. Furthermore, research consistently indicates that lower education and higher stress increase the chance of becoming obese. Moderate to mild food insecurity also contributes to stress and probably alters eating patterns in ways that encourage weight gain.

There is also solid evidence that living in poor urban and rural areas can limit access, both economic and physical, to high-nutrient, low-calorie foods, frequently leaving residents with little choice but to eat calorie-dense foods. Poor neighborhoods also often lack facilities for physical activity and in some cases suffer levels of social disorder that limit time spent outdoors. Poverty not only influences neighborhood characteristics that affect food intake and physical activity but may also increase individuals' focus on the present and decrease the value that they place on the future, thereby increasing their time preference. Simply put, managing frequent immediate crises interferes with long-term thinking. Three studies find correlations between measures of time preference and BMI or obesity, so it's possible that poverty also contributes to obesity by increasing time preference. In sum, part of the association between public assistance and obesity arises because poverty raises the risks both of becoming poor enough to qualify for aid and of becoming obese.

Finally, factors other than poverty also appear to raise the likelihood of public assistance and obesity. To the extent that disabilities and mental illness result from factors other than obesity, they present a separate possible pathway to both public assistance programs and obesity. There is stronger evidence that childhood abuse and domestic violence are likely additional independent contributors to both public assistance and obesity.

Besharov's assertion that public assistance contributes to obesity may be true for women who are long–term participants in the FSP, but public assistance certainly isn't the only reason, or the most influential reason, why obesity is more prevalent among the poor. Furthermore, I find little evidence that giving participants cash rather than food stamps will reduce their risk of obesity. The association between program participation and obesity has many pathways, often with feedback between factors, so no single change in public assistance will produce significant reductions in obesity among low-income Americans. Furthermore, given that the prevalence of obesity is rising faster among higher-income groups than among lower-income groups, focusing policy discussions only on low-income Americans may further stigmatize them and distract policy makers from opportunities to improve the overall health of the entire nation.

What Can We Do to Reduce Obesity Prevalence?

Reducing obesity prevalence could save the government a considerable amount of money, slow the growth in health care costs in general, and improve labor productivity. Rising medical expenditures lead to higher insurance premiums for everyone and increase the financial claims on publicly funded medical programs, particularly Medicaid and Medicare. Reduced labor productivity can adversely affect the macroeconomy and lessen the amount of tax revenues collected. To the degree that obesity contributes to caseloads, its reduction could also lead to savings on public assistance programs. While it is difficult to precisely measure the costs caused by obesity, most estimates run in the tens of billions of dollars annually. Thus, government has a considerable interest in developing policies to improve Americans' weight status.

An additional, less discussed incentive to reduce obesity involves national security. In the late 1950s aides presented President Eisenhower with evidence that American children were less fit than their European counterparts and that about half of the men examined by draft boards were physically unfit (Department of Health and Human Services 2007). Seeing a connection between national physical fitness and national security, Eisenhower initiated the President's Council on Youth Fitness, now known as the President's Council on Physical Fitness and Sports. If government can develop policies that reduce obesity, the nation may benefit from a more fit pool of citizens to serve in the armed forces.

What can policy makers do to reduce obesity? Since the evidence suggests that long-term participation in the FSP is associated with greater BMI in women, we need to explore possible changes in this program. Researchers need to experiment with varying benefits levels and payment frequency to determine whether such changes will lead to improved weight outcomes. Experiments using the Electronic Benefit Transfer system to discount high-nutrient, low-calorie foods among food stamp recipients would also help determine whether nutritional intake and BMI respond to lower prices as predicted.

Expanding the availability of health and nutrition education among public assistance participants could improve their choices regarding food and physical activity, but only if coupled with programs to expand the availability and affordability of high-nutrient, low-calorie foods in low-income areas. Evaluations of the Farmers' Market Nutrition Program, which enables WIC participants to acquire fresh produce at local farmers' markets, will offer insights into how expanding access to fresh fruits and vegetables to low-income areas can affect BMI and health. Part of the education and access efforts should focus on people and institutions that provide child care to low-income families, so that when mothers are on the job their children will have access to proper nutrition and develop healthy eating habits.

The review of the "Obesity Causes Public Assistance" model indicates that one way to reduce public assistance caseloads is to reduce obesity among the general population. Government can affect neighborhood features that influence physical activity, such as sidewalks, bike paths, parks, public safety, pollution levels, and the design of new neighborhoods. Government can and does influence the relative prices of different types of food through agricultural subsidies; that influence could be changed to encourage the consumption of healthier foods.

Government also has considerable influence over school environments and thus has options to help children, in particular, avoid obesity (Haskins et al. 2006; Leviton 2008). Improvements in the quantity and quality of physical education could help children develop the habit of regular physical activity. Increased class time devoted to health, nutrition, and media literacy may help students make better choices about food and leisure-time activities. Devoting resources to social and emotional learning curricula and counseling for students struggling with difficult home situations, teasing, and mental illness could help them learn to cope more successfully with stress and get needed treatments, which could improve both their physical and mental health. Finally, government can control the amount of advertising of high-calorie foods and sedentary leisure-time activities in public schools and the types of foods available for purchase. Teaching children about health and nutrition will prove useless if schools allow the promotion of sugary drinks and fast foods and make them widely available for purchase. Allowing private companies to use public facilities to advertise high-calorie, low-nutrient foods to a captive audience whose welfare at school is a public responsibility is unethical and likely leads to higher future health costs. We should fund our schools adequately so they don't have to resort to beverage and food contracts to acquire needed revenue.

We need to rethink policy regarding advertising to children outside of school as well. Does the First Amendment really guarantee the right of advertisers to promote products to human beings unable to discern commercial and persuasive content? Is using advertising to engage children in the effort to nag their parents into purchasing products constitutionally protected? Childhood is the time to establish healthy habits, but the pervasive influence of marketing makes this difficult. The development of "stealth marketing," particularly using electronic means such as text messaging and chat rooms, raises further legal and ethical concerns about advertising to children.

Government can also improve access to information to help consumers make better food consumption decisions. Nutrition labeling has helped health conscious consumers in their grocery selections, and requiring large restaurants to provide nutritional information would help consumers in their purchases of foods prepared away from home. Government could sponsor public service ad campaigns to promote healthy lifestyles and the social acceptance of all people regardless of body size. Finally, government can take action to lessen the impoverishing impacts of obesity by adopting and enforcing legislation prohibiting discrimination against individuals on the basis of body weight. All of the possible actions to reduce obesity have the potential to both improve health and reduce public assistance caseloads.

Just as anti-obesity efforts have the potential to reduce poverty and welfare caseloads, anti-poverty efforts have the potential to reduce obesity. Chapter 4 described several pathways from poverty to obesity. Income determines where we can live and thus the features of our immediate environment, which influence our health behaviors. Working on new funding strategies for public schools could reduce the variability in school quality across neighborhood socioeconomic measures. Lower-quality education for poor students diminishes their chances of developing the necessary coping skills and knowledge sets to make healthy choices and to effectively deal with life's challenges. Providing subsidized intensive preschool programs can help economically disadvantaged children become more prepared for school and more successful in both the short and long term (Duncan et al. 2007). Poorer nutrition among low-income children can compromise not only physical development but also cognitive development, impairing their ability to benefit from available educational opportunities. We will all benefit via improved health and productivity if we can identify ways to make sure all children receive good nutrition and education regardless of their SES. School breakfasts and lunches are an important part of this effort.

Reducing poverty's limiting impact on access to nutritious foods and facilities for physical activities will help individuals make better health choices. Programs to bring supermarkets and farmers' markets to poor areas could enable low-income Americans to purchase and consume more nutritious foods. Assuring good street lighting, maintaining sidewalks and parks, providing adequate public safety, and opening public school gyms after school hours in low-income areas could encourage physical activity. Offering nutrition and health education in poor communities might also reduce adverse impacts of poverty on body weight. All of these strategies offer opportunities for successful partnerships between government and local community groups.

Finally, government programs designed to prevent and treat mental illness, childhood abuse, and domestic violence likely generate benefits not only in terms of improved psychological well-being but also in terms of better physical health. Helping the mentally ill and victims of abuse cope with psychological problems can diffuse self-destructive behaviors, such as overeating.

What can academics do to help stem the rise in obesity? I encourage us all to venture out of our particular disciplines and develop a broader understanding of the causes and consequences of obesity. Interdisciplinary teams of researchers stand a better chance of advancing our understanding of obesity and the possible steps to reduce it. We must also venture off our campuses and into our communities to share what we've learned both at the grassroots level and with policy makers at various levels of government.

Notes

Introduction

1. Raebel et al. (2004) report evidence that higher direct medical costs for the obese relative to the non-obese arise mostly from higher prescription medication expenses.

2. They also find underweight to be associated with increased mortality. The NHANES data are collected by the National Center for Health Statistics to track the health and nutrition of a nationally representative sample of children and adults in the United States. The NHANES data include measured, rather than self-reported, height and weight, but are not longitudinal as the same people aren't examined in each survey wave. Tucker et al. (2006) use figures from the NHANES and a semi-Markov model to simulate life expectancy adjusting for weight gain over the life course. Their simulations suggest that in younger cohorts (both white and black) higher body mass index is associated with lower life expectancies. However, in older black cohorts the reverse is true, with heavier people expected to live longer. Gronniger (2005) argues that obesity-mortality estimates are generally biased upward due to omitted factors that influence both obesity and mortality.

3. Too little fat, dyslipodemia, also poses serious health risks. I thank Dr. Charles Burant, director of the Michigan Metabolomics and Obesity Center, for his guidance on this section.

4. Additional evidence consistent with fat as a cause of disease comes from follow-up evaluations of laparoscopic gastric banding patients, which find improvements in diabetes, hypertension, and sleep apnea (Champault et al. 2006; Spivak et al. 2005).

5. In addition to these health concerns, researchers are beginning to examine the implications of greater body weight on fuel consumption. For example, industrial engineers estimate that the growth in Americans' body mass index has lead to a small rise in fuel consumption in noncommercial vehicles. Using aggregate data Jacobson and McLay (2006) estimate that body weight gain since 1960 has led to an average increase in annual gasoline usage of 1 to 3.4 gallons per car and 1.6 to 5.5 gallons per light truck. This adds up to between 272 and 938 million additional gallons of gasoline per year, about 0.7 percent of total passenger vehicle consumption. A team of medical doctors at the Centers for Disease Control and Prevention esti-

mates that weight gain during the 1990s raised airline fuel consumption in 2000 by 350 million gallons, costing the airlines an additional $275 million.

6. Preliminary research suggests that childhood obesity among girls may cause an early onset of puberty, which is associated with psychological problems, earlier initiation of sexual intercourse, and teen pregnancy (Kaplowitz et al. 2001; Davison et al. 2003; Lee et al. 2007).

Chapter 1

1. BMI equals weight in kilograms divided by height in meters squared, or weight in pounds multiplied by 703 divided by height in inches squared.

2. Details on these data sets are available at the following websites: NHANES, *www.cdc.gov/nchs/nhanes.htm*; BRFSS, *www.cdc.gov/brfss*; and NLSY, *www.bls.gov/nls*.

3. Childhood obesity is officially defined as a BMI at or above the ninety-fifth percentile on gender- and age-specific revised Centers for Disease Control and Prevention growth charts. Researchers now often refer to this category as "overweight" rather than "obese," but it is analogous to the adult obese category (BMI of 30 or higher) in that it indicates the likelihood of a degree of body fatness which may compromise health. Since this book focuses on obesity, I continue to refer to this category of children as "obese." Similarly, I refer to children with a BMI between the 85th and 95th percentiles as "overweight," but other researcher often call them "at risk of overweight."

4. Marmot (2004) notes that in the Whitehall Study of British civil servants only women exhibited a relationship between BMI and social status, but both genders showed a social gradient in the waist-hip ratio, which measures central fatness.

5. "Poor" is defined as family income below the official poverty line; "near poor" means a family income above the poverty line but below 200 percent of the poverty line; and "not poor" means a family income greater than or equal to 200 percent of the poverty line.

6. Obesity here is defined as a BMI of 27.8 or higher for men and 27.3 or higher for women.

7. In October 2008, the Food Stamp Program was renamed the Supplemental Nutrition Assistance Program (SNAP). For consistency with the cited research, however, I have referred to the program as the Food Stamp Program, or FSP, throughout.

8. State rankings by obesity rates based on the Behavioral Risk Factor Surveillance System are available in United Health Foundation (2005).

Chapter 2

1. I've found no published research on a connection between WIC and women's weight, although the provision of infant formula in this program might allow mothers to retain body fat rather than expend it nursing.

2. The PSID-CDS is a nationally representative sample with 1,449 children in the six-to-twelve age group.
3. Jones et al. include children ages five to twelve in their sample, while Hofferth and Curtain study children ages six to twelve.
4. They also find that girls whose families began FSP had somewhat improved math and reading scores.
5. Other non-emergency feeding programs for adults include Child and Adult Care Food Program; WIC; Commodity Supplemental Food Program; Food Distribution on Indian Reservations; Nutrition Program for the Elderly; Food Distribution Programs for Charitable Institutions and Summer Camps; and Food Donation Programs to Soup Kitchens and Food Banks.
6. Baum (2007), Bitler and Currie (2004), Chen et al. (2005), Dunifon and Kowaleski-Jones (2004), Frongillo et al. (2006), Gibson (2006), Jones and Frongillo (2006), Meyerhoefer and Pylypchuk (2007), Ver Ploeg et al. (2006, 2007), Schanzenbach (2005), and Zagorsky and Smith (2008).
7. TANF's predecessor, AFDC, did not set any work requirements.
8. Similar results have been found in Britain (Hawkins et al. 2007).
9. Heavily dependent households are those for whom Social Security benefits constitute 70 percent or more of income.
10. Self-efficacy refers to the belief in one's ability to control events and outcomes, while self-esteem deals with self-approval or disapproval.

Chapter 3

1. The authors define "at risk of overweight" as a BMI of 27.8 or higher for men and 27.3 or higher for women.
2. Burton et al. (1999) examined telephone-customer-service workers, so their productivity was measured by how much time they took in handling a call and how much time they were unavailable to answer phones calls during working hours.
3. They also find that greater physical activity is associated with lower health care costs in all weight categories.
4. Houston et al. (2007) report that in the Health, Aging, and Body Composition study, obesity at age twenty-five is associated with lower scores on physical functioning tests at ages seventy to seventy-nine, which suggests that obesity can cause disability in later years.
5. Obesity was removed from the Social Security Administration's Listing of Impairments in 1999. According to the Federal Register of May 15, 2000 (vol. 65, no. 94, pp. 31039–43), obesity can qualify a person for disability benefits if a physician finds that obesity constitutes a "severe impairment" to their work, alone or in concert with other listed diseases.
6. Rand and MacGregor (1990) find that the frequency of self-reported weight-based discrimination drops dramatically following weight-loss surgery in a sample of fifty-seven morbidly obese patients.
7. Crandall's theory of the basis of weight-based discrimination draws on Ryan's work on the "Blame the Victim" ideology (Ryan 1971).
8. The situation may be improving, however. More retailers are beginning to

recognize the economic potential of serving the increasing number of plus-size consumers (Fetto 2001).

9. Similar results have been observed in longitudinal studies in Britain (Sargent and Blanchflower 1994). Brunello and D'Hombres (2007) find evidence that a 10 percent rise in BMI modestly depresses real earnings in nine European Union countries, but the impact is larger for men (3.3 percent) than for women (1.9 percent).

10. The Institute of Medicine (2005) and Brescoll et al. (2008) present an expanded discussion of recommendations to reduce childhood obesity, while the review by Swinburn and Egger (2002) summarizes recommendations for both adults and children.

Chapter 4

1. Interview on NPR's Day to Day program, April 27, 2007.
2. Rose et al. define food insufficiency as sometimes or often not getting enough food to eat.
3. While there is convincing evidence that depression can cause obesity, there is also evidence of the reverse causal flow (Chapter 3). Stunkard et al. (2004) summarize the state of current knowledge by saying that "depression influences obesity under some circumstances and obesity influences depression under others."
4. They measure neighborhood disadvantage using an index accounting for the rates of poverty, female headed households, home ownership, and college education. Neighborhood disorder is measured using the Ross-Mirowsky scale and includes both criminal and noncriminal activities and measures of both physical (graffiti, abandoned buildings) and social (drug use) disorder.
5. For more information on this program, go to *www.thefoodtrust.org*.

Chapter 5

1. Community living arrangements include living in a group home, with a relative, or in a semi-independent residential setting.
2. The PSID doesn't include disability information on women in enough survey waves to be included in the analysis.
3. DALYs measure the years of potential life lost because of premature death and years lived with a disability. The second leading cause of DALYs is cardiovascular disease, followed by cancer.

Chapter 6

1. The title for this section derives from the "Health Effects of Non-health Policy" conference sponsored by the National Poverty Center in February 2006.

References

Abraham, L. K. 1993. *Mama Might Be Better Off Dead: The Failure of Health Care in Urban America.* Chicago: University of Chicago Press.

ACOG (American College of Obstetricians and Gynecologists) Committee on Obstetric Practice. 2005. "Obesity in Pregnancy." *Obstetrics and Gynecology* 106 (3): 671–75.

Acs, Z., and Lyles, A. 2007. *Obesity, Business and Public Policy.* Northhampton, MA: Edward Elgar.

Adelaja, A., and Nayga, R. 1997. "Income and Racial Differentials in Selected Nutrient Intakes." *American Journal of Agricultural Economics* 79 (5): 1452–61.

Adler, N., Boyce, T., Chesney, M., Cohen, S., Folkman, S., Kahn, R., and Syme, S. 1994. "Socioeconomic Status and Health: The Challenge of the Gradient." *American Psychologist* 49 (1): 15–24.

Alaimo, K., Olson, C., and Frongillo, E. 2001. "Low Family Income and Food Insufficiency in Relation to Overweight in U.S. Children." *Archives of Pediatric and Adolescent Medicine* 155 (10): 1161–67.

———. 2002. "Family Food Insufficiency, but Not Low Family Income, Is Positively Associated with Dysthymia and Suicide Symptoms in Adolescents." *Journal of Nutrition* 132 (4): 719–25.

Alaimo, K., Packnett, E., Miles, R., and Kruger, D. 2008. "Fruit and Vegetable Intake among Urban Community Gardeners." *Journal of Nutrition Education and Behavior* 40 (2): 94–101.

Alcaly, R., and Klevorick, A. 1971. "Food Prices in Relation to Income Levels in New York City." *Journal of Business* 44 (4): 380–97.

Altonji, J., and Blank, R. 1999. "Race and Gender in the Labor Market." In *Handbook of Labor Statistics,* ed. O. Ashenfelter and D. Card, 3: 3143–259. Amsterdam: Elsevier.

Alvarez, J., Pavao, J., Baumrind, N., and Kimerling, R. 2007. "The Relationship between Child Abuse and Adult Obesity among California Women." *American Journal of Preventive Medicine* 33 (1): 28–33.

Alwitt, L., and Donley, T. 1997. "Retail Stores in Poor Urban Neighborhoods." *Journal of Consumer Affairs* 31 (1): 139–64.

Al-Zahrani, M., Bissada, N., and Borawskit, E. 2003. "Obesity and Periodontal Disease in Young, Middle-Aged, and Older Adults." *Journal of Periodontology* 74 (5): 610–15.

American Academy of Pediatrics. 2006. "Policy Statement: Children, Adolescents, and Advertising." *Pediatrics* 118 (6): 2563–69.

American Lung Assocation. 2001. "Urban Air Pollution and Health Inequalities: A Workshop Report." *Environmental Health Perspectives* 109 (Suppl. 3): 357–74.

American Obesity Association. "AOA Fact Sheets: Obesity in the U.S." Available at *obesity1.tempdomainname.com.*

American Psychological Association. 2004. "Report of the APA Task Force on Advertising and Children: Summary of Findings and Conclusions." Available at *www. apa.org.*

American Public Health Association. 2003. "Food Marketing and Advertising Directed at Children and Adolescents: Implications for Overweight." Policy No. 200317. Available at *www.apha.org.*

Anderson, D., and Saunders, D. 2007. "The Postseparation Psychological Recovery of Domestic Abuse Survivors." In *Intimate Partner Violence*, ed. K. Kendall-Tackett and S. Giacomoni. Kingston, NJ: Civic Research Institute.

Anderson, J., Bybee, D., Brown, R., McLean, D., Garcia, E., Breer, M., and Schillo, B. 2001. "5 a Day Fruit and Vegetable Intervention Improves Consumption in a Low Income Population." *Journal of the American Dietetic Association* 101: 195–202.

Anderson, P., Butcher, K., and Levine, P. 2003a. "Economic Perspectives on Childhood Obesity." *Economic Perspectives* 27 (3): 30–48.

———. 2003b. "Maternal Employment and Overweight Children." *Journal of Health Economics* 22 (3): 477–504.

Anderson, S., Cohen, P., Naumova, E., and Must, A. 2006. "Association of Depression and Anxiety Disorders with Weight Change in a Prospective Community-Based Study of Children Followed Up into Adulthood." *Archives of Pediatric and Adolescent Medicine* 160 (3): 285–91.

Angell, M., and Kassirer, J. 1998. "Losing Weight—An Ill-Fated New Year's Resolution." *New England Journal of Medicine* 338 (Jan. 1): 52–54.

APA. *See* American Psychological Association

Arena, V., Padiyar, K., Burton, W., and Schwerha, J. 2006. "The Impact of Body Mass Index on Short-Term Disability in the Workplace." *Journal of Occupational and Environmental Medicine* 48 (11): 1118–24.

Armstrong, D. 2000. "A Survey of Community Gardens in Upstate New York: Implications for Health Promotion and Community Development." *Health and Place* 6: 319–27.

Arnade, C., and Gopinath, M. 2006. "The Dynamics of Individuals' Fat Consumption." *American Journal of Agricultural Economics* 88 (4): 836–50.

Associated Press. 2006. "Michigan Grocers Seek Twice-Monthly Food Stamp Distributions." *New York Times.* May 13.

Averett, S., and Korenman, S. 1996. "The Economic Reality of the Beauty Myth." *Journal of Human Resources* 31 (2): 304–30.

———. 1999. "Black-White Differences in Social and Economic Consequences of Obesity." *International Journal of Obesity* 23: 166–73.

Axinn, W., Duncan, G., and Thornton, A. 1997. "The Effects of Parents' Income, Wealth, and Attitudes on Children's Completed Schooling and Self-Esteem." In *Consequences of Growing Up Poor*, ed. G. Duncan and J. Brooks-Gunn, 518–40. New York: Russell Sage Foundation.

Bacolor, J., Guzmán, L., and Waller, A. 2007. "Availability and Accessibility of Healthy Food in Ypsilanti, Michigan." Ypsilanti, MI: Washtenaw County Public Health Department.

Balasubramanian, S., and Cole, C. 2002. "Consumers' Search and Use of Nutrition Information: The Challenge and Promise of the Nutrition Labeling and Education Act." *Journal of Marketing* 66 (3): 112–27.

Baltrus, P., Lynch, J., Everson-Rose, S., Raghunathan, T., and Kaplan, G. 2005. "Race/Ethnicity, Life-Course Socioeconomic Position, and Body Weight Trajectories over 34 Years: The Alameda County Study." *American Journal of Public Health* 95 (9): 1595–1601.

Barefoot, J., Heitman, B., Helms, M., Williams, R., Surwit, R., and Siegler, I. 1998. "Symptoms of Depression and Changes in Body Weight from Adolescence to Mid-Life." *International Journal of Obesity* 22: 688–94.

Barker, D. 1997. "Maternal Nutrition, Fetal Nutrition, and Disease in Later Life." *Nutrition* 13 (9): 807–13.

Basiotis, P. 2002. "In the U.S., Food Insufficient or Insecure Persons Are More Likely to Be Overweight, Why?" Consumer Federation of America Food Policy Conference, Washington, DC, April 23.

Basiotis, P., Kramer-LeBlanc, C., and Kennedy, E. 1998. "Maintaining Nutrition Security and Diet Quality: The Role of the Food Stamp Program and WIC." *Family Economics and Nutrition Review* 11 (1–2): 4–16.

Basiotis, P., and Lino, M. 2002. "Food Insufficiency and Prevalence of Overweight among Adult Women." *Nutrition Insights* 26: 1–2.

Batty, G., Deary, I., and Macintyre, S. 2007. "Childhood IQ in Relation to Risk Factors for Premature Mortality in Middle-Aged Persons: The Aberdeen Children of the 1950s Study." *Journal of Epidemiology and Community Health* 61: 241–47.

Baum, A., Garofalo, J., and Yali, A. 1999. "Socioeconomic Status and Chronic Stress: Does Stress Account for the SES Effects on Health?" *Annals of the New York Academy of Sciences* 896: 131–44.

Baum, C. 2007. "The Effects of Food Stamps on Obesity." USDA, Economic Research Service, Contractor and Cooperator Report No. 34.

Baum, C., and Ford, W. 2004. "The Wage Effects of Obesity: A Longitudinal Study." *Health Economics* 13: 885–99.

Baumeister, R., and Vohs, K. 2003. "Willpower, Choice, and Self-Control." In *Time and Decision: Economic and Psychological Perspectives on Intertemporal Choice*, ed. G. Lowenstein, D. Read, and R. Baumeister, 201–16. Russell Sage Foundation: New York.

Beaudoin, C., Fernandez, C., Wall, J., and Farley, T. 2007. "Promoting Healthy Eating and Physical Activity: Short-Term Effects of a Mass Media Campaign." *American Journal of Preventive Medicine* 32 (3): 217–23.

Becker, G., and Mulligan, C. 1997. "The Endogenous Determination of Time Preference." *Quarterly Journal of Economics* 112 (3): 729–58.

Beckett, W., Jacobs, D., Yu, X., Iribarren, C., and Williams, O. 2001. "Asthma Is Associated with Weight Gain in Females but Not Males, Independent of Physical Activity." *American Journal of Respiratory Critical Care Medicine* 164 (11): 2045–50.

Belle, D., and Doucet, J. 2003. "Poverty, Inequality, and Discrimination as Sources of Depression among U.S. Women." *Psychology of Women Quarterly* 27 (2): 101–13.

Besharov, D. 2002. "We're Feeding the Poor As If They're Starving." *WashingtonPost.com*, December 8.

———. 2003. "Growing Overweight and Obesity in America: The Potential Role of Federal Nutrition Programs." Testimony before the Committee on Agriculture, Nutrition, and Forestry, April 2.

Besharov, D., and Germanis, P. 2000. "Evaluating WIC." *Evaluation Policy* 24 (2): 123–90.

Bhattacharya, J., and Currie, J. 2001. "Youths at Nutritional Risk: Malnourished or Misnourished?" In *Youths as Risk*, ed. J. Gruber. Chicago: University of Chicago Press.

———. 2004. "Poverty, Food Insecurity, and Nutritional Outcomes for Children and Adults." *Journal of Health Economics* 23 (4): 839–62.

Bhattacharya, J., Currie, J., and Haider, S. 2004a. "Breakfast of Champions? The School Breakfast Program and the Nutrition of Children." NBER Working Paper No. W10608.

———. 2004b. "Evaluating the Impact of School Nutrition Programs: Final Report." USDA, Economic Research Service, Electronic Publications from the Food Assistance and Nutrition Research Program, E-FAN-04-008, July.

———. 2004c. "Poverty, Food Insecurity, and Nutritional Outcomes in Children and Adults." *Journal of Health Economics* 23: 839–62.

Biggs, J. 2004. "Few Food Dollars Often Lead to Many Unhealthy Extra Pounds." *HealthyMemphis.org*, September 27.

Bitler, M., and Currie, J. 2004. "Medicaid at Birth, WIC Takeup, and Children's Outcomes." Institute for Research on Poverty Discussion Paper No. 1286-04.

———. 2005. "Does WIC Work? The Effects of WIC on Pregnancy and Birth Outcomes." *Journal of Policy Analysis and Management* 24 (1): 73–91.

Björntorp, P. 2001. "Do Stress Reactions Cause Abdominal Obesity and Comorbidities?" *Obesity Reviews* 2: 73–86.

Björntorp, P., and Rosmond, R. 2000. "Obesity and Cortisol." *Nutrition* 16: 924–36.

Black, D., Goldstein, R., and Mason, E. 1992. "Prevalence of Mental Disorders in 88 Morbidly Obese Bariatric Clinic Patients." *American Journal of Psychiatry* 149: 227–34.

Black, D., Sciacca, J., and Coster, D. 1994. "Extremes in Body Mass Index: Probabilities in Healthcare Expenditures." *Preventive Medicine* 23: 385–93.

Blau, F., Ferber, M., and Winkler, A. 2006. *The Economics of Women, Men, and Work*. 5th ed. Upper Saddle River, NJ: Pearson Prentice Hall.

Block, J., Scribner, R., and DeSalvo, K. 2004. "Fast Food, Race/Ethnicity, and Income: A Geographic Analysis." *American Journal of Preventive Medicine* 27 (3): 211–17.

Boarnet, M., Anderson, C., Day, K., McMillan, T., and Alfonzo, M. 2005. "Evaluation of the California Safe Routes to School Legislation." *American Journal of Preventive Medicine* 28 (2, Suppl. 2): 134–40.

Bogin, B. 1999. *Patterns of Human Growth*. 2nd ed. Cambridge: Cambridge University Press.

Bogost, I. 2005. "Frame and Metaphor in Political Games." Proceedings of the DiGRA 2005 Conference.

Boone, J., Gordon-Larsen, P., Adair, L., and Popkin, B. 2007. "Screen Time and Physical Activity during Adolescence: Longitudinal Effects on Obesity in Young Adulthood." *International Journal of Behavioral Nutrition and Physical Activity* 4 (26), doi:10.1186/1479-5868-4-26.

Borghans, L., and Golsteyn, B. 2006. "Time Discounting and the Body Mass Index: Evidence from the Netherlands." *Economics and Human Biology* 4: 39–61.

Borjas, G. 2004. "Food Insecurity and Public Assistance." *Journal of Public Economics* 88: 1421–43.

Bove, C., and Olson, C. 2006. "Obesity in Low-Income Rural Women: Qualitative

Insights about Physical Activity and Eating Patterns." *Women and Health* 44 (1): 57–78.

Bowman, S., Gortmaker, S., Ebbling, C., Pereira, M., Ludwig, D. 2004. "Effects of Fast-Food Consumption on Energy Intake and Dietary Quality among Children in a National Household Survey." *Pediatrics* 113 (1): 112–18.

Bradbard S., Michaels, E., Fleming, F., and Campbell, M. 1997. "Understanding the Food Choices of Low-Income Families." Report from Lisboa Associates to USDA, Food and Consumer Service.

Brady, S., and Matthews, K. 2002. "The Influence of Socioeconomic Status and Ethnicity on Adolescents' Exposure to Stressful Life Events." *Journal of Pediatric Psychology* 27 (7): 575–83.

Brescoll, V., Kersh, R., and Brownell, K. 2008. "Assessing the Feasibility and Impact of Federal Childhood Obesity Policies." *Annals of the American Academy of Political and Social Science* 615: 178–94.

Breunig, R., and Dasgupta, I. 2005. "Do Intra-household Effects Generate the Food Stamp Cash-Out Puzzle?" *American Journal of Agricultural Economics* 87 (3): 552–68.

Breunig, R., Dasgupta, I., Gundersen, C., and Pattanaik, P. 2001. "Explaining the Food Stamp Cash-Out Puzzle." USDA, Economic Research Service, Food Assistance and Nutrition Research Report No. 12.

Britz, B., Siegfried, W., Ziegler, A., Lamertz, C., Herpertz-Dahlmann, B., Remschmidt, H., Wittchen, H., and Hebebrand, J. 2000. "Rates of Psychiatric Disorder in a Clinical Study Group of Adolescents with Extreme Obesity and in Obese Adolescents Ascertained via Population Based Study." *International Journal of Obesity* 24 (12): 1707–14.

Brooks-Gunn, J., and Duncan, G. 1997. "The Effects of Poverty on Children." *Future of Children* 7 (2): 55–71.

Brown, G., and Harris, T. 1978. *Social Origins of Depression*. London: Tavistock.

Brown, G., and Moran, P. 1997. "Single Mothers, Poverty and Depression." *Psychological Medicine* 27: 21–33.

Brown, P. 1991. "Culture and the Evolution of Obesity." *Human Nature* 2 (1): 31–57.

Brownell, K. 2005. "The Chronicling of Obesity: Growing Awareness of Its Social, Economic, and Political Contexts." *Journal of Health Politics, Policy and Law* 30 (5): 955–64.

Bruce, M., Takeuchi, D., and Leaf, P. 1991. "Poverty and Psychiatric Status." *Archives of General Psychiatry* 48: 470–74.

Brunello, G., and D'Hombres, B. 2007. "Does Body Weight Affect Wages? Evidence from Europe." *Economics and Human Biology* 5: 1–19.

Bullard, R. 2005. *The Quest for Environmental Justice: Human Rights and the Politics of Pollution*. San Francisco: Sierra Club Books.

Bullock, H., Wyche, K., and Williams, W. 2001. "Media Images of the Poor." *Journal of Social Issues* 57 (2): 229–46.

Burdette, H., Wadden, T., and Whitaker, R. 2006. "Neighborhood Safety, Collective Efficacy, and Obesity in Women with Young Children." *Obesity* 14 (3): 518–25.

Burdette, H., and Whitaker, R. 2004. "Neighborhood Playgrounds, Fast Food Restaurants, and Crime: Relationships to Overweight in Low-Income Preschool Children." *Preventive Medicine* 38: 57–63.

Burkhauser, R., and Cawley, J. 2004. "Obesity, Disability, and Movement onto the

Disability Insurance Rolls." University of Michigan Retirement Research Center Working Paper No. 2004-089.

Burney, J., and Haughton, B. 2002. "EFNEP: A Nutrition Education Program That Demonstrates Cost-Benefit." *Journal of the American Dietetic Association* 102 (1): 39–45.

Burstein, N., Fox, M. K., Hiller, J., Kornfeld, R., Lam, K., Price, C., and Rodda, D. 2000. "WIC General Analysis Project: Profile of WIC Children." Cambridge, MA: Abt Associates, Inc.

Burtless, G. 2004. "The Labor Force Status of Mothers Who Are Most Likely to Receive Welfare: Changes Following Reform." Brookings Institution Web Editorial, March 30. Available at *www.brookings.edu*.

Burton, W., Chen, C., Schultz, A., and Edington, D. 1998. "The Economic Costs Associated with Body Mass Index in a Workplace." *Journal of Occupational and Environmental Medicine* 40 (9): 786–92.

Burton, W., Conti, D., Chen, C., Schultz, A., and Edington, D. 1999. "The Role of Health Risk Factors and Disease on Worker Productivity." *Journal of Occupational and Environmental Medicine* 41 (10): 863–77.

Butler, J., and Raymond, J. 1996. "The Effect of the Food Stamp Program on Nutrient Intake." *Economic Inquiry* 34 (4): 781–98.

Cao, J. 1996. "Welfare Recipiency and Welfare Recidivism: An Analysis of the NLSY Data." Institute for Research on Poverty Discussion Paper No. 1081-96.

Caraher, M., Landon, J., Dalmeny, K. 2006. "Television Advertising and Children: Lessons from Policy Development." *Public Health Nutrition* 9 (5): 596–605.

Carlson, A., and Senauer, B. 2003. "The Impact of the Special Supplemental Nutrition Program for Women, Infants, and Children on Child Health." *American Journal of Agricultural Economics* 85 (2): 479–91.

Carpenter, C. 2006. "The Effects of Employment Protection for Obese People." *Industrial Relations* 45 (3): 393–415.

Carr, D., and Friedman, M. 2005. "Is Obesity Stigmatizing? Body Weight, Perceived Discrimination, and Psychological Well-Being in the United States." *Journal of Health and Social Behavior* 46: 244–59.

Cartwright, M., Wardle, J., Steggles, N., Simon, A., Croker, H., and Jarvis, M. 2003. "Stress and Dietary Practices in Adolescents." *Health Psychology* 22 (4): 362–69.

Case, A., Lubotsky, D., Paxson, C. 2002. "Economic Status and Health in Childhood: The Origins of the Gradient." *American Economics Review* 92 (5): 1308–34.

Casey, P., Simpson, P., Gossett, J., Bogle, M., et al. 2006. "The Association of Child and Household Food Insecurity with Childhood Overweight Status." *Pediatrics* 118 (5): 2206–7.

Casey, P., Szeto, K., Lensing, S., Bogle, M., and Weber, J. 2001. "Children in Food-Insufficient, Low-Income Families: Prevalence, Health, and Nutrition Status." *Archives of Pediatric and Adolescent Medicine* 155 (4): 508–14.

Castner, L., and Schirm, A. 2004. "State Food Stamp Participation Rates for the Working Poor in 2001." Final report submitted to the USDA, Mathematica Policy Research Reference No. 6044-714.

Cawley, J. 2000. "An Instrumental Variables Approach to Measuring the Effect of Body Weight on Employment Disability." *Health Services Research* 35 (5, pt. 2): 1159–79.

———. 2001. "Body Weight and the Dating and Sexual Behaviors of Young Adolescents." In *Social Awakenings: Adolescent Behavior as Adulthood Approaches*, ed. R. T. Michael, 174–98. New York: Russell Sage Foundation.

———. 2004a. "An Economic Framework for Understanding Physical Activity and Eating Behaviors." *American Journal of Preventive Medicine* 27 (3, Suppl. 1): 117–25.

———. 2004b. "The Impact of Obesity on Wages." *Journal of Human Resources* 39 (2): 452–74.

Cawley, J., and Danziger, S. 2005. "Morbid Obesity and the Transition from Welfare to Work." *Journal of Policy Analysis and Management* 24 (4): 727–43.

Cawley, J., Joyner, K., and Sobal, J. 2006. "Size Matters: The Influence of Adolescents' Weight and Height on Dating and Sex." *Rationality and Society* 18 (1): 67–94.

Cawley, J., Meyerhoefer, C., and Newhouse, D. 2007. "The Impact of State Physical Education Requirements on Youth Physical Activity and Overweight." *Health Economics* 16 (12): 1287–1301.

CDC. *See* Centers for Disease Control and Prevention

Center for Science in the Public Interest. 2007. "British Crackdown on Junk Food Ads Praised." CSPI Newsroom, February 23. Available at *www.cspinet.org.*

Center on Hunger and Poverty. 2002. "The Consequences of Hunger and Food Insecurity: Evidence from Recent Scientific Studies." June. Available at *www. centeronhunger.org.*

Centers for Disease Control and Prevention. n.d. *Physical Activity and Health: Persons with Disabilities; A Report of the Surgeon General.* Available at *www.cdc.gov.*

———. 1995. "Nutritional Status of Children Participating in the Special Supplemental Nutrition Program for Women, Infants, and Children—United States, 1988–91." *Morbidity and Mortality Weekly Report* 45 (3): 65–69.

———. 1996. *Physical Activity and Health: A Report of the Surgeon General.* Atlanta: National Center for Chronic Disease Prevention and Health Promotion.

———. 1999. "Neighborhood Safety and the Prevalence of Physical Activity— Selected States, 1996." *Morbidity and Mortality Weekly Report* 48: 143–46.

———. 2000. "Prevalence of Leisure-Time and Occupational Physical Activity among Employed Adults—United States, 1990." *Morbidity and Mortality Weekly Report* 49 (19): 420–24.

———. 2002. "State-Specific Prevalence of Obesity among Adults with Disabilities—Eight States and the District of Columbia, 1998–1999." *Morbidity and Mortality Weekly Report* 51 (36): 805–8.

———. 2003. "Physical Activity Levels among Children Aged 9–13 Years—United States, 2002." *Morbidity and Mortality Weekly Report* 52 (33): 785–88.

Chadwick Center on Children and Families. 2004. *Closing the Quality Chasm in Child Abuse Treatment: Identifying and Disseminating Best Practices.* San Diego, CA: Chadwick Center on Children and Families.

Champault, A., Duwat, O., Polliand, C., Rizk, N., and Champault, G. 2006. "Quality of Life after Laparoscopic Gastric Banding: Prospective Study with a Follow-Up of 2 Years." *Surgical Laparoscopy, Endoscopy, and Percutaneous Techniques* 16 (3): 131–36.

Chandola, T., Deary, I., Blane, D., Batty, G. 2006. "Childhood IQ in Relation to Obesity and Weight Gain in Adult Life: The National Child Development (1958) Study." *International Journal of Obesity* 30: 1422–32.

Chang, V., and Lauderdale, D. 2005. "Income Disparities in Body Mass Index and

Obesity in the United States, 1971–2002." *Archives of Internal Medicine* 165: 2122–28.

Chapman, G. 2003. "Time Discounting of Health Outcome." In *Time and Decision: Economic and Psychological Perspectives on Intertemporal Choice*, ed. G. Lowenstein, D. Read, and R. Baumeister, 395–417. New York: Russell Sage Foundation.

Chase-Lansdale, P., Moffitt, R., Lohman, B., Cherlin, A., Coley, R., Pittman, L., Roff, J., and Votruba-Drzal, E. 2003. "Mother's Transitions from Welfare to Work and the Well Being of Preschoolers and Adolescents." *Science* 299 (5612): 1548–52.

Cheadle, A., Psaty, B., Curry, S., Wagner, E., Diehr, P., Koepsell, T., and Kristal, A. 1991. "Community-Level Comparisons between the Grocery Store Environment and Individual Dietary Practices." *Preventive Medicine* 20 (2): 250–61.

Chen, Z., Yen, S., and Eastwood, D. 2005. "Effects of Food Stamp Participation on Body Weight and Obesity." *American Journal of Agricultural Economics* 87 (5): 1167–73.

Chernin, K. 1981. *The Obsession: Reflections on the Tyranny of Slenderness*. New York: Harper Collins.

Chou, S., Rashad, I., and Grossman, M. 2005. "Fast-Food Restaurant Advertising on Television and Its Influence on Childhood Obesity." NBER Working Paper No. 11879.

Chowdhary, U., and Beale, N. 1988. "Plus-Size Women's Clothing Interest, Satisfactions and Dissatisfactions with Ready-to-Wear Apparel." *Perceptual and Motor Skills* 66 (3): 783–88.

Chrousos, G. 2000. "The Role of Stress and the Hypothalamic-Pituitary-Adrenal Axis in the Patheogenesis of Metabolic Syndrome: Neuro-endocrine and Target Tissue-Related Causes." *International Journal of Obesity* 24 (Suppl. 2): S50–S55.

Chung, C., and Myers, S. 1999. "Do the Poor Pay More for Food? An Analysis of Grocery Store Availability and Food Price Disparities." *Journal of Consumer Affairs* 33 (2): 276–96.

Classen, T., and Hokayem, C. 2005. "Childhood Influences on Youth Obesity." *Economics and Human Biology* 3: 165–87.

Cody, S., Gleason, P., Schechter, B., Satake, M., and Sykes, J. 2005. "Food Stamp Program Entry and Exit: An Analysis of the Participation Trends of the 1990s." USDA, Economic Research Service, Contractor and Cooperator Report No. 8.

Cohen, D., and Farley, T. 2008. "Eating as an Automatic Behavior." *Preventing Chronic Disease* 5 (1): 1–7.

Coiro, M. 2001. "Depressive Symptoms among Women Receiving Welfare." *Women and Health* 32 (1–2): 1–23.

Colditz, G. 1992. "Economic Costs of Obesity." *American Journal of Clinical Nutrition* 55: 503S–75.

Cole, N., and Fox, M. K. 2004. "Nutrition and Health Characteristics of Low-Income Populations. Vol. 2, WIC Program Participants and Nonparticipants." USDA, Economic Research Service, Electronic Publications from the Food Assistance and Nutrition Program, E-FAN-04-014-2.

Commission on Positive Youth Development. 2005. "The Positive Perspective on Youth Development." In *Treating and Preventing Adolescent Mental Health Disorders*, ed. D. Evans, E. Foa, R. Gur, H. Hendin, C. O'Brien, M. Seligman, and B. Walsh. New York: Oxford University Press.

Conley, D., and Glauber, R. 2005. "Gender, Body Mass, and Socioeconomic Status." NBER Working Paper No. 11343.

Cooley, E., Toray, T., Valdez, N., and Tee, M. 2007. "Risk Factors for Maladaptive Eating Patterns in College Women." *Eating and Weight Disorders* 12 (3): 132–39.

Coon, K., and Tucker, K. 2002. "Television and Children's Consumption Patterns." *Minerva Pediatrica* 54 (5): 423–36.

Corburn, J., Osleeb, J., and Porter, M. 2006. "Urban Asthma and the Neighborhood Environment in New York City." *Health and Place* 12: 167–79.

Corcoran, M., Danziger, S., Kalil, A., and Seefeldt, K. 2000. "How Welfare Reform is Affecting Women's Work." *Annual Review of Sociology* 26: 241–69.

Cotton Incorporated, Inc. 1999. "The Forgotten (Young) Woman: Plus-Size Young Women Want Choice and Fit Too." January 28. Available at *www.cottoninc.com*.

Coulter, M. 2004. *The Impact of Domestic Violence on the Employment of Women on Welfare.* U.S. Department of Justice, award no. 1998-WT-VX-0020.

Cozzarelli, C., Wilkinson, A., and Tagler, M. 2001. "Attitudes toward the Poor and Attributions of Poverty." *Journal of Social Issues* 57 (2): 207–27.

Crandall, C. 1991. "Do Heavy-Weight Students Have More Difficulty Paying for College?" *Personality and Social Psychology Bulletin* 17: 606–11.

———. 1994. "Prejudice against Fat People: Ideology and Self-Interest." *Journal of Personality and Social Psychology* 66 (5): 882–94.

———. 1995. "Do Parents Discriminate against Their Heavyweight Daughters?" *Personality and Social Psychology Bulletin* 21: 724–35.

Crepinsek, M., and Burstein, N. 2004. "Maternal Employment and Children's Nutrition. Vol. 2, Other Nutrition-Related Outcomes." USDA, Economic Research Service, Electronic Publications from the Food Assistance and Nutrition Research Program, E-FAN-04-006-2.

Cristofar, S., and Basiotis, P. 1992. "Dietary Intakes and Selected Characteristics of Women Ages 19–50 Years and Their Children Ages 1–5 Years by Reported Perception of Food Sufficiency." *Journal of Nutrition Education* 134: 1432–38.

Crosnoe, R. 2007. "Gender, Obesity, and Education." *Sociology of Education* 80: 241–60.

Cummins, S., and Macintyre, S. 2005. "Food Environments and Obesity—Neighborhood or Nation?" *International Journal of Epidemiology* 35: 100–104.

Currie, J. 2003. "U.S. Food and Nutrition Programs." In *Means-Tested Transfer Programs in the United States*, ed. R. Moffitt. Chicago: University of Chicago Press.

Currie, J., and Cole, N. 1993. "Welfare and Child Health: The Link between AFDC Participation and Birth Weight." *American Economic Review* 8 (4): 971–85.

Curtis, K., and McClellan, S. 1995. "Falling through the Safety Net: Poverty, Food Assistance, and Shopping Constraints in an American City." *Urban Anthropology* 24 (1–2): 93–135.

Cutler, D., Glaeser, E., and Shapiro, J. 2003. "Why Have Americans Become More Obese?" *Journal of Economic Perspectives* 17 (3): 93–118.

Dallman, M., la Fleur, S., Pecoraro, N., Gomez, F., Houshyar, H., and Akana, S. 2004. "Minireview: Glucocorticoids—Food Intake, Abdominal Obesity, and Wealthy Nations in 2004." *Endocrinology* 145 (6): 2633–38.

Dallman, M., Pecoraro, N., Akana, S., la Fleur, S., Gomez, F., Houshyar, H., Bell, M., Bhatnagar, S., Laugero, K., and Manalo, S. 2003. "Chronic Stress and Obesity: A New View of 'Comfort Food.'" *Proceedings of the National Academy of Science* 100 (20): 11696–701.

Dallman, M., Pecoraro, N., and la Fleur, S. 2005. "Chronic Stress and Comfort Foods: Self-Medication and Abdominal Obesity." *Brain, Behavior, and Immunity* 19: 275–80.

Damon, A., King, R., and Leibtag, E. 2006. "Household Food Expenditures across Income Groups: Do Poor Households Spend Differently than Rich Ones?" Paper presented at the American Agricultural Economics Association Annual Meetings, Long Beach, CA, July 23–26.

Daniel, M., Moore, D., Decker, S., Belton, L., DeVellis, B., Doolen, A., and Campbell, M. 2006. "Associations among Education, Cortisol Rhythm, and BMI in Blue-Collar Women." *Obesity* 14 (2): 327–35.

Dannenberg, A. L., Burton, D. C., and Jackson, R. J. 2004. "Economic and Environmental Costs of Obesity: The Impact on Airlines." *American Journal of Preventive Medicine* 27 (3): 264.

Danziger, S. 2002. "Approaching the Limits: Early Lessons from Welfare Reform." Joint Center for Poverty Research Working Paper No. 195.

Danziger, S., Corcoran, M., Danziger, S., Heflin, C., Kalil, A., Levine, J., Rosen, D., Seefeldt, K., Siefert, K., and Tolman, R. 2000. "Barriers to the Employment of Recipients." In *Prosperity for All? The Economic Boom and African-Americans*, ed. R. Cherry and W. Rodgers, 245–78. New York: Russell Sage Foundation.

Danziger, S., Corcoran, M., and Heflin, C. 2000. "Work, Income, and Material Hardship after Welfare Reform." *Journal of Consumer Affairs* 34 (1): 6–30.

Darmon, N., Briend, A., and Drewnowski, A. 2004. "Energy-Dense Diets Are Associated with Lower Diet Costs: A Community Study of French Adults." *Public Health Nutrition* 17 (1): 21–27.

Darmon, N., Ferguson, E., and Briend, A. 2002. "A Cost Constraint Alone Has Adverse Effects on Food Selection and Nutrient Density: An Analysis of Human Diets by Linear Programming." *Journal of Nutrition* 132: 3764–71.

———. 2003. "Do Economic Constraints Encourage the Selection of Energy Dense Diets?" *Appetite* 41: 315–22.

Datar, A., and Sturm, R. 2004. "Physical Education in Elementary School and Body Mass Index: Evidence from the Early Childhood Longitudinal Study." *American Journal of Public Health* 94 (9): 1501–6.

Davidow, J. 2004. "The Obesity Crisis: A Health Diet Often beyond the Means of Poor, Hungry." *Seattle Post-Intelligencer*, September 9. Available at *seattlepi. nwsource.com*.

Davison, K., Susman, E., and Birch, L. 2003. "Percent Body Fat at Age 5 Predicts Earlier Pubertal Development among Girls at Age 9." *Pediatrics* 111 (4): 815–21.

Degher, D., and Hughes, G. 1999. "The Adoption and Management of a 'Fat' Identity." In *Interpreting Weight: The Social Management of Fatness and Thinness*, ed. J. Sobal and D. Maurer. New York: Aldine de Gruyter.

DeLeire, T., and Levy, H. 2005. "The Material Well-Being of Single Mother Households in the 1980s and 1990s: What Can We Learn from Food Spending?" National Poverty Center Working Paper No. 01-05.

Delva, J., Johnston, L., and O'Malley, P. 2007. "The Epidemiology of Overweight and Related Lifestyle Behaviors." *American Journal of Preventive Medicine* 33 (4, Suppl. 1): S178–S186.

Delva, J., O'Malley, P., and Johnston, L. 2007. "Availability of More-Healthy and Less-Healthy Food Choices in American Schools." *American Journal of Preventive Medicine* 33 (4, Suppl. 1): S226–39.

Department of Health and Human Services. 2007. "History of the President's Council on Physical Fitness and Sports (1956–2006)." *PCPFS 50th Anniversary Toolkit*. Available at *www.fitness.gov*.

Devaney, B., Gordon, A., and Burghardt, J. 1993. *The School Nutrition Dietary Assessment Study: Dietary Intakes of Program Participants and Nonparticipants*. Washington, DC: Mathematica Policy Research, Inc.

Devaney, B., and Moffitt, R. 1991. "Dietary Effects of the Food Stamp Program." *American Journal of Agricultural Economics* 73 (1): 202–11.

Devlin, M., Yanovski, S., and Wilson, G. 2000. "Obesity: What Mental Health Professionals Need to Know." *American Journal of Psychiatry* 157: 854–66.

Dietz, W. 1995. "Does Hunger Cause Obesity?" *Pediatrics* 95 (5): 766–67.

———. 1998. "Health Consequences of Obesity in Youth: Childhood Predictors of Adult Disease." *Pediatrics* 101 (3, Suppl.): 518–25.

Diez Roux, A., Nieto, F., Caulfield, L., Tyroler, H., Watson, R., and Szklo, M. 1999. "Neighborhood Differences in Diet: The Atherosclerosis Risk in Communities (ARIC) Study." *Journal of Epidemiology and Community Health* 53: 55–63.

DiPietro, L., Anda, R., Williamson, D., and Stunkard, A. 2002. "Depressive Symptoms and Weight Change in a National Cohort of Adults." *International Journal of Obesity* 16: 745–53.

Dixon, L., Winkleby, M., and Radimer, K. 2001. "Dietary Intakes and Serum Nutrients Differ between Adults from Food-Insufficient and Food-Sufficient Families: Third National Health Nutrition Examination Survey, 1988–1994." *Journal of Nutrition* 131 (4): 1232–46.

Dohrenwend, B., Levav, I., Shrout, P., Schwartz, S., Naveh, G., Link, B., Skodol, A., and Stueve, A. 1992. "Socioeconomic Status and Psychiatric Disorders: The Causation-Selection Issue." *Science* 255 (5047): 946–52.

Dollahite, J., Kenkel, D., and Thompson, C. 2008. "An Economic Evaluation of the Expanded Food and Nutrition Education Program." *Journal of Nutrition Education and Behavior* 40 (3): 134–43.

Downey, G., and Moen, P. 1987. "Personal Efficacy, Household Income, and Family Transitions: A Longitudinal Study of Women Heading Households." *Journal of Health and Social Behavior* 28 (3): 320–33.

Draheim, C., Stanish, H., Williams, D., and McCubbin, J. 2007. "Dietary Intake of Adults with Mental Retardation Who Reside in Community Settings." *American Journal of Mental Retardation* 112 (5): 392–400.

Drapeau, V., Therrien, D., Richard, D., and Tremblay, A. 2003. "Is Visceral Obesity a Physiological Adaptation to Stress?" *Panminerva Medica* 45: 189–95.

Drewnowski, A. 2004. "Obesity and the Food Environment: Dietary Energy Density and Diet Costs." *American Journal of Preventive Medicine* 27 (3, Suppl.): 154–62.

Drewnowski, A., Almiron-Roig, E., Marmonier, C., and Lluch, A. 2004. "Dietary Energy Density and Body Weight: Is There a Relationship?" *Nutrition Reviews* 62 (11): 403–13.

Drewnowski, A., and Darmon, N. 2005. "The Economics of Obesity: Dietary Energy Density and Energy Cost." *American Journal of Clinical Nutrition* 82 (Suppl.): S265—S273.

Drewnowski, A., Darmon, N., and Briend, A. 2004. "Replacing Fats and Sugars with Vegetables and Fruit—A Question of Cost." *American Journal of Public Health* 94 (9): 1555–59.

Drewnowski, A., and Spector, S. 2004. "Poverty and Obesity: The Role of Energy Density and Energy Costs." *American Journal of Clinical Nutrition* 79 (1): 6–16.

Driscoll, A., and Moore, K. 1999. "The Relationship of Welfare Receipt to Child Outcomes." *Journal of Family and Economics Issues* 20 (1): 85–113.

Dubois, L., Farmer, A., Girard, M., and Porcherie, M. 2006. "Family Food Insufficiency Is Related to Overweight among Preschoolers." *Social Science and Medicine* 63: 1503–16.

Dugan, L. 2003. "Domestic Violence Legislation: Exploring Its Impact on the Likelihood of Domestic Violence, Police Involvement, and Arrest." *Criminology and Public Policy* 2 (2): 283–312.

Duncan, G. 2005. "Income and Child Well-Being." Geary Lecture delivered at the Economics and Social Research Institute, Dublin, Ireland, December 12.

Duncan, G., and Brooks-Gunn, J. 1997. *Consequences of Growing Up Poor.* New York: Russell Sage Foundation.

Duncan, G., Dunifon, R., Doran, M., and Yeung, W. 1998. "How Different Are Welfare and Working Families? And Do Those Differences Matter for Children's Achievement?" Joint Center for Poverty Research Working Paper No. 38.

Duncan, G., and Hoffman, S. 1985. "A Reconsideration of the Economic Consequences of Marital Dissolution." *Demography* 22 (4): 485–96.

Duncan, G., Ludwig, J., and Magnuson, K. 2007. "Reducing Poverty through Preschool Interventions." *Future of Children* 17 (2): 143–60.

Duncan, G., Yeung, W., Brooks-Gunn, J., and Smith, J. 1998. "How Much Does Childhood Poverty Affect the Life Chances of Children?" *American Sociological Review* 63 (3): 406–23.

Duncan, S., Duncan, T., Strycker, L., and Chaumeton, N. 2002. "Neighborhood Physical Activity Opportunity: A Multilevel Contextual Model." *Research Quarterly for Exercise and Sport* 73 (4): 457–63.

Dunifon, R., and Kowaleski-Jones, L. 2004. "Exploring the Influence of the National School Lunch Program on Children." Institute for Research on Poverty Discussion Paper No. 1277-04.

Dunnewind, S. 2004. "Teen Recruits Create Word-of-Mouth 'Buzz' to Hook Peers on Products." *Seattle Times*, Nov. 29. Available at *seattletimes.nwsource.com.*

Edin, K., and Lein, L. 1997. *Making Ends Meet: How Single Mothers Survive Welfare and Low-Wage Work.* New York: Russell Sage Foundation.

Edmonds, J., Baranowski, T., Baranowski, J., Cullen, K., and Myres, D. 2001. "Ecological and Socioeconomic Correlates of Fruit, Juice, and Vegetable Consumption among African-American Boys." *Preventive Medicine* 32: 476–81.

Ehrenreich, B. 2001. *Nickel and Dimed: On (Not) Getting By in America.* New York: Metropolitan Books.

Eisenberg, M., Neumark-Sztainer, D., and Perry, C. 2003. "Peer Harassment, School Connectedness, and Academic Achievement." *Journal of School Health* 73 (8): 311–16.

Eisenberg, M., Neumark-Sztainer, D., and Story, M. 2003. "Associations of Weight-Based Teasing and Emotional Well-Being among Adolescents." *Archives of Pediatric and Adolescent Medicine* 157: 733–38.

Eisenhauer, E. 2001. "In Poor Health: Supermarket Redlining and Urban Nutrition." *Geo Journal* 53 (2): 125–33.

Eliassen, A. H., Colditz, G., Rosner, B., Willett, W., and Hankinson, S. 2006. "Adult Weight Change and Risk of Postmenopausal Breast Cancer." *JAMA* 296 (2): 193–201.

Elliot, M. 1996. "Impact of Work, Family, and Welfare Receipt on Women's Self-Esteem in Young Adulthood." *Social Psychology Quarterly* 59 (1): 80–95.

Ennis, N., Hobfoll, S., and Schröder, K. 2000. "Money Doesn't Talk, It Swears: How Economic Stress and Resistance Resources Impact Inner-City Women's Depressive Mood." *American Journal of Community Psychology* 28 (2): 149–73.

Ensel, W., and Lin, N. 1991. "The Life Stress Paradigm and Psychological Distress." *Journal of Health and Social Behavior* 32 (4): 321–41.

Ensminger, M. 1995. "Welfare and Psychological Distress: A Longitudinal Study of African American Urban Mothers." *Journal of Health and Social Behavior* 36 (4): 346–59.

Epel, E., Lapidus, R., McEwen, B., and Brownell, K. 2001. "Stress May Add Bite to Appetite in Women: A Laboratory Study of Stress-Induced Cortisol and Eating Behavior." *Psychoneuroendocrinology* 26: 37–49.

Epstein, L., Wu, Y., Paluch, R., Cerny, F., and Dorn, J. 2000. "Asthma and Maternal Body Mass Index Are Related to Pediatric Body Mass Index and Obesity: Results from the Third National Health and Nutrition Examination Survey." *Obesity Research* 8 (8): 575–81.

Ernsberger, P. 1989. "Obesity Is Hazardous to Your Health." *Debates in Medicine* 2: 102–37.

Estabrook, P., Lee, R., and Gyurcsik, N. 2003. "Resources for Physical Activity Participation: Does Availability and Accessibility Differ by Neighborhood Socioeconomic Status?" *Annals of Behavioral Medicine* 25 (2): 100–104.

Evans, G. 2004. "The Environment of Childhood Poverty." *American Psychologist* 59 (2): 77–92.

Evans, G., and English, K. 2002. "The Environment of Poverty: Multiple Stressor Exposure, Psychophysiological Stress, and Socioemotional Adjustment." *Child Development* 73 (4): 1238–48.

Evans, G., and Kim, P. 2007. "Childhood Poverty and Health: Cumulative Risk Exposure and Stress Dysregulation." *Psychological Science* 18 (11): 953–57.

Evans, W., Finkelstein, E., Kamerow, D., and Renaud, J. 2005. "Public Perceptions of Childhood Obesity." *American Journal of Preventive Medicine* 28 (1): 26–32.

Everson, S., Siobhan, M., Lynch, J., Kaplan, G. 2002. "Epidemiological Evidence for the Relation between Socioeconomic Status and Depression, Obesity, and Diabetes." *Journal of Psychosomatic Research* 53: 891–95.

Ewing, R., Schmid, T., Killingsworth, R., Zlot, A., and Raudenbush, S. 2003. "Relationship between Urban Sprawl and Physical Activity, Obesity, and Morbidity." *American Journal of Health Promotion* 18 (1): 47–57.

Eyler, A., Baker, E., Cromer, L., King, A., Brownson, R., and Donatelle, R. 1998. "Physical Acticity and Minority Women: A Qualitative Study." *Health Education and Behavior* 25 (5): 640–52.

Eyler, A., Matson-Koffman, D., Young, D., Wilcox, S., Wilbur, J., Thompson, J., Sanderson, B., and Evenson, K. 2003. "Quantitative Study of Correlates of Physical Activity in Women from Diverse Racial/Ethnic Groups." *American Journal of Preventive Medicine* 25 (3, Suppl. 1): 93–103.

Faith, M., and Allison, D. 1997. "Assessment of Psychological Status among Obese Persons." In *Body Image, Eating Disorders, and Obesity*, ed. J. Thompson. Washington, DC: American Psychological Association.

Farrell, P., and Fuchs, V. 1982. "Schooling and Health: The Cigarette Connection." *Journal of Health Economics* 1: 217–30.

Farrington, D., and Welsh, B. 2005. "Randomized Experiments in Criminology:

What Have We Learned in the Last Two Decades?" *Journal of Experimental Criminology* 1 (1): 9–38.

Fauth, R., Leventhal, T., and Brooks-Gunn, J. 2004. "Short-Term Effects of Moving from Public Housing in Poor and Middle-Class Neighborhoods on Low-Income, Minority Adults' Outcomes." *Social Science and Medicine* 59: 2271–84.

Fedler, J., and Tanzer, Z. 2000. "A World in Denial: International Perspectives on Violence against Women." In *Reclaiming Women's Spaces*, ed. Y. Park, J. Fedler, and Z. Dangor, 17–46. Johannesburg: Nisaa Institute for Women's Development.

Felitti, V., Anda, R., Nordenberg, D., Williamson, D., Spitz, A., Edwards, V., Koss, M., and Marks, J. 1998. "Relationship of Childhood Abuse and Household Dysfunction to Many of the Leading Causes of Death in Adults." *American Journal of Preventive Medicine* 14 (4): 245–58.

Fellowes, M. 2006. "From Poverty, Opportunity: Putting the Market to Work for Lower Income Families." Brookings Institution, Metropolitan Policy Program.

Felson, D., and Zhang, Y. 1998. "An Update on the Epidemiology of Knee and Hip Osteoarthritis with a View to Prevention." *Arthritis and Rheumatology* 41: 1343–55.

Fertig, A., Glomm, G., and Tchernis, R. 2006. "The Connection between Maternal Employment and Childhood Obesity." COEPR Working Papers No. 2006-020.

Fetto, J. 2001. "More Is More." *American Demographics*, June 1: 8.

Field, A., Coakley, E., Must, A., Spandano, J., Laird, N., Dietz, W., Rimm, E., and Colditz, G. 2001. "Impact of Overweight on the Risk of Developing Common Chronic Diseases during a 10-Year Period." *Archives of Internal Medicine* 161 (13): 1581–86.

Finke, M., Chern, W., and Fox, J. 1997. "Do the Urban Poor Pay More for Food? Issues in Measurement." *Advancing the Consumer Interest* 9 (1): 13–17.

Finkelstein, E., Fiebelkorn, I., and G. Wang. 2003. "National Medical Spending Attributable to Overweight and Obesity: How Much and Who's Paying?" *Health Affairs* (Web Exclusive), May 14. Available at *www.healthaffairs.org*.

———. 2004. "State-Level Estimates of Annual Medical Expenditures Attributable to Obesity." *Obesity Research* 12: 18–24.

Fischer, C., Hout, M., Jankowski, M., Lucas, S., Swidler, A., and Voss, K. 1996. *Inequality by Design: Cracking the Bell Curve Myth*, Princeton, NJ: Princeton University Press.

Fisher, I. 1961. *The Theory of Interest: Reprints of Economic Classics.* New York: Augustus M. Kelley.

Fisher, J., and Birch, L. 1999. "Restricting Access to Palatable Foods Affects Children's Behavioral Response, Food Selection, and Intake." *American Journal of Clinical Nutrition* 69: 1264–72.

Fisher, M., and Weber, B. 2002. "The Importance of Place in Welfare Reform: Common Challenges for Central Cities and Remote Rural Areas." Center on Urban and Metropolitan Policy, Brookings Institution Research Brief.

Fitchen, J. 1988. "Hunger, Malnutrition, and Poverty in the Contemporary United States: Some Observations on Their Social and Cultural Context. *Food and Foodways* 2 (3): 309–33.

Flanagan, S. 1996. "Obesity: The Last Bastion of Prejudice." *Obesity Surgery* 6 (5): 430–37.

Flegal, K., Graubard, B., Williamson, D., and Gail, M. 2005. "Excess Deaths Associated with Underweight, Overweight, and Obesity." *JAMA* 293 (15): 1861–67.

Fogel, R. 2003. "Secular Trends in Physiological Capital." *Perspectives in Biology and Medicine* 46 (3, Suppl.): S24–S38.

Fontaine, K., Redden, D., Wang, C., Westfall, A., and Allison, D. 2003. "Years of Life Lost Due to Obesity." *JAMA* 289 (2): 187–93.

Food Research and Action Center (FRAC). 2004. *Proceedings of the Roundtable on Understanding the Paradox of Hunger and Obesity.* November 22. Available at *www.frac.org.*

———. 2005. *Obesity, Food Insecurity, and the Federal Child Nutrition Programs: Understanding the Linkages.* October. Available at *www.frac.org.*

Fox, M., and Cole, N. 2004. "Nutrition and Health Characteristics of Low-Income Populations. Vol. 1, Food Stamp Program Participants and Nonparticipants." USDA, Economic Research Service, Electronic Publications from the Food Assistance and Nutrition Research Program, E-FAN=04-014-1, Dec.

FRAC. *See* Food and Research Action Center

Fraker, T. 1990. "The Effects of Food Stamps on Food Consumption: A Review of the Literature." USDA, Food and Consumer Services, Office of Analysis and Evaluation, Oct.

Fraker, T., Martini, A., and Ohls, J. 1995. "The Effect of Food Stamp Cashout on Food Expenditure: An Assessment of Findings from Four Demonstrations." *Journal of Human Resources* 30 (4): 633–49.

Frank, L., Andersen, M., and Schmid, T. 2004. "Obesity Relationships with Community Design, Physical Activity, and Time Spent in Cars." *American Journal of Preventive Medicine* 27 (2): 87–96.

Frankel, D., and Gould, E. 2001. "The Retail Price of Inequality." *Journal of Urban Economics* 49 (2): 219–39.

Frederick, S., Loewenstein, G., and O'Donoghue, T. 2002. "Time Discounting and Time Preference: A Critical Review." *Journal of Economic Literature* 11 (June): 351–401.

French, J., Jeffery, R., and Oliphant, A. 1994. "Facility Access and Self-Reward as Methods to Promote Physical Activity among Health Sedentary Adults." *American Journal of Health Promotion* 8 (4): 257–59.

French, S. 2003. "Pricing Effects on Food Choices." *Journal of Nutrition* 133 (3): 841S–843S.

French, S., Harnack, L., and Jeffery, R. 2000. "Fast Food Restaurant Use among Women in the Pound Prevention Study: Dietary, Behavioral and Demographic Correlates." *International Journal of Obesity and Related Metabolic Disorders* 24 (10): 1353–59.

French, S., and Wechsler, H. 2004. "School-Based Research and Initiatives: Fruit and Vegetable Environment, Policy, and Pricing Workshop." *Preventive Medicine* 39 (Suppl. 2): S101–S107.

Friedman, H., Schwartz, J., Tomlinson-Keasey, C., Tucker, J., Martin, L., Wingard, D., and Criqui, M. 1995. "Childhood Conscientiousness and Longevity: Health Behaviors and Cause of Death." *Journal of Personality and Social Psychology* 68 (4): 696–703.

Friedman, M., and Brownell, K. 1995. "Psychological Correlates of Obesity: Moving to the Next Generation of Research." *Psychological Bulletin* 117: 3–20.

Friedman, M., Powell, K., Hutwagner, L., Graham, L., and Teague, W. 2001. "Impact of Changes in Transportation and Commuting Behaviors during the 1996 Summer Olympic Games in Atlanta on Air Quality and Childhood Asthma." *JAMA* 285 (7): 897–905.

Frongillo, E. 2003. "Understanding Obesity and Program Participation in the Context of Poverty and Food Insecurity." *Journal of Nutrition* 133 (7): 2117–18.

Frongillo, E., Jyoti, D., and Jones, S. 2006. "Food Stamp Participation Is Associated with Better Academic Learning among School Children." *Journal of Nutrition* 136 (4): 1077–80.

Frongillo, E., Olson, C., Rauschenbach, B., and Kendall, A. 1997. "Nutritional Consequences of Food Insecurity in a Rural New York State County." Institute for Research on Poverty Discussion Paper No. 1120–97.

Frumkin, H. 2002. "Urban Sprawl and Public Health." *Public Health Reports* 117 (3): 201–18.

Fu, H., and Goldman, N. 1996. "Incorporating Health into Marriage Choice Models." *Journal of Marriage and the Family* 58 (3): 740–58.

———. 2000. "The Association between Health-Related Behaviors and the Risk of Divorce in the USA." *Journal of Biosocial Science* 32: 63–88.

Fuchs, V. 1986. *The Health Economy*. Cambridge, MA: Harvard University Press.

———. 1991. "Time Preference and Health: An Exploratory Study." In *The Economics of Health*, ed. A. J. Culyer, 1: 93–150. Great Yarmouth, UK: Edward Elgar.

Fulkerson, J., Sherwood, N., Perry, C., Neumark-Sztainer, D., and Story, M. 2004. "Depressive Symptoms and Adolescent Eating and Health Behaviors: A Multifaceted View in a Population-Based Sample." *Preventive Medicine* 38 (6): 865–75.

Furey, S., Strugnell, C., and McIlveen, H. 2001. "An Investigation of the Potential Existence of 'Food Deserts' in Rural and Urban Areas of Northern Ireland." *Agriculture and Human Values* 18 (4): 447–57.

Gaesser, G. 2002. *Big Fat Lies: The Truth about Your Weight and Your Health.* Carlsbad, CA: Gürze Books.

Gallagher, M. 2006. "Examining the Impact of Food Deserts on Public Health in Chicago." Report sponsored by LaSalle Bank. Available at *www.lasallebank.com*.

Gallup Organization. 2003. "Poll Analyses: Smoking Edges Out Obesity as Employment Liability." August 7. Available at *www.galluppoll.com*.

General Accounting Office. 2000. *Public Education: Commercial Activities in Schools.* Publication HEHS-00-156.

Garn, S., and Clark, D. 1976. "Trends in Fatness and the Origins of Obesity." *Pediatrics* 57 (4): 443–56.

Gibson, D. 2003. "Food Stamps Program Participation Is Positively Related to Obesity in Low Income Women." *Journal of Nutrition* 133: 2225–31.

———. 2004. "Long-Term Food Stamp Program Participation Is Differentially Related to Overweight in Young Girls and Boys." *Journal of Nutrition* 134 (2): 372–79.

———. 2006. "Long-Term Food Stamp Participation Is Positively Related to Simultaneous Overweight in Young Daughters and Obesity in Mothers." *Journal of Nutrition* 136 (4): 1081–85.

Glantz, L. 1997. "Controlling Tobacco Advertising: The FDA Regulations and the First Amendment." *American Journal of Public Health* 87 (3): 446–51.

Glanz, K., Basil, M., Maibach, E., Goldberg, J., and Snyder, D. 1998. "Why Americans Eat What They Do: Taste, Nutrition, Cost, Convenience, and Weight Control Concerns as Influences on Food Consumption." *Journal of the American Dietetic Association* 98 (10): 1118–26.

Gleason, P., and Suitor, C. 2003. "Eating and School: How the National School

Lunch Program Affects Children's Diets." *American Journal of Agricultural Economics* 85 (4): 1047–61.

Gluckman, P., Hanson, M., and Beedle, A. 2007. "Early Life Events and Their Consequences for Later Disease: A Life History and Evolutionary Perspective." *American Journal of Human Biology* 19: 1–19.

Goldberg, R., and Steury, R. 2001. "Depression in the Workplace: Costs and Barriers to Treatment." *Psychiatric Services* 52 (12): 1639–43.

Goldman, D., and Smith, J. 2002. "Can Patient Self-Management Help Explain the SES Health Gradient?" *PNAS* 99 (16): 10929–34.

Goleman, G. 1995. *Emotional Intelligence.* Bantam Books: New York.

Goodman, E., Slap, G., and Huang, B. 2003. "The Public Health Impact of Socioeconomic Status on Adolescent Depression and Obesity." *American Journal of Public Health* 93 (11): 1844–50.

Goodman, E., and Whitaker, R. 2002. "A Prospective Study of the Role of Depression in the Development and Persistence of Adolescent Obesity." *Pediatrics* 109 (3): 497–504.

Gordon, A., Devaney, B., and Burghardt, J. 1995. "Dietary Effects of the National School Lunch Program and the School Breakfast Program." *American Journal of Clinical Nutrition* 61 (1): 221S–231S.

Gordon, C., Ghai, N., Purciel, M., Talwalkar, A., and Goodman, A. 2007. *Eating Well in Harlem: How Available Is Healthy Food?* New York: New York City Department of Health and Mental Hygiene.

Gordon-Larsen, P., McMurray, R., and Popkin, B. 2000. "Determinants of Adolescent Physical Activity and Inactivity Patterns." *Pediatrics* 105 (6): e83.

Gordon-Larsen, P., Nelson, M., Page, P., and Popkin, B. 2006. "Inequality in the Built Environment Underlies Key Health Disparities in Physical Activity and Obesity." *Pediatrics* 117 (2): 417–24.

Gore, S., Foster, J., DiLillo, V., Kirk, K., and West, D. 2003. "Television Viewing and Snacking." *Eating Behaviors* 4: 399–405.

Gorely, T., Marshall, S., and Biddle, S. 2004. "Couch Kids: Correlates of Television Viewing among Youth." *International Journal of Behavioral Medicine* 11 (3): 152–63.

Gorman, R. 2006. "Miracle Up North." *Eating Well* 5 (3): 32–38.

Gortmaker, S., Must, A., Perrin, J., Sobal, A., and Dietz, W. 1993. "Social and Economic Consequences of Overweight in Adolescence and Young Adulthood." *New England Journal of Medicine* 329 (14): 1008–12.

Gottschalk, P. 2005. "Can Work Alter Welfare Recipients' Beliefs?" *Journal of Policy Analysis and Management* 2 (3): 485–98.

Government Accountability Office. 2006. *Food Stamp Trafficking: FNS Could Enhance Program Integrity by Better Targeting Stores Likely to Traffic and Increasing Penalties.* GAO-07-53. Washington, DC: Government Accountability Office.

Greenberg, B., Eastin, M., Hofshire, L., Lachlin, K., and Brownell, K. 2003. "The Portrayal of Overweight and Obese Persons in Commercial Television." *American Journal of Public Health* 93 (8): 1342–48.

Greenberg, M., Weissberg, R., O'Brien, M., Zins, J., Fredericks, L., Resnik, H., and Elias, M. 2003. "Enhancing School-Based Prevention and Youth Development through Coordinated Social, Emotional, and Academic Learning." *American Psychologist* 58 (6–7): 466–74.

Greenlund, K., Liu, K., Dyer, A., Kiefe, C., Burke, G., and Yunis, C. 1996. "Body

Mass Index in Young Adults: Associations with Parental Body Size and Education in the CARDIA Study." *American Journal of Public Health* 86 (4): 480–85.

Griffiths, L., Wolke, D., Page, A., and Horwood, J. 2006. "Obesity and Bullying: Different Effects for Boys and Girls." *Archives of Diseases of Childhood* 91: 121–25.

Gronniger, J. 2005. "Familial Obesity as a Proxy for Omitted Variables in the Obesity-Mortality Relationship." *Demography* 42 (4): 719–35.

Grzywacz, J., Almeida, D., Neupert, S., and Ettner, S. 2004. "Socioeconomic Status and Health: A Micro-level Analysis of Exposure and Vulnerability to Daily Stressors." *Journal of Health and Social Behavior* 45 (1): 1–16.

Gundersen, C., and Oliveira, V. 2001. "The Food Stamp Program and Food Insufficiency." *American Journal of Agricultural Economics* 83 (4): 875–87.

Gustafson, T., and Sarwer, D. 2004. "Childhood Sexual Abuse and Obesity." *Obesity Reviews* 5 (3): 129–35.

Guthrie, J., Lin, B., and Frazao, E. 2002. "Role of Food Prepared Away from Home in the American Diet, 1977–78 versus 1994–96: Changes and Consequences." *Journal of Nutrition Education and Behavior* 34 (3): 140–50.

Guthrie, J., Lin, B., Reed, J., and Stewart, H. 2005. "Understanding Economic and Behavioral Influences on Fruit and Vegetable Choices." *Amber Waves* 3 (2): 36–41.

Guttman, N., and Ressler, W. 2001. "On Being Responsible: Ethical Issues in Appeals to Personal Responsibility in Health Campaigns." *Journal of Health Communication* 6 (2): 117–36.

Gwynn, R., and Thurston, G. 2001. "The Burden of Air Pollution: Impacts among Racial Minorities." *Environmental Health Perspectives* 109 (4): 501–6.

Gyamfi, P., Brooks-Gunn, J., and Jackson, A. 2001. "Associations between Employment and Financial and Parental Stress in Low-Income Black Mothers." *Women and Health* 32 (1–2): 119–35.

Haider, S., Jacknowitz, A., and Schoeni, R. 2003. "Welfare Work Requirements and Child Well-Being: Evidence from the Effects on Breast-Feeding." *Demography* 40 (3): 479–97.

Haines, J., Neumark-Sztainer, D., Eisenberg, M., and Hannan, P. 2006. "Weight Teasing and Disordered Eating Behaviors in Adolescents: Longitudinal Findings from Project EAT (Eating among Teens)." *Pediatrics* 117 (2): e209–e215.

Halkjær, J., Holst, C., and Sørensen, T. 2003. "Intelligence Test Score and Educational Level in Relation to BMI Changes and Obesity." *Obesity Research* 11 (10): 1238–45.

Hall, M., Bromberger, J., and Matthews, K. 1999. "Socioeconomic Status as a Correlate of Sleep in African-American and Caucasian Women." *Annals of the New York Academy of Sciences* 896 (1): 427–30.

Hall, R. 1978. "Stochastic Implications of the Life Cycle–Permanent Income Hypothesis: Theory and Evidence." *Journal of Political Economy* 86 (6): 971–87.

Halpern, D., and Bates, C. 2004. "Personal Responsibility and Changing Behaviour: The State of Knowledge and Its Implications for Public Policy." Issue paper prepared for the Prime Minister's Strategy Unit. Available at *www.number10. gov.uk*.

Hannan, P., French, S., Story, M., and Fulkerson, J. 2002. "A Pricing Strategy to Promote Purchase of Lower Fat Foods in a High School Cafeteria: Acceptability and Sensitivity Analysis." *American Journal of Health Promotion* 17: 1–6.

Hanson, K., Sobal, J., and Frongillo, E. 2007. "Gender and Marital Status Clarify

Associations between Food Insecurity and Body Weight." *Journal of Nutrition* 137 (6): 1460–65.

Harder, T., Bergmann, R., Kallischnigg, G., and Plagamann, A. 2005. "Duration of Breastfeeding and Risk of Overweight: A Meta-Analysis." *American Journal of Epidemiolgy* 162 (5): 397–403.

Hardesty, D., and Krakow, B. 2000. "Potential Sleep Disorders in a Welfare-to-Work Population." *Sleep* 23 (Abstract Suppl. 2): A228.

Harris, M. 1990 "Is Love Seen as Different for the Obese?" *Journal of Applied Social Psychology* 20: 1209–24.

Harris Interactive. 2007. "WSJ.com/Harris Interactive Survey Finds That Most Adults Believe Parents, Schools and Food Industry Can Make Difference in Battling Childhood Obesity." Available at *www.harrisinteractive.com.*

Harrison, G., Lau, M., and Williams, M. 2002. "Estimating Individual Discount Rates for Denmark: A Field Experiment." *American Economics Review* 92 (5): 1606–17.

Harrison, K. 2005. "Is 'Fat Free' Good for Me? A Panel Study of Television Viewing and Children's Nutritional Knowledge and Reasoning." *Health Communication* 17 (2): 117–32.

Harrykissoon, S., Rickert, V., and Wiemann, C. 2002. "Prevalence and Patterns of Intimate Partner Violence among Adolescent Mothers during the Postpartum Period." *Archives of Pediatrics and Adolescent Medicine* 156: 325–30.

Harsanyi, D. 2007. *Nanny State.* New York: Broadway Books.

Hart, C., Taylor, M., Davey Smith, G., Whalley, L., Starr, J., and Hole, D. 2003. "Childhood IQ, Social Class, Deprivation, and Their Relationships with Mortality and Morbidity Risk in Later Life: Prospective Observational Study Linking the Scottish Mental Survey 1932 and the Midspan Studies." *Psychosomatic Medicine* 65: 877–83.

Haskins, R., Paxson, C., and Donahue, E. 2006. "Fighting Obesity in the Public Schools: Policy Brief." *Future of Children Policy Brief,* Spring.

Hasler, G., Pine, D., Gamma, A., Milos, G., Ajdacic, V., Eich, D., Rössler, J., and Angst, J. 2004. "The Associations between Psychopathology and Being Overweight: A 20-Year Prospective Study." *Psychological Medicine* 34: 1047–57.

Hasler, G., Pine, D., Kleinbaum, D., Gamma, A., Luckenbaugh, D., Ajdacic, V., Eich, D., Rössler, W., and Angst, J. 2005. "Depressive Symptoms during Childhood and Adult Obesity: The Zurich Cohort Study." *Molecular Psychiatry* 10: 842–50.

Hastings, G., Stead, M., McDermott, L., Forsyth, A., MacKintosh, A., Rayner, M., Godfrey, C., Caraher, M., and Angus, K. 2003. "Review of Research on the Effects of Food Promotion to Children." Final report prepared for the Food Standards Agency, University of Strathclyde, Centre for Social Marketing.

Hawkins, S., Cole, T., and Law, C. 2007. "Maternal Employment and Early Childhood Overweight: Findings from the UK Millennium Cohort Study." *International Journal of Obesity,* July 17, advance online publication, doi:10.1038/sj/ijo.0803682.

Hayes, L. 2000. "Are Prices Higher for the Poor in New York City?" *Journal of Consumer Policy* 23: 127–52.

Hayes, S. 2003. *Flat Broke with Children: Women in the Age of Welfare Reform.* New York: Oxford University Press.

Hayne, C., Moran, P., and Ford, M. 2004. "Regulating Environments to Reduce Obesity." *Journal of Public Health Policy* 25 (3–4): 391–407.

Heath, G., Brownson, R., Kruger, J., Miles, R., Powell, K., and Ramsey, L. 2006. "The Effectiveness of Urban Design and Land Use and Transport Policies and Practices to Increase Physical Activity: A Systematic Review." *Journal of Physical Activity and Health* 3 (Suppl. 1): S55–S76.

Heckman, J. 1995. "Lessons from the Bell Curve." *Journal of Political Economy* 103 (5): 1091–120.

Hedley, A., Ogden, C., Johnson, C., Carroll, M., Curtain, L., and Flegal, K. 2004. "Prevalence of Overweight and Obesity among U.S. Children, Adolescents, and Adults, 1999–2002." *JAMA* 291 (23): 2847–50.

Heflin, C., Siefert, K., and Williams, D. 2005. "Food Insufficiency and Women's Mental Health: Findings from a 3-Year Panel of Welfare Recipients." *Social Science and Medicine* 61: 1971–82.

Heflin, C., and Ziliak, J. 2006. "Does Food Stamp Receipt Mediate the Relationship between Food Insufficiency and Mental Health?" University of Kentucky Center for Poverty Research Working Paper No. 2006-03.

Herpertz, S., Kielmann, R., Wolf, A., Langkafel, M., Senf, W., and Hebebrand, J. 2003. "Does Obesity Surgery Improve Psychosocial Functioning? A Systematic Review." *International Journal of Obesity* 27: 1300–14.

Herrnstein, R., and Murray, C. 1994. *The Bell Curve: Intelligence and Class Structure in American Life.* Free Press: New York.

Hersen, M., and Thomas, J. 2006. *Comprehensive Handbook of Personality and Psychopathology.* Vol. 2, *Adult Psychopathology.* Hoboken, NJ: John Wiley.

Hersen, M., and Turner, S. 2003. *Adult Psychopathology and Diagnosis.* 4th ed. Hoboken, NJ: John Wiley.

Hill, J., and Peters, J. 1998. "Environmental Contributions to the Obesity Epidemic." *Science* 280 (5368): 1371–74.

Hillier, A., Foster, G., Vander Veur, S., Grundy, K., and Culhane, D. 2007. "The Impact of Poverty, Crime, and the Physical Environment on Overweight and Obesity in Elementary School Children." Department of City and Regional Planning Working Paper, University of Pennsylvania.

Hobfoll, S., Ritter, C., Lavin, J., Hulsizer, M., and Cameron, R. 1995. "Depression Prevalence and Incidence among Inner-City Pregnant and Postpartum Women." *Journal of Consulting and Clinical Psychology* 63: 445–53.

Hofferth, S., and Curtain, S. 2005. "Poverty, Food Programs, and Childhood Obesity." *Journal of Policy Analysis and Management* 24 (4): 703–26.

Hoffman, S., and Duncan, G. 1988. "What Are the Economic Consequences of Divorce?" *Demography* 25 (4): 641–45.

Holden, K., and Smock, P. 1991. "The Economic Costs of Marital Dissolution: Why Do Women Bear a Disproportionate Cost?" *Annual Review of Sociology* 17: 51–78.

Holmes, M., and Newman, M. 2006. "Generalized Anxiety Disorder." In *Adult Psychopathology and Diagnosis* (4th ed.), ed. M. Hersen, S. Turner, 101–20. Hoboken, NJ: John Wiley.

Holt, D., Ippolito, P., Desrochers, D., and Kelley, C. 2007. "Children's Exposure to TV Advertising in 1977 and 2004." Federal Trade Commission, Bureau of Economics Staff Report.

Holzer, H., Schanzenbach, D., Duncan, G., and Ludwig, J. 2007. "The Economic Costs of Poverty in the United States: Subsequent Effects of Children Growing Up Poor." National Poverty Center Working Paper No. 07-04.

Horowitz, C., Colson, K., Herbert, P., and Lancaster, K. 2004. "Barriers to Buying

Healthy Foods for People with Diabetes: Evidence of Environmental Disparities." *American Journal of Public Health* 94 (9): 1549–54.

Houston, D., Ding, J., Nicklas, B., Harris, T., Lee, J., Nevitt, M., Rubin, S., Tylavsky, F., and Kritchevsky, S. 2007. "The Association between Weight History and Physical Performance in the Health, Aging, and Body Composition Study." *International Journal of Obesity*, May 22, advance online publication, doi:10.1038/sj.ijo.0803652.

Hu, F., Li, T., Colditz, G., Willet, W., and Manson, J. 2003. "Television Watching and Other Sedentary Behaviors in Relation to Risk of Obesity and Type 2 Diabetes Mellitus in Women." *JAMA* 289 (14): 1785–91.

Hubbard, V. 2000. "Defining Overweight and Obesity: What Are the Issues?" *American Journal of Clinical Nutrition* 72: 1067–68.

Huhman, M., Potter, L., Wong, F., Banspach, S., Duke, J., and Heitzler, C. 2005. "Effects of a Mass Media Campaign to Increase Physical Activity among Children: Year-1 Results of the VERB Campaign." *Pediatrics* 116 (2): e277–e284.

Humpel, N., Owen, N., and Leslie, E. 2002. "Environmental Factors Associated with Adult's Participation in Physical Activity." *American Journal of Preventive Medicine* 22 (3): 188–99.

Hussey, J., Chang, J., and Kotch, J. 2006. "Child Maltreatment in the United States: Prevalence, Risk Factors, and Adolescent Health Consequences." *Pediatrics* 118 (3): 933–42.

Huston, S., Evenson, K., Bors, P., and Gizlice, Z. 2003. "Neighborhood Environment, Access to Places for Activity, and Leisure-Time Physical Activity in a Diverse North Carolina Population." *American Journal of Health Promotion* 18 (1): 58–69.

Huston, S., and Finke, M. 2003. "Diet Choice and the Role of Time Preference." *Journal of Consumer Affairs* 37 (1): 143–60.

Institute of Medicine. 1999. *Toward Environmental Justice: Research, Education, and Health Policy Needs.* Washington, DC: National Academies Press.

———. 2005. *Preventing Childhood Obesity: Health in the Balance.* Washington, DC: National Academies Press.

———. 2006. *Food Marketing to Children and Youth: Threat or Opportunity?* Washington, DC: National Academies Press.

International Obesity Task Force. 1999. "PHAPO Causal Web." *International Association for the Study of Obesity Newsletter*, Spring. Available at *www.iaso.org*.

Jackson, L. 1992. *Physical Appearance and Gender: Sociobiological and Sociocultural Perspectives.* Albany: State University of New York.

Jacobson, S. H., and McLay, L. A. 2006. "The Economic Impact of Obesity on Automobile Fuel Consumption." *Engineering Economist* 51 (4): 307–23.

Jayakody, R., Danziger, S., and Pollack, H. 2000. "Welfare Reform, Substance Use and Mental Health." *Journal of Health, Politics, Policy and Law* 25 (4): 623–35.

Jeffery, R., and French, S. 1998. "Epidemic Obesity in the United States: Are Fast Food and Television Viewing Contributing?" *American Journal of Public Health* 88 (2): 277–80.

Jeffery, R., French, S., Raether, C., and Baxter, J. 1994. "An Environmental Intervention to Increase Fruit and Salad Purchases in a Cafeteria." *Preventive Medicine* 23: 788–92.

Jerrett, M., Burnett, R., Kanaroglou, P., Eyles, J., Finkelstein, N., Giovis, C., and Brook, J. 2001. "A GIS–Environmental Justice Analysis of Particulate Air Pollution in Hamilton, Canada." *Environment and Planning A* 33: 955–73.

Jetter, K., and Cassady, D. 2006. "The Availability and Cost of Healthier Food Alternatives." *American Journal of Preventive Medicine* 30 (1): 38–44.

Joanisse, L., and Synnott, A. 1999. "Fighting Back: Reactions and Resistance to the Stigma of Obesity." In *Interpreting Weight: The Social Management of Fatness and Thinness*, ed. J. Sobal and D. Maurer. New York: Aldine de Gruyter.

Johnson, J., Cohen, P., Kasen, S., and Brook, J. 2002. "Childhood Adversities Associated with Risk for Eating Disorders or Weight Problems during Adolescence or Early Adulthood." *American Journal of Psychiatry* 159 (3): 394–400.

Johnston, L., Delva, J., and O'Malley, P. 2007. "Soft Drink Availability, Contracts, and Revenues in American Secondary Schools." *American Journal of Preventive Medicine* 33 (4, Suppl. 1): S209–S225.

Jolliffe, D. 2004. "Extent of Overweight among U.S. Children and Adolescents from 1971 to 2000." *International Journal of Obesity* 28: 4–9.

Jones, J., and Frongillo, E. 2006. "The Modifying Effects of Food Stamp Program Participation on the Relation between Food Insecurity and Weight Change in Women." *Journal of Nutrition* 136 (4): 1091–94.

Jones, S. 2004. "Research Needs to Better Understand the Relationship between Hunger and Obesity and to Develop Sensitive and Effective Policy Solutions." *Proceedings of the Roundtable on Understanding the Paradox of Hunger and Obesity, Food Research and Action Center, November 22, 2004*. Washington, DC: Food Research and Action Center.

Jones, S., Jahns, L., Laraia, B., and Haughton, B. 2003. "Lower Risk of Overweight in School-Aged Food Insecure Girls Who Participate in Food Assistance." *Archives of Pediatric and Adolescent Medicine* 157: 780–84.

Jones, S., Merkle, S., Fulton, J., Wheeler, L., and Mannino, D. 2006. "Relationship between Asthma, Overweight, and Physical Activity among U.S. High School Students." *Journal of Community Health* 31 (6): 469–78.

Jordan, A., and Robinson, T. 2008. "Children Television Viewing, and Weight Status: Summary and Recommendations from an Expert Panel Meeting." *Annals of the American Academy of Political and Social Science* 615: 119–32.

Jung, S., Østbye, T., and Park, K. 2006. "A Longitudinal Study of the Relationship between Health Risk Factors and Dependence in Activities of Daily Living." *Journal of Preventive Medicine and Public Health* 39 (3): 211–28.

Jyoti, D., Frongillo, E., and Jones, S. 2005. "Food Insecurity Affects School Children's Academic Performance, Weight Gain, and Social Skills." *Journal of Nutrition* 135 (12): 2831–39.

Kaaks, R., Lukanova, A., and Kurzer, M. 2002. "Obesity, Endogenous Hormones, and Endometrial Cancer Risk: A Synthetic Review." *Cancer, Epidemiology, Biomarkers and Prevention* 11: 1531–43.

Kabbani, N., and Yazbeck, M. 2004. "The Role of Food Assistance Programs and Employment Circumstances in Helping Households with Children Avoid Hunger." Institute for Research on Poverty Discussion Paper No. 1280-04.

Kabbani, N., and Yazbeck-Kmeid, M. 2005. "The Role of Food Assistance in Helping Food Insecure Households Escape Hunger." *Review of Agricultural Economics* 27 (3): 439–45.

Kaestner, R., and Tarlov, E. 2006. "Changes in the Welfare Caseload and the Health of Low-Educated Mothers." *Journal of Policy Analysis and Management* 25 (3): 623–43.

Kahn, E., and the Task Force on Community Preventive Services. 2002. "The Effectiveness of Interventions to Increase Physical Activity: A Systematic Review." *American Journal of Preventive Medicine* 22 (4, Suppl.): 73–107.

Kahn, R., Wise, P., Kennedy, P., and Kawachi, I. 2000. "State Income Inequality, Household Income, and Maternal Mental and Physical Health: A Cross Sectional National Survey." *British Medical Journal* 321 (7272): 1311–15.

Kallen, D., and Doughty, A. 1984. "The Relationship of Weight, the Self-Perception of Weight, and Self-Esteem with Courtship Behavior." *Marriage and Family Review* 7: 93–114.

Kaplan, G. 2007. "Health Status Disparities in the United States." Presentation given April 4, 2007, at the Woodrow Wilson International Center for Scholars, transcript available at *www.wilsoncenter.org*.

Kaplowitz, P., Slora, E., Wasserman, R., Pedlow, S., and Herman-Giddens, M. 2001. "Earlier Onset of Puberty in Girls: Relation to Increased Body Mass Index and Race." *Pediatrics* 108: 347–53.

Kaufman, L., and Karpati, A. 2007. "Understanding the Sociocultural Roots of Childhood Obesity: Food Practices among Latino Families of Bushwick, Brooklyn." *Social Science and Medicine* 64: 2177–88.

Kaufman, P., MacDonald, J., Lutz, S., and Smallwood, D. 1997. "Do the Poor Pay More for Food? Item Selection and Price Differences Affect Low-Income Household Food Costs." USDA, Economic Research Service, Agricultural Economics Report No. 759.

Kaushal, N. 2007. "Do Food Stamps Cause Obesity? Evidence from Immigrant Experience." *Journal of Health Economics* 26: 968–91.

Kelly, L., and Patterson, B. 2006. "Childhood Nutrition: Perceptions of Caretakers in a Low-Income Urban Setting." *Journal of School Nursing* 22 (6): 345–51.

Kempson, K., Keenan, D., Sadani, P., Ridlen, S., and Rosato, N. 2002. "Food Management Practices Used by People with Limited Resources to Maintain Food Sufficiency as Reported by Nutrition Educators." *Journal of the American Dietetic Association* 102 (12): 1795–99.

Kendall, A., Olson, C., and Frongillo, E. 1996. "Relationship of Hunger and Food Insecurity to Food Availability and Consumption." *Journal of the American Dietetic Association* 96 (10): 1019–24.

Kennedy, E., Ohls, J., Carlson, S., Fleming, K. 1995. "The Healthy Eating Index: Design and Applications." *Journal of the American Dietetic Association* 95 (10): 1103–8.

Kessler, R., Barber, C., Birnbaum, H., and Frank, R. 1999. "Depression in the Workplace: Effects on Short-Term Disability." *Health Affairs* 18 (5): 163–71.

Kessler, R., Berglund, P., Demler, O., Jin, R., Koretz, D., Merikangas, K., Rush, A., Walters, E., and Wang, P. 2003. "The Epidemiology of Major Depressive Disorder: Results from the National Comorbidity Survey Replication." *JAMA* 289 (23): 3095–105.

Kessler, R., Berglund, P., Demler, O., Jin, R., Merikangas, K., and Walters, E. 2005. "Lifetime Prevalence and Age-of-Onset Distributions of DSM-IV Disorders in the National Comorbidity Survey Replication." *Archives of General Psychiatry* 62 (6): 593–602.

Kessler, R., Chiu, W., Demler, O., Merikangas, K., and Walters, E. 2005. "Prevalence, Severity, and Comorbidity of 12-Month DSM-IV Disorders in the National Comorbidity Survey Replication." *Archives of General Psychiatry* 62 (6): 617–27.

Kessler, R., Greenberg, P., Mickelson, K., Meneades, L., and Wang, P. 2001. "The

Effects of Chronic Medical Conditions on Work Loss and Work Cutback." *Journal of Occupational and Environmental Medicine* 43: 218–25.

Kieffer, E., Willis, S., Arellano, N., and Guzman, R. 2002. "Perspectives of Pregnant and Postpartum Latino Women on Diabetes, Physical Activity, and Health." *Health Education and Behavior* 29 (5): 542–56.

Kieffer, E., Willis, S., Odoms-Young, A., Guzman, R., Allen, A., Two Feathers, J., and Loveluck, J. 2004. "Reducing Disparities in Diabetes among African-American and Latino Residents of Detroit: The Essential Role of Community Planning Focus Groups." *Ethnicity and Disease* 14 (Suppl. 1): S1-27–S1-37.

Kim, K., and Frongillo, E. 2007. "Participation in Food Assistance Programs Modifies the Relation of Food Insecurity with Weight and Depression in Elders." *Journal of Nutrition* 137 (4): 1005–10.

Kim, S., and Willis, L. 2007. "Talking about Obesity: News Framing of Who is Responsible for Causing and Fixing the Problem." *Journal of Health Communication* 12 (4): 359–76.

Kind, K., and Hathcote, J. 2000. "Specialty-Size College Females: Satisfaction with Retail Outlets and Apparel Fit." *Journal of Fashion Marketing and Management* 4 (4): 315–24.

King, A., Castro, C., Wilcox, S., Eyler, A., Sallis, J., and Brownson, R. 2000. "Personal and Environmental Factors Associated with Physical Inactivity among Different Racial-Ethnic Groups of U.S. Middle-Aged and Older-Aged Women." *Health Psychology* 19 (4): 354–64.

King, E., Shapiro, J., Hebl, M., Singletary, S., and Turner, S. 2006. "The Stigma of Obesity in Customer Service: A Mechanism for Remediation and Bottom-Line Consequences of Interpersonal Discrimination." *Journal of Applied Psychology* 91 (3): 579–93.

Kipke, M., Iverson, E., Moore, D., Booker, C., Ruelas, V., Peters, A., and Kaufman, F. 2007. "Food and Park Environments: Neighborhood-Level Risks for Childhood Obesity in East Los Angeles." *Journal of Adolescent Health* 40: 325–33.

Klein, R. 2000. "Health Inequalities: Bringing the Hidden Assumptions into the Open." *Health Economics* 9: 569–70.

Kling, J., Liebman, J., and Katz, L. 2007. "Experimental Analysis of Neighborhood Effects." *Econometrica* 75 (1): 83–119.

Kling, J., Liebman, J., Katz, L., and Sanbonmatsu, L. 2004. "Moving to Opportunity and Tranquility: Neighborhood Effects on Adult Economic Self-Sufficiency and Health from a Randomized Housing Voucher Experiment." Princeton University, Department of Economics, Industrial Relations Section, Working Paper No. 860.

Knab, J., Garfinkel, I., and McLanahan, S. 2007. "The Effects of Welfare and Child Support Policies on Maternal Health and Wellbeing." Center for Research on Child Wellbeing Working Paper No. 2006-04-FF.

Knitzer, J. 2007. "Testimony of Jane Knitzer, Ed.D., Director, National Center for Chidren in Poverty, Mailman School of Public Health Columbia University." U.S. Congress, House Ways and Means Committee, Hearing on Economic and Societal Costs of Poverty, January 24.

Knowles, J. 1977. "The Responsibility of the Individual." In *Doing Better and Feeling Worse*, ed. John H. Knowles. New York: W. W. Norton.

Komlos, J., Smith, P., and Bogin, B. 2004. "Obesity and the Rate of Time Preference: Is There a Connection?" *Journal of Biosocial Science* 36 (2): 209–19.

Kowaleski-Jones, L., and Duncan, G. 2002. "Effects of Participation in the WIC

Program on Birthweight: Evidence from the National Longitudinal Survey of Youth." *American Journal of Public Health* 92 (5): 799–804.

Krebs-Smith, S., Cook, A., Subar, A., Cleveland, L., and Friday, J. 1995. "U.S. Adults' Fruit and Vegetable Intakes, 1989 to 1991: A Revised Baseline for the Healthy People 2000 Objective." *American Journal of Public Health* 85 (12): 1623–29.

Krueger, P., Rogers, R., Ridao-Cano, C., and Hummer, R. 2004. "To Help or To Harm? Food Stamp Receipt and Mortality Risk Prior to the 1996 Welfare Reform Act." *Social Issues* 82 (4): 1573–99.

Kuchler, F., and Ballenger, N. 2002. "Societal Costs of Obesity: How Can We Assess When Federal Interventions Will Pay?" *Food Review* 25 (3): 33–37.

Kuczmarski, R., and Flegal, K. 2000. "Criteria for Definition of Overweight in Transition: Background and Recommendations for the United States." *Journal of Clinical Nutrition* 72: 1074–81.

Kufahl, P. 2005. "We Failed Them, Too." *Fitness Business Pro*, Oct. 1, p. 4.

Kumanyika, S. 2001. "Minisymposium on Obesity: Overview and Some Strategic Considerations." *Annual Review of Public Health* 22: 293–308.

Kumanyika, S., and Grier, S. 2006. "Targeting Interventions for Ethnic Minority and Low-Income Populations." *Future of Children* 16 (1): 187–207.

Kunkel, M., Luccia, B., and Moore, A. 2003. "Evaluation of the South Carolina Seniors Farmers' Market Nutrition Education Program." *Journal of the American Dietetic Association* 103: 880–83.

Kunreuther, H. 1973. "Why the Poor Pay More for Food: Theoretical and Empirical Evidence." *Journal of Business* 46: 368–83.

Kunz, J., and Kalil, A. 1999. "Self-Esteem, Self-Efficacy, and Welfare Use." *Social Work Research* 23: 119–26.

Kunz-Ebrecht, S., Kirschbaum, C., and Steptoe, A. 2004. "Work Stress, Socioeconomic Status and Neuroendocrine Activation over the Working Day." *Social Science and Medicine* 58 (8): 1523–30.

Kuo, L., Kitlinska, J., Tilan, J., Li, L., Baker, S., Johnson, M., Lee, E., Burnett, M., Fricke, S., Kvetnansky, R., Herzog, H., and Zukowska, Z. 2007. "Neuropeptide Y Acts Directly in the Periphery on Fat Tissue and Mediates Stress-Induced Obesity and Metabolic Syndrome." *Nature Medicine*, 13 (7): 803–11.

Laibson, D. 1997. "Golden Eggs and Hyperbolic Discounting." *Quarterly Journal of Economics* 112 (2): 443–77.

Lakdawalla, D., Bhattacharya, J., and Goldman, D. 2004. "Are the Young Becoming More Disabled?" *Health Affairs* 23 (1): 168–76.

Laraia, B., Siega-Riz, A., Kaufman, J., and Jones, S. 2004. "Proximity of Supermarkets Is Positively Associated with Diet Quality Index for Pregnancy." *Preventive Medicine* 39: 869–75.

Latham, J., and Moffat, T. 2007. "Determinants of Variation in Food Cost and Availability in Two Socioeconomically Contrasting Neighborhoods of Hamilton, Ontario, Canada." *Health and Place* 13: 273–87.

Latkin, C., and Curry, A. 2003. "Stressful Neighborhoods and Depression: A Prospective Study of the Impact of Neighborhood Disorder." *Journal of Health and Social Behavior* 44 (1): 34–44.

Latner, J., and Stunkard, A. 2003. "Getting Worse: The Stigmatization of Obese Children." *Obesity Research* 11 (3): 452–56.

Lawlor, D., Clark, H., Davey Smith, G., and Leon, D. 2006. "Childhood Intelligence, Educational Attainment and Adult Body Mass Index: Findings from a

Prospective Cohort and within Sibling-Pairs Analysis." *International Journal of Obesity* 30: 1758–65.

Lawrance, E. 1991. "Poverty and the Rate of Time Preference: Evidence from Panel Data." *Journal of Political Economy* 99 (1): 54–77.

Lawrence, V., and Kopelman, P. 2004. "Medical Consequences of Obesity." *Clinics in Dermatology* 22: 296–302.

Lee, B. 2007. "Congresswoman Barbara Lee Joins the Food Stamp Challenge." Posted to the website of the Congressional Food Stamp Challenge (*foodstamp-challenge.typepad.com*), June 5.

Lee, J., Appulgliese, D., Kaciroti, N., Corwyn, R., Bradley, R., and Lumeng, J. 2007. "Weight Status of Young Girls and the Onset of Puberty." *Pediatrics* 119: 624–30.

Leibtag, E., and Kaufman, P. 2003. "Exploring Food Purchase Behavior of Low-Income Households." *Current Issues in Economics of Food Markets.* USDA, Economic Research Service, Agriculture Information Bulletin No. 747-07.

Leibtag, E., and Mancino, L. 2005. "Food Market Dynamics and USDA's New Dietary Guidelines." U.S. Department of Agriculture, Economic Research Service, EIB-5.

Leichter, H. 2003. "'Evil Habits' and 'Personal Choices': Assigning Responsibility for Health in the 20th Century." *Milbank Quarterly* 81 (4): 603–26.

Lennon, M. 2001. "Foreword: Mental Health of Poor Women in an Era of Devolution." *Women and Health* 32 (1–2): xv–xxi.

Lennon, M., Blome, J., and English, K. 2002. "Depression among Women on Welfare: A Review of the Literature." *Journal of the American Medical Women's Association* 57: 27–31.

Leonetti, D., Fujimoto, W., Wahl, P., Harrison, G., and Jenner, D. 1995. "Educational Attainment, Stress Hormones, Body Fat and Health: A Sociocultural Neuroendocrine Pathway?" In *Social Aspects of Obesity*, ed. I. Garine and N. Pollock. Amsterdam: Gordon and Breach.

Leventhal, T., and Brooks-Gunn, J. 2003. "Moving to Opportunity: An Experimental Study of Neighborhood Effects on Mental Health." *American Journal of Public Health* 93 (9): 1576–82.

Leviton, L. 2008. "Children's Healthy Weight and the School Environment." *Annals of the American Academy of Political and Social Science* 615: 38–55.

Lewin Group. 2000. "Access and Utilization of New Antidepressant and Antipsychotic Medications." Report submitted to the Office of the Assistant Secretary for Planning and Evaluation and the National Institute of Mental Health, U.S. Department of Health and Human Services.

Lewis, L., Sloane, D., Nascimento, L., Diamant, A., Guinyard, J., Yancey, A., and Flynn, G. 2005. "African Americans' Access to Healthy Food Options in South Los Angeles Restaurants." *American Journal of Public Health* 95 (4): 668–73.

Lievense, A., Bierma-Zeinstra, S., Verhagen, A., van Baar, M., Verhaar, J., and Koes, B. 2002. "Influence of Obesity on the Development of Osteoarthritis of the Hip: A Systematic Review." *Rheumatology* 41: 1155–62.

Light, A. 2004. "Gender Difference in the Marriage and Cohabitation Income Premium." *Demography* 41 (2): 263–84.

Lin, B. 2005. "Nutrition and Health Characteristics of Low-Income Populations: Healthy Eating Index." USDA, Economic Research Service, Agricultural Information Bulletin 796-1.

Linn, S. 2004. "Food Marketing to Children in the Context of a Marketing Mael-strom." *Journal of Public Health Policy* 25 (3–4): 367–78.

Linn, S., and Novosat, C. 2008. "Calories for Sale: Food Marketing to Children in the Twenty-First Century." *Annals of the American Academy of Political and Social Science* 615: 133–55.

Linz, P., Lee, M., and Bell, L. 2005. "Obesity, Poverty, and Participation in Nutrition Assistance Programs." USDA, Food and Nutrition Services, Report No. FSP-04-PO.

Lissau, I., and Sorensen, T. 1994. "Parental Neglect during Childhood and Increased Risk of Obesity in Young Adulthood." *Lancet* 343 (8893): 324–27.

Lleras-Muney, A. 2005. "The Relationship between Education and Adult Mortality in the United States." *Review of Economic Studies* 72 (1): 189–221.

Logio, K. 2003. "Gender, Race, Childhood Abuse, and Body Image among Adolescents." *Violence against Women* 9 (8): 931–54.

Lott, B. 2002. "Cognitive and Behavioral Distancing from the Poor." *American Psychologist* 57 (2): 100–110.

Lovett, L. 2005. "The Popeye Principle: Selling Child Health in the First Nutrition Crisis." *Journal of Health Politics, Policy and Law* 30 (5): 803–38.

Lupien, S., King, S., Meaney, M., and McEwen, B. 2000. "Child's Stress Hormone Levels Correlate with Mother's Socioeconomic Status and Depressive State." *Biological Psychiatry* 48 (10): 976–80.

Lumeng, J., Appugliese, D., Cabral, H., Bradley, R., and Zuckerman, B. 2006. "Neighborhood Safety and Overweight Status in Children." *Archives of Pediatric and Adolescent Medicine* 160: 25–31.

Lumeng, J., Gannon, K., Appugliese, D., Cabral, H., and Zuckerman, B. 2005. "Preschool Child Care and Risk of Overweight in 6- to 12-Year-Old Children." *International Journal of Obesity* 29: 60–66.

Lumeng, J., Somashekar, D., Appugliese, D., Kaciroti, N., Corwyn, R., and Bradley, R. 2007. "Shorter Sleep Duration Is Associated with Increased Risk for Being Overweight at Ages 9 to 12 Years." *Pediatrics* 120 (5): 1020–29.

Lutz, S., Blaylock, J., and Smallwood, D. 1993. "Household Characteristics Affect Food Choices." *Food Review* 16 (2): 12–17.

Lynch, J., Kaplan, G., and Shema, S. 1997. "Cumulative Impact of Sustained Economic Hardship on Physical, Cognitive, Psychological and Social Functioning." *New England Journal of Medicine* 337: 1889–95.

MacDonald, J., and Nelson, P. 1991. "Do the Poor Still Pay More? Food Price Variations in Large Metropolitan Areas." *Journal of Urban Economics* 30: 344–59.

Macera, C., Ham, S., Yore, M., Jones, D., Ainsworth, B., Kimsey, C., and Kohl, H. 2005. "Prevalence of Physical Activity in the United States: Behavioral Risk Factor Surveillance System, 2001." *Preventing Chronic Disease* 2 (2): 1–10.

Macintyre, S., McKay, L., Cummins, S., and Burns, C. 2005. "Out-of-Home Food Outlets and Area Deprivation: Case Study in Glasgow, UK." *International Journal of Behavioral Nutrition and Physical Activity* 2: 16, doi:10.1186/1479-5868-2-16.

Maheshwari, N., Robinson, J., Kohatsu, N., and Zimmerman, B. 2005. "Obesity Prevalence Increasing 3 Times Faster in High than Low Income Groups: National Health and Nutrition Examination Surveys 1971 to 2002." *Circulation* 111 (14): 190.

Maillot, M., Darmon, N., Darmon, M., Lafay, L., and Drewnowski, A. 2007.

"Nutrient-Dense Food Groups Have High Energy Costs: An Econometric Approach to Nutrient Profiling." *Journal of Nutrition* 137 (7): 1815–20.

Malik, V., Schulze, M., and Hu, F. 2006. "Intake of Sugar-Sweetened Beverages and Weight Gain: A Systematic Review." *American Journal of Clinical Nutrition* 84: 274–88.

Mamun, A., Lawlor, D., Alati, R., O'Callaghan, M., Williams, G., and Najman, J. 2007. "Increasing Body Mass Index from Age 5 to 14 Years Predicts Asthma among Adolescents: Evidence from a Birth Cohort Study." *International Journal of Obesity* 31: 578–83.

Marmot, M. 2000. "Multilevel Approaches to Understanding Social Determinants." In *Social Epidemiology*, ed. L. Berkman and I. Kawachi, 349–67. Oxford: Oxford University Press.

———. 2004. *The Status Syndrome: How Social Standing Affects Our Health and Longevity.* New York: Times Books.

Marshall, S., Biddle, S., Gorely, T., Cameron, N., and Murdey, I. 2004. "Relationships between Media Use, Body Fatness, and Physical Activity in Children and Youth: A Meta-Analysis." *International Journal of Obesity* 28 (10): 1238–46.

Marshall, S., Jones, D., Ainsworth, B., Reis, J., Levy, S., and Macera, C. 2007. "Race/Ethnicity, Social Class, and Leisure-Time Physical Inactivity." *Medicine and Science in Sports and Exercise* 39 (1): 44–51.

Matheson, D., Varady, J., Varady, A., and Killen, J. 2002. "Household Food Security and Nutritional Status of Hispanic Children in the Fifth Grade." *American Journal of Clinical Nutrition* 76: 210–17.

Maxwell, C. 2005. "Prosecuting Domestic Violence." *Criminology and Public Policy* 4 (3): 527–34.

McDonough, P., Duncan, G., Williams, D., and House, J. 1997. "Income Dynamics and Adult Mortality in the United States, 1972 through 1989." *American Journal of Public Health* 87 (9): 1476–83.

McElroy, S., Kotwal, R., Malhotra, S., Nelson, E., Keck, P., and Nemeroff, C. 2004. "Are Mood Disorders and Obesity Related? A Review for the Mental Health Professional." *Journal of Clinical Psychology* 65 (5): 634–51.

McEwen, B. 2001. "From Molecules to Mind: Stress, Individual Differences, and the Social Environment." *Annals of the New York Academy of Sciences* 935: 42–49.

McGinnis, J., and Foege, W. 1993. "Actual Causes of Death in the United States." *JAMA* 270 (18): 2207–12.

McGinnis, J., Grootman, J., and Kraak, V. 2006. *Food Marketing to Children: Threat or Opportunity?* Washington, DC: National Academies Press.

McIntyre, L., Glanville, N., Raine, K., Dayle, J., Anderson, B., and Battaglia, N. 2003 "Do Low-Income Lone Mothers Compromise Their Nutrition to Feed Their Children?" *Canadian Medical Association Journal* 168 (6): 686–91.

McNeil, J. 2000. "Employment, Earnings, and Disability." Paper presented at the Western Economics Association Meetings, Vancouver.

Mears, D. 2003. "Research and Interventions to Reduce Domestic Violence Revictimization." *Trauma, Violence, and Abuse* 4 (2): 127–47.

Measelle, J., Stice, E., and Hogansen, J. 2006. "Developmental Trajectories of Co-occurring Depressive, Eating, Antisocial, and Substance Abuse Problems in Female Adolescents." *Journal of Abnormal Psychology* 115 (3): 524–38.

Mello, M., Studdert, D., and Brennan, T. 2006. "Obesity—The New Frontier of Public Health Law." *New England Journal of Medicine* 354 (24): 2601–10.

Menard, A. 2001. "Domestic Violence and Housing: Key Policy and Program Changes." *Violence against Women* 7 (6): 707–20.

Meyer, B., and Mok, W. 2006. "Disability, Earnings, Income and Consumption." Working paper, Harris Graduate School of Public Policy Studies, University of Chicago.

Meyer, B., and Sullivan, J. 2004. "The Effects of Welfare and Tax Reform: The Material Well-Being of Single Mothers in the 1980s and 1990s." *Journal of Public Economics* 88 (7–8): 1387–420.

Meyerhoefer, C., and Pylypchuk, Y. 2008. "Does Participation in the Food Stamp Program Increase the Prevalence of Obesity and Health Care Spending?" *American Journal of Agricultural Economics* 90 (2): 287–305.

Miech, R., Caspi, A., Moffitt, T., Wright, B., and Silva, P. 1999. "Low Socioeconomic Status and Mental Disorders: A Longitudinal Study of Selection and Causation during Young Adulthood." *American Journal of Sociology* 104 (4): 1096–131.

Miech, R., Kumanyika, S., Stettler, N., Link, B., Phelan, J., and Chang, V. 2006. "Trends in the Association of Poverty with Overweight among U.S. Adolescents, 1971–2004." *JAMA* 295 (20): 2385–93.

Minkler, M. 1999. "Personal Responsibility for Health? A Review of the Arguments and the Evidence at the Century's End." *Health Education and Behavior* 26 (1): 121–40.

Mintz, S. 1985. *Sweetness and Power: The Place of Sugar in Modern History.* Viking: New York.

Mirowsky, J., and Ross, C. 1986. "Social Patterns of Distress." *Annual Review of Sociology* 12: 23–45.

———. 2003. *Education, Social Status, and Health.* New York: Aldine de Gruyter.

Mitra, A. 2001. "Effects of Physical Attributes on the Wages of Males and Females." *Applied Economic Letters* 8: 731–35.

Mock, C. N., Grossman, D. C., Kaufman, R. P., Mack, C. D., and Rivara, F. P. 2002. "The Relationship between Body Weight and Risk of Death and Serious Injury in Motor Vehicle Crashes." *Accident Analysis and Prevention* 34 (2): 221–28.

Moffitt, R. 1999. "The Effect of Pre-PRWORA Waivers on AFDC Caseloads and Female Earnings, Income, and Labor Force Behavior." In *Economic Conditions and Welfare Reform,* ed. S. Danziger, 91–118. Kalamazoo, MI: Upjohn Institute.

Molnar, A. 2003. "School Commercialism Hurts All Children, Ethnic Minority Group Children Most of All." *Journal of Negro Education* 72 (4): 371–78.

Molnar, B., Gortmaker, S., Bull, F., and Buka, S. 2004. "Unsafe to Play? Neighborhood Disorder and Lack of Safety Predict Reduced Physical Activity among Urban Children and Adolescents." *American Journal of Health Promotion* 18 (5): 378–86.

Montgomery, S., and Willis, W. 2006. "Fiscal Year 2005 Impact and Review of the Expanded Food and Nutrition Education Program." U.S. Department of Agriculture, Cooperative State Research Education and Extension Service, May 2006.

Moore, L., and Diez Roux, A. 2006. "Associations of Neighborhood Characteristics with the Location and Type of Food Stores." *American Journal of Public Health* 96 (2): 325–31.

Moore, P., Adler, N., Williams, D., and Jackson, J. 2002. "Socioeconomic Status and Health: The Role of Sleep." *Psychosomatic Medicine* 64: 337–44.

Moorman, C. 1996. "A Quasi Experiment to Assess the Consumer and Informational Determinants of Nutrition Information Processing Activities: The Case of the Nutritional Labeling and Education Act." *Journal of Public Policy and Marketing* 15 (1): 28–44.

Morenoff, J., Diez Roux, A., Osypuk, T., and Hansen, B. 2006. "Residential Environments and Obesity: What Can We Learn about Policy Interventions from Observational Studies?" Paper presented at the National Poverty Center conference "Health Effects of Non-health Policy," Bethesda, MA, February 9–10.

Morland, K., Diez Roux, A., and Wing, S. 2006. "Supermarkets, Other Food Stores, and Obesity: The Atherosclerosis Risk in Communities Study." *American Journal of Preventive Medicine* 30 (4): 333–39.

Morland, K., Wing, S., and Diez Roux, A. 2002. "The Contextual Effect of the Local Food Environment on Residents' Diets: The Atherosclerosis Risk in Communities Study." *American Journal of Public Health* 92 (11): 1761–67.

Morland, K., Wing, S., Diez Roux, A., and Poole, C. 2002. "Neighborhood Characteristics Associated with the Location of Food Stores and Food Services Places." *American Journal of Preventive Medicine* 22 (1): 23–29.

Mosley, J. 1995. "Poverty, Welfare Receipt, and Adolescent Self-Esteem." NSFH Working Paper No. 69.

Moyer, D., DiPietro, L., Berkowitz, R., and Stunkard, A. 1997. "Childhood Sexual Abuse and Precursors of Binge Eating in an Adolescent Female Population." *International Journal of Eating Disorders* 21 (1): 23–30.

Mujahid, M., Diez Roux, A., Borrell, L., and Nieto, F. 2005. "Cross-Sectional and Longitudinal Associations of BMI with Socioeconomic Characteristics." *Obesity Research* 13 (8): 1412–21.

Murphy, J., Wehler, C., Pagano, M., Little, M., Kleinman, R., and Jellinek, M. 1998. "Relationship between Hunger and Psychosocial Functioning in Low-Income American Children." *Journal of the American Academy of Child and Adolescent Psychiatry* 37 (2): 163–70.

Must, A., and Tybor, D. 2005. "Physical Activity and Sedentary Behavior: A Review of Longitudinal Studies of Weight and Adiposity in Youth." *International Journal of Obesity* 299 (Suppl. 2): S84–S96.

Mustillo, S., Worthman, C., Erkanli, A., Keeler, G., Angold, A., and Costello, E. 2003. "Obesity and Psychiatric Disorder: Developmental Trajectories." *Pediatrics* 111 (4): 851–59.

National Center for Health Statistics. 2001. *Health, United States, 2001, Urban and Rural Health Chartbook.* Hyattsville, MD: National Center for Health Statistics.

———. 2002. "Leisure-Time Physical Activity among Adults: United States, 1997–98." Advance Data No. 325, April 7.

———. 2005. *Health, United States, 2005.* Hyattsville, MD: National Center for Health Statistics.

———. 2006. "Prevalence of Overweight among Children and Adolescents: United States, 2003–2004." Available at *www.cdc.gov/nchs.*

———. 2007. *Health, United States, 2007.* Hyattsville, MD: National Center for Health Statistics.

National Conference of State Legislatures. 2007. "Childhood Obesity—2006 Policy Options, Nutrition and Physical Activity." Available at *www.ncsl.org.*

National Institute for Mental Health. Revised 2007. "Depression." National Institutes of Health Publication No. 00-3561. Available at *www.nimh.nih.gov.*

National Institutes of Health. 1998. "Clinical Guidelines on the Identification,

Evaluation, and Treatment of Overweight and Obesity in Adults: The Evidence Report." National Institutes of Health Publication No. 98-4083.

National Research Council and Institute of Medicine. 2000. *From Neurons to Neighborhoods: The Science of Early Childhood Development*, ed. J. Shonkoff and D. Phillips. Washington, DC: National Academies Press.

National Scientific Council on the Developing Child. 2005. "Excessive Stress Disrupts the Architecture of the Developing Brain." Working Paper No. 3. Available at *www.developingchild.net*.

Nayga, R. 2001. "Effect of Schooling on Obesity: Is Health Knowledge a Moderating Factor?" *Education Economics* 9 (2): 129–37.

Neault, N., Cook, J., Morris, V., and Frank, D. 2005. "The Real Cost of a Healthy Diet: Healthful Foods Are Out of Reach for Low-Income Families in Boston, Massachusetts." Boston Medical Center Department of Pediatrics.

Neel, J. 1962. "Diabetes Mellitus: A Thrifty Genotype Rendered Detrimental by Progress?" *American Journal of Human Genetics* 14: 353–62.

———. 1999. "The Thrifty Genotype in 1998." *Nutrition Reviews* 57 (5): S2–S9.

Nelson, K., Brown, M., and Lurie, N. 1998. "Hunger in an Adult Patient Population." *JAMA* 279 (15): 1211–14.

Nestle, M. 2002. *Food Politics: How the Food Industry Influences Nutrition and Health*. Berkeley: University of California Press.

Neumark, D., and Stock, W. 2001. "The Effects of Race and Sex Discrimination Laws." NBER Working Paper No. 8215.

Neumark-Sztainer, D., Falkner, N., Story, M., Perry, C., Hannan, P., and Mulert, S. 2002. "Weight-Teasing among Adolescents: Correlations with Weight Status and Disordered Eating Behaviors." *International Journal of Obesity* 26 (1): 123–31.

Newman, C. 2006. "Bipolar Disorder." In *Adult Psychopathology and Diagnosis* (4th ed.), ed. M. Hersen and S. Turner, 244–61. Hoboken, NJ: John Wiley.

New York Department of Health and Hygiene. 2006. "Eating In, Eating Out, Eating Well: Access to Healthy Food in North and Central Brooklyn." Available at *www.nyc.gov*.

Nichols-Casebolt, A. 1986. "The Psychological Effects of Income: Testing Income Support Benefits." *Social Service Review* 60: 287–302.

Nord, M., Andrews, M., and Carlson, S. 2006. "Household Food Security in the United States, 2005." USDA, Economic Research Service, Report No. ERR-29.

Ogden, C., Carroll, M., Curtin, L., McDowell, M., Tabak, C., and Flegal, K. 2006. "Prevalence of Overweight and Obesity in the United States, 1999–2004." *JAMA* 295 (13): 1549–55.

Ogden, C., Flegal, K., Carroll, M., and Johnson, C. 2002. "Prevalence and Trends in Overweight among U.S. Children and Adolescents, 1999–2000." *JAMA* 288: 1728–32.

Ohls, J., Ponza, M., Moreno, L., Zambrowski, A., and Cohen, R. 1999. "Food Stamp Participants' Access to Food Retailers: Final Report." USDA, Food and Nutrition Service, July 1999.

O'Keefe J., and Cordain, L. 2004. "Cardiovascular Disease Resulting from a Diet and Lifestyle at Odds with Our Paleolithic Genome: How to Become a 21st-Century Hunter-Gatherer." *Mayo Clinic Proceedings* 79 (1): 101–8.

Oliver, G., and Wardle, J. 1999. "Perceived Effects of Stress on Food Choice." *Physiology and Behavior* 6 (3): 511–15.

Oliver, J. 2006. *Fat Politics: The Real Story behind America's Obesity Epidemic*. New York: Oxford University Press.

Oliver, J., and Lee, T. 2005. "Public Opinion and the Politics of Obesity in America." *Journal of Health Politics, Policy and Law* 30 (5): 923–54.

Oliver, L., and Hayes, M. 2008. "Effects of Neighborhood Income on Reported Body Mass Index: An Eight Year Longitudinal Study of Canadian Children." *BMC Public Health* 8 (16): doi:10.1186/1471-2458-8-16.

Olson, C. 2005. "Food Insecurity in Women: A Recipe for Unhealthy Trade-Offs." *Topics in Clinical Nutrition* 20 (4): 321–28.

O'Malley, P., Johnston, L., Delva, J., Bachman, J., and Schulenberg, J. 2007. "Variation in Obesity among American Secondary School Students by School and School Characteristics." *American Journal of Preventive Medicine* 33 (4, Suppl. 1): S187–S194.

Orr, L., Feins, J., Jacob, R., and Beecroft, E. 2003. "Moving to Opportunity Interim Impacts Evaluation." U.S. Department of Housing and Urban Development, Office of Policy Development and Research.

Østbye, T., Dement, J., and Krause, K. 2007. "Obesity and Workers' Compensation: Results from the Duke Health and Safety Surveillance System." *Archives of Internal Medicine* 167: 766–73.

Owen, C., Martin, R., Whincup, P., Davey-Smith, G., Gillman, M., and Cook, D. 2005. "The Effect of Breastfeeding on Mean Body Mass Index throughout Life: A Quantitative Review of Published and Unpublished Observational Evidence." *American Journal of Clinical Nutrition* 82 (6): 1298–307.

Pagán, J., and Dávila, A. 1997. "Obesity, Occupational Attainment and Earnings." *Social Science Quarterly* 78: 756–70.

Painter, R., Roseboom, T., and Bleker, O. 2005. "Prenatal Exposure to the Dutch Famine and Disease in Later Life: An Overview." *Reproductive Toxicology* 20 (3): 345–52.

Paluska, S., and Schwenk, T. 2000. "Physical Activity and Mental Health: Current Concepts." *Sports Medicine* 29 (3): 167–80.

Parker, L. 1994. "The Role of Workplace Support in Facilitating Self-Sufficiency among Single Mothers on Welfare." *Family Relations* 43 (2): 168–73.

Parker, S., and Keim, K., 2004. "Emic Perspectives of Body Weight in Overweight and Obese White Women with Limited Income." *Journal of Nutrition Education and Behavior* 36: 282–89.

Parks, S., Houseman, R., and Brownson, R. 2003. "Differential Correlates of Physical Activity in Urban and Rural Adults of Various Socioeconomics Backgrounds in the United States." *Journal of Epidemiology and Community Health* 57: 29–35.

Patterson, E. 1991. "Poverty, Income Inequality, and Community Crime Rates." *Criminology* 29 (4): 755–76.

Pavetti, L., Holcomb, P., and Duke, A. 1995. "Increasing Participation in Work and Work-Related Activities: Lessons from Five State Demonstration Projects." Urban Institute Press, Washington, DC. Available at *www.urban.org*.

Pereira, M., Kartashov, A., Ebbling, C., Van Horn, L., Slattery, M., Jacobs, D., and Ludwig, D. 2005. "Fat-Food Habits, Weight Gain, and Insulin Resistance (the CARDIA Study): 15-Year Prospective Analysis." *Lancet* 365 (9453): 36–42.

Perry, C., Bishop, D., Taylor, G., Davis, M., Story, M., et al. 2004. "A Randomized School Trial of Environmental Strategies to Encourage Fruit and Vegetable Consumption among Children." *Health Education and Behavior* 131 (1): 65–76.

Petterson, S., and Friel, L. 2001. "Psychological Distress, Hopelessness, and Welfare." *Women and Health* 32 (1–2): 79–99.

Pierce, J., Wardle, J. "Cause and Effect Beliefs and Self-Esteem of Overweight Children." *Journal of Childhood Psychology and Psychiatry* 38: 645–50.

Pignatti, R., Bertella, L., Albani, G., Mauro, A., Molinari, E., and Semenza, C. 2006. "Decision-Making in Obesity: A Study Using the Gambling Task." *Eating and Weight Disorders* 11 (3): 126–32.

Pine, D., Goldstein, R., Wolk, S., and Weissman, M. 2001. "The Association between Childhood Depression and Adult Body Mass Index." *Pediatrics* 107 (5): 1049–56.

Pingitore, R., Dugoni, B., Tindale, R. S., and Springs, B. 1994. "Bias against Overweight Job Applicants in a Simulated Employment Interview." *Journal of Applied Psychology* 79 (6): 909–17.

Pi-Sunyer, F. 2002. "Medical Complications of Obesity in Adults." In *Eating Disorders and Obesity: A Comprehensive Handbook* (2nd ed.), ed. C. G. Fairburn and K. D. Brownell. New York: Guilford Press.

Poikolainen, A. 2005. "Characteristics of Food Stamps Households: Fiscal Year 2004." Prepared by Mathematica Policy Research, Inc., for the USDA, Food and Nutrition Service.

Polit, D., London, A., and Martinez, J. 2001. "The Health of Poor Urban Women: Findings from the Project on Devolution and Urban Change." Manpower Demonstration Research Corporation.

Polivy, J. 1996. "Psychological Consequences of Food Restriction." *Journal of the American Dietetic Association* 96 (6): 589–94.

Pollan, M. 2006. *The Omnivore's Dilemma: A Natural History of Four Meals.* New York: Penguin Press.

Popenoe, R. 2005. "Ideal." In *Fat: The Anthropology of an Obsession*, ed. D. Kulick and A. Meneley, 9–28. New York: Jeremy P. Tarcher/Penguin.

Popkin, S. 1990. "Welfare: Views from the Bottom." *Social Problems* 37 (1): 64–79.

Poulton, R., Caspi, A., Milne, B., Thomson, W., Taylor, A., Sears, M., and Moffitt, T. 2002. "Association between Children's Experience of Socioeconomic Disadvantage and Adult Health: A Life-Course Study." *Lancet* 360: 1640–45.

Powdermaker, H. 1997. "An Anthropological Approach to the Problem of Obesity." In *Food and Culture: A Reader*, ed. C. Counihan and P. Van Esterik. New York: Routledge.

Powell, L., Auld, C., Chaloupka, F., O'Malley, P., and Johnston, L. 2007. "Associations between Access to Food Stores and Adolescent Body Mass Index." *American Journal of Preventive Medicine* 33 (4, Suppl. 1): S301–S307.

Powell, L., Chaloupka, F., and Bao, Y. 2007. "The Availability of Fast-Food and Full-Service Restaurants in the United States: Associations with Neighborhood Characteristics." *American Journal of Preventive Medicine* 33 (4, Suppl. 1): S240–S245.

Powell, L., Slater, S., and Chaloupka, F. 2004. "The Relationship between Community Physical Activity Settings and Race, Ethnicity, and Socioeconomic Status." *Evidence-Based Preventive Medicine* 1: 135–44.

Powell, L., Slater, S., Chaloupka, F., and Harper, D. 2006. "Availability of Physical Activity–Related Facilities and Neighborhood Demographic and Socioeconomic Characteristics: A National Study." *American Journal of Public Health* 96 (9): 1676–80.

Power, C., Manor, O., and Matthews, S. 2003. "Child and Adult Socioeconomic Conditions and Obesity in a National Cohort." *International Journal of Obesity* 27: 1081–86.

Prather, R., and Williamson, D. 1988. "Psychopathology Associated with Bulimia, Binge Eating, and Obesity." *International Journal of Eating Disorders* 7: 177–84.

Puhl, R., and Brownell, K. 2001. "Bias, Discrimination, and Obesity." *Obesity Research* 9 (12): 788–805.

Puska, P., Tuomilehto, J., Nissinen, A., and Vartiainen, E. 1995. *The North Karelia Project: 20 Year Results and Experiences.* Finland: National Public Health Institute (KTL).

Putnam, J., Allshouse, J., and Kantor, L. 2002. "U.S. Per Capita Food Supply Trends: More Calories, Refined Carbohydrates, and Fats." *Food Review* 25 (3): 2–15.

Quesenberry, C., Caan, B., and Jacobson, A. 1998. "Obesity, Health Services Use, and Health Care Costs among Members of a Health Maintenance Organization." *Archives of Internal Medicine* 158: 466–72.

Raebel, M., Malone, D., Conner, D., Xu, S., Porter, J., and Lanty, F. 2004. "Health Services Use and Health Care Costs of Obese and Nonobese Individuals." *Archives of Internal Medicine* 164 (Oct. 24): 2135–40.

Rand, C., and MacGregor, A. 1990. "Morbidly Obese Patients' Perceptions of Social Discrimination Before and After Surgery for Obesity." *Southern Medical Journal* 83: 1390–5.

Rank, M. 1994. *Living on the Edge: The Realities of Welfare in America.* New York: Columbia University Press.

Raphael, J. 1996. "Domestic Violence and Welfare Receipt: Toward a New Feminist Theory of Welfare Dependency." *Harvard Women's Law Journal* 19: 201–27.

———. 1997. "Trapped by Poverty/Trapped by Abuse: New Evidence Documenting the Relationship between Domestic Violence and Welfare." Report for the Project for Research on Welfare, Work, and Domestic Violence. Available at *www. ssw.umich.edu/trapped*.

———. 2000. *Saving Bernice: Battered Women, Welfare, and Poverty.* Boston: Northeastern University Press.

Ravelli, A., van der Meulen, J., Osmond, C., Barker, D., and Bleker, O. 1999. "Obesity at the Age of 50 Years in Men and Women Exposed to Famine Prenatally." *American Journal of Clinical Nutrition* 70: 811–16.

Reagan, P. 1996. "Sexual Outcasts: The Perceived Impact of Body Weight and Gender on Sexuality." *Journal of Applied Social Psychology* 26: 1803–15.

Register, C., and Williams, D. 1990. "Wage Effects of Obesity among Young Workers." *Social Science Quarterly* 71 (1): 130–41.

Reicks, M., Randall, J., and Haynes, B. 1994. "Factors Affecting Vegetable Consumption in Low-Income Households." *Journal of the American Dietetic Association* 94 (11): 1309–11.

Reidpath, D., Burns, C., Garrard, J., Mahoney, M., and Townsend, M. 2002. "An Ecological Study of the Relationship between Social and Environmental Determinants of Obesity." *Health and Place* 8: 141–45.

Richardson, L., Davis, R., Poulton, R., McCauley, E., Moffitt, T., Caspi, A., and Connell, F. 2003. "A Longitudinal Evaluation of Adolescent Depression and Adult Obesity." *Archives of Pediatric and Adolescent Medicine* 157: 739–45.

Richardson, S., Goodman, N., Hastorf, A., and Dornbusch, S. 1961. "Cultural Uniformity in Reaction to Physical Disabilities." *American Sociological Review* 26 (2): 241–47.

Riger, S., and Staggs, S. 2004. "Welfare Reform, Domestic Violence, and Employment." *Violence against Women* 10 (9): 961–90.

Riger, S., Staggs, S., and Schewe, P. 2004. "Intimate Partner Violence as an Obstacle to Employment among Mothers Affected by Welfare Reform." *Journal of Social Issues* 60 (4): 801–17.

Riolo, S., Nguyen, T., Greden, J., and King, C. 2005. "Prevalence of Depression by Race/Ethnicity: Findings from the National Health and Nutrition Examination Survey III." *American Journal of Public Health* 95 (6): 998–1000.

Ritchey, F., LaGory, M., Fitzpatrick, K., and Mullis, J. 1990. "A Comparison of Homeless, Community-Wide, and Selected Distressed Samples on the CES-Depression Scale." *Journal of Public Health* 80 (11): 1384–86.

Ritenbaugh, C. 1982. "Obesity as a Culture Bound Syndrome." *Culture, Medicine and Psychiatry* 6: 347–61.

Roberts, R., Deleger, S., Strawbridge, W., and Kaplan, G. 2003. "Prospective Association between Obesity and Depression: Evidence from the Alameda County Study." *International Journal of Obesity* 27: 514–21.

Robinson, L., McIntyre, L., and Officer, S. 2005. "Welfare Babies: Poor Children's Experiences Informing Healthy Peer Relationships in Canada." *Health Promotion International* 20 (4): 342–50.

Robinson, T. 1999. "Reducing Children's Television Viewing to Prevent Obesity." *JAMA* 282 (16): 1561–67.

Rodriguez, E., Frongillo, E., and Chandra, P. 2001. "Do Social Programmes Contribute to Mental Well-Being? The Long-Term Impact of Unemployment on Depression in the United States." *International Journal of Epidemiology* 30: 163–70.

Roehling, M. 1999. "Weight-Based Discrimination in Employment: Psychological and Legal Aspects." *Personnel Psychology* 52 (4): 969–1016.

Roemmich, J., Epstein, L., Raja, S., Yin, L., Robinson, J., and Winiewicz, D. 2006. "Association of Access to Parks and Recreational Facilities with the Physical Activity of Young Children." *Preventive Medicine* 43 (6): 437–41.

Rogers, J., and Gray, M. 1994. "CE Data: Quintiles of Income versus Quintiles of Outlays." *Monthly Labor Review*, Dec.: 32–37.

Ronti, T., Lupattelli, G., and Mannarino, E. 2006. "The Endocrine Function of Adipose Tissue: An Update." *Clinical Endocrinology* 64 (4): 355–65.

Rose, D. 1999. "Economic Determinants and Dietary Consequences of Food Insecurity in the United States." *Journal of Nutrition* 129 (2, Suppl.): 517S–520S.

Rose, D., and Bodor, J. 2006. "Household Food Insecurity and Overweight Status in Young School Children: Results from the Early Childhood Longitudinal Study." *Pediatrics* 117 (2): 464–73.

Rose, D., Bodor, J., and Chilton, M. 2006. "Has the WIC Incentive to Formula-Feed Led to an Increase in Overweight Children?" *Journal of Nutrition* 136 (4): 1086–90.

Rose, D., Gundersen, C., and Oliveira, V. 1998. "Socio-economic Determinants of Food Insecurity in the United States: Evidence from the SIPP and CSFII Datasets." USDA, Economic Research Service Technical Bulletin 1869.

Rose, D., Habicht, J., and Devaney, B. 1998. "Household Participation in the Food

Stamp and WIC Programs Increases Nutrient Intake of Preschool Children." *Journal of Nutrition* 128: 548–55.

Roseboom, T., de Rooij, S., and Painter, R. 2006. "The Dutch Famine and Its Long-Term Consequences for Adult Health." *Early Human Development* 82: 485–91.

Rosmond, R., and Björntorp, P. 1998. "Endocrine and Metabolic Aberrations in Men with Abdominal Obesity in Relation to Anxio-Depressive Infirmity." *Metabolism* 47 (10): 1187–93.

———. 2000. "Occupational Status, Cortisol Secretory Pattern, and Visceral Obesity in Middle-Aged Men." *Obesity Research* 8 (6): 445–50.

Ross, C. 2000. "Neighborhood Disadvantage and Adult Depression." *Journal of Health and Social Behavior* 41 (June): 177–87.

Ross, C., and Mirowsky, J. 2001. "Neighborhood Disadvantage, Disorder, and Health." *Journal of Health and Social Behavior* 42 (Sept.): 258–76.

Ross, C., and Wu, C. 1995. "The Links between Education and Health." *American Sociological Review* 60: 719–45.

Rothblum, E., Brand, P., Miller, C., and Oetjen, H. 1990. "The Relationship between Obesity, Employment Discrimination, and Employment-Related Victimization." *Journal of Vocational Behavior* 37: 251–66.

Rush, D. 1986. "The National WIC Evaluation: An Examination of the Special Supplemental Food Program for Women, Infants, and Children. Vol. 1: Summary." USDA, Food and Nutrition Service, Office of Analysis and Evaluation.

Ruskin, G. 2005. "Request for Investigation of Companies That Engage in 'Buzz' Marketing." Letter to Donald Clark, Secretary of the Federal Trade Commission, Oct. 18, 2005, from Gary Ruskin, Executive Director of Consumer Alert. Available at *www.commercialalert.org/buzzmarketing.pdf.*

Ryan, W. 1971. *Blaming the Victim.* New York: Pantheon Books.

Saelens, B., Sallis, J., Black, J., and Chen, D. 2003. "Neighborhood-Based Differences in Physical Activity: An Environment Scale Evaluation." *American Journal of Public Health* 93 (9): 1552–58.

Sallis, J. 2004. "Obesity: Is Personal Responsibility the Answer?" *San Diego Union-Tribune,* April 9.

Sallis, J., Bauman, A., and Pratt, M. 1998. "Environmental and Policy Interventions to Promote Physical Activity." *American Journal of Preventive Medicine* 15 (4): 379–97.

Sallis, J., and Glanz, K. 2006. "The Role of Built Environments in Physical Activity, Eating, and Obesity in Childhood." *The Future of Children* 16 (1): 89–108.

Sallis, J., Hovell, M., Hofstetter, C., Elder, J., Hackley, M., Caspersen, C., and Powell, K. 1990. "Distance between Homes and Exercise Facilities Related to Frequency of Exercise among San Diego Residents." *Public Health Reports* 105 (2): 179–85.

Sallis, J., Prochaska, J., and Taylor, W. 2000. "A Review of Correlates of Physical Activity of Children and Adolescents." *Medicine and Science in Sports and Exercise* 32 (5): 963–75.

Samwick, A., 1998. "Discount Rate Heterogeneity and Social Security Reform." *Journal of Development Economics* 57: 117–46.

Sansone, R., Sansone, L., Wiederman, D., Shaffer, P., and Koplan, J. 1998. "The Relationship between Obesity and Medical Utilization among Women in a Primary Care Setting." *International Journal of Eating Disorders* 23: 161–67.

Sargent, J., and Blanchflower, D. 1994. "Obesity and Stature in Adolescence and

Earnings in Young Adulthood." *Archives of Pediatric and Adolescent Medicine* 148: 681–87.

Schanzenbach, D. 2002. "What Are Food Stamps Worth?" Princeton University Industrial Relations Section Working Paper No. 468.

———. 2005. "Do School Lunches Contribute to Childhood Obesity?" University of Chicago Working Paper.

Schor, J. 2004. *Born to Buy.* Scribner: New York.

Schwartz, H. 1986. *Never Satisfied: A Cultural History of Diets, Fantasies and Fat.* New York: Free Press.

Schwartz, T., Nihalani, N., Jindal, S., Virk, S., and Jones, N. 2004. "Psychiatric Medication-Induced Obesity: A Review." *Obesity Reviews* 5: 115–21.

Schwimmer, J., Burwinkle, T., and Varni, J. 2003. "Health-Related Quality of Life of Severely Obese Children and Adolescents." *JAMA* 289 (14): 1813–19.

Seiders, K., and Berry, L. 2007. "Should Business Care about Obesity?" *MIT Sloan Management Review* 48 (2): 15–17.

Seiders, K., and Petty, R. 2004. "Obesity and the Role of Food Marketing: A Policy Analysis of Issues and Remedies." *Journal of Public Policy and Marketing* 23 (2): 153–69.

Seifert, K., Heflin, C., Corcoran, M., and Williams, D. 2001. "Food Insufficiency and the Physical and Mental Health of Low-Income Women." *Women and Health* 32 (1–2): 159–77.

Selway, J. 2006. "Childhood Maltreatment and Adult Obesity." *Bariatric Nursing and Surgical Patient Care* 1 (4): 273–82.

Shalla, V., and Schellenberg, G. 1998. "The Value of Words: Literacy and Economic Security in Canada." Statistics Canada report no. 89-552-MPE.

Shapin, S. 2006. "Eat and Run: Why We're So Fat." *New Yorker*, Jan. 16: 76–82.

Shapiro, J. 2005. "Is There a Daily Discount Rate? Evidence from the Food Stamp Nutrition Cycle." *Journal of Public Economics* 89: 303–25.

Shapiro, J., King, E., and Quinones, M. 2007. "Expectations of Obese Trainees: How Stigmatized Trainee Characteristics Influence Training Effectiveness." *Journal of Applied Psychology* 92 (1): 239–49.

Shaw, C. 1996. "Controversial Options." *Online NewsHour*, Feb. 20. Transcript available at *www.pbs.org/newshour*.

Sherry, B. 2005. "Food Behaviors and Other Strategies to Prevent and Treat Pediatric Overweight." *International Journal of Obesity* 29 (2, Suppl.): S116–S126.

Sherwood, N., Morton, N., Jeffery, R., French, S., Neumark-Sztainer, D., and Falkner, N. 1998. "Consumer Preferences in Format and Type of Community-Based Weight Control Programs." *American Journal of Health Promotion* 13 (1): 12–18.

Shoda, Y., Mischel, W., and Peake, P. 1990. "Predicting Adolescent Cognitive and Self-Regulatory Competencies from Preschool Delay of Gratification: Identifying Diagnostic Conditions." *Developmental Psychology* 26 (6): 978–86.

Siefert, K., Bowman, P., Heflin, C., Danziger, S., and Williams, D. 2000. "Social and Environmental Predictors of Maternal Depression in Current and Recent Welfare Recipients." *American Journal of Orthopsychiatry* 70 (4): 510–22.

Siefert, K., Heflin, C., Corcoran, M., and Williams, D. 2001. "Food Insufficiency and Physical and Mental Health of Low-Income Women." *Women and Health* 32 (1–2): 159–77.

———. 2004. "Food Insufficiency and Physical and Mental Health in a Longitudinal Survey of Welfare Recipients." *Journal of Health and Social Behavior* 45 (2): 171–86.

Siegrist, J., and Marmot, M. 2004. "Health Inequalities and the Psychosocial Environment—Two Scientific Challenges." *Social Science and Medicine* 58: 1463–73.

Simon, G., Von Korff, M., Saunders, K., Miglioretti, D., Crane, P., van Belle, G., and Kessler, R. 2006. "Associations between Obesity and Psychiatric Disorders in the U.S. Adult Population." *Archives of General Psychiatry* 63 (7): 8824–30.

Skalicky, A., Meyers, A., Adams, W., Yang, Z., Cook, J., and Frank, D. 2006. "Child Food Insecurity and Iron Deficiency Anemia in Low-Income Infants and Toddlers in the United States." *Maternal and Child Health Journal* 10 (2): 177–85.

Sloane, D., Diamant, A., Lewis, L., Yancey, A., Flynn, G., Nascimento, L., McCarthy, W., Guinyard, J., and Cousineau, M. 2003. "Improving the Nutritional Resource Environment for Healthy Living through Community-Based Participatory Research." *Journal of General Internal Medicine* 18: 568–75.

Smith, C., Shah, I., Pell, J., Crossley, J., and Dobbie, R. 2007. "Maternal Obesity in Early Pregnancy and Risk of Spontaneous and Elective Preterm Deliveries: A Retrospective Cohort Study." *American Journal of Public Health* 97 (1): 157–62.

Smith, E. 2001. "Obesity Bias Weighs against Job Seekers." Posted to the website of Magellan Health Services (*www.magellanassist.com/mem/library*), May 21.

Smith, J. 1999. "Healthy Bodies and Thick Wallets: The Duel Relation between Health and Economic Status." *Journal of Economic Perspectives* 13 (2): 145–66.

Smith, P., Bogin, B., and Bishai, D. 2005. "Are Time Preference and Body Mass Index Associated? Evidence from the National Longitudinal Survey of Youth." *Economics and Human Biology* 3: 259–70.

Smith, P., Bogin, B., Varela-Silva, M. I., and Gossiaux, B. 2006. "Prospects for Welfare Alleviation in an Obesogenic Environment." In *Trends in Poverty and Welfare Alleviation Issues*, ed. M. Lane, 1–31. New York: Nova Science Publishers.

Smith, P., Bogin, B., Varela-Silva, M. I., Orden, B., and Loucky, J. 2002. "Does Immigration Help or Harm Children's Health: The Mayan Case." *Social Science Quarterly* 83 (4): 994–1002.

Smith, P., and Zagorsky, J. 2006. "Does Public Assistance Contribute to Adult Recipients' Weight Problems?" University of Michigan–Dearborn Working Paper No. 101.

Smith, T. 2006. "Reconciling Psychology with Economics: Obesity, Behavioral Biology, and Rational Overeating." Washington State University School of Economics Working Paper No. 2006-4.

Smolak, L., and Murnen, S. 2002. "A Meta-analytic Examination of the Relationship between Child Sexual Abuse and Eating Disorders." *International Journal of Eating Disorders* 31 (2): 136–50.

Smolensky, E., and Gootman, J. 2003. *Working Families and Growing Kids: Caring for Children and Adolescents.* Committee on Family and Work Policies. Washington, DC: National Academies Press.

Sobal, J. 1984. "Marriage, Obesity, and Dieting." *Marriage and Family Review* 7: 115–39.

Sobal, J., and Bursztyn, M. 1998. "Dating People with Anorexia Nervosa and Bulimia Nervosa: Attitudes and Beliefs of University Students." *Women and Health* 27 (3): 73–88.

Sobal, J., Nicolopoulos, V., and Lee, J. 1995. "Attitudes about Weight and Dating among Secondary School Students." *International Journal of Obesity* 19: 376–81.

Sobal, J., Rauschenbach, B., and Frongillo, E. 1995. "Obesity and Marital Quality: Analysis of Weight, Marital Unhappiness, and Marital Problems in a U.S. National Sample." *Journal of Family Issues* 16: 746–64.

Sobal, J., and Stunkard, A. 1989. "Socioeconomic Status and Obesity: A Review of the Literature." *Psychological Bulletin* 105 (2): 260–75.

Social Security Administration. 2000. Social Security Ruling (SSR) 00–39, Titles II and XVI: Evaluation of Obesity. Federal Register, May 15 (vol. 65, no. 94): 31039–43.

———. 2006. "Social Security Bulletin: Annual Statistical Supplement, 2005." Available at *www.ssa.gov*.

Spiegel, K., Tasali, E., Penev, P., and Van Cauter, E. 2004. "Sleep Curtailment in Healthy Young Men Is Associated with Decreased Leptin Levels, Elevated Ghrelin Levels, and Increased Hunger and Appetite." *Annals of Internal Medicine* 141 (11): 846–50.

Spilsbury, J., Storfer-Isser, A., Kirchner, H., Nelson, L., Rosen, C., Drotar, D., and Redline, S. 2006. "Neighborhood Disadvantage as a Risk Factor for Pediatric Obstructive Sleep Apnea." *Journal of Pediatrics* 149 (3): 342–47.

Spivak, H., Hewitt, M., Onn, A., and Half, E. 2005. "Weight Loss and Improvement of Obesity-Related Illness in 500 Patients following Laparoscopic Adjustable Gastric Banding Procedure." *American Journal of Surgery* 189 (1): 27–32.

Staunton, C., Hubsmith, D., and Kallins, W. 2003. "Promoting Safe Walking and Biking to School: The Marin County Success Story." *American Journal of Public Health* 93 (9): 1431–34.

Stearns, P. 1997. *Fat History: Bodies and Beauty in the Modern West*. New York: New York University Press.

Stephens, M. 2003. "3rd of Tha Month: Do Social Security Recipients Smooth Consumption between Checks?" *American Economic Review* 93 (1): 406–22.

Steptoe, A., and Feldman, P. 2001. "Neighborhood Problems Add Sources of Chronic Stress: Development of a Measure of Neighborhood Problems, and Associations with Socioeconomic Status and Health." *Annals of Behavioral Medicine* 23 (3): 177–85.

Sterling, P., and Eyer, J. 1988. "Allostasis: A New Paradigm to Explain Arousal Pathology." In *Handbook of Life Stress, Cognition and Health*, ed. S. Fisher and J. Reason, 629–49. New York: John Wiley.

Stevens, J. 2005. "Targeting Obesity at Its Roots: Adverse Childhood Experience." *Sacramento Bee*, July 31.

Stewart, H., Blisard, N., Bhuyan, S., and Nayga, R. 2004. "The Demand for Food Away from Home: Full-Service or Fast Food?" USDA, Economic Research Service Research Brief, Jan.

Stewart, W., Ricci, J., Chee, E., Hahn, S., and Morganstein, D. 2003. "Cost of Lost Productive Work Time among U.S. Workers with Depression." *JAMA* 289: 3135–44.

Stice, E., Presnell, K., Shaw, H., and Rohde, P. 2005. "Psychological and Behavioral Risk Factors for Obesity Onset in Adolescent Girls: A Prospective Study." *Journal of Consulting and Clinical Psychology* 73 (2): 195–202.

Story, M., and French, S. 2004. "Food Advertising and Marketing Directed at Children and Adolescents in the U.S." *International Journal of Behavioral Nutrition and Physical Activity* 1 (3). Available at *www.ijbnpa.org*.

Strauss, R. 2000. "Childhood Obesity and Self-Esteem." *Pediatrics* 105 (1): 15–19.

Stunkard, A., and Allison, K. 2003. "Two Forms of Disordered Eating in Obesity: Binge Eating and Night Eating." *International Journal of Obesity and Related Metabolic Disorders* 27: 1–12.

Stunkard, A., Faith, M., and Allison, K. 2003. "Depression and Obesity." *Biological Psychiatry* 54: 330–37.

———. 2004. "Depression and Obesity: A Complex Relationship." *Psychiatric Times* 21 (11).

Sturm, R. 2002. "The Effects of Obesity, Smoking, and Drinking on Medical Problems and Costs." *Health Affairs* 21 (2): 245–53.

Sturm, R., and Datar, A. 2005. "Body Mass Index in Elementary School Children, Metropolitan Area Food Prices and Food Outlet Density." *Public Health* 119 (12): 1059–68.

Sturm, R., Ringel, J., and Andreyeva, T. 2004. "Increasing Obesity Rates and Disability Trends." *Health Affairs* 23 (2): 199–205.

Subar, A., Heimmendinger, J., Patterson, B., Krebs-Smith, S., Pivonka, E., and Kessler, R. 1992. "Fruit and Vegetable Intake in the United States: The Baseline Survey of the 5 a Day for Better Health Program." Division of Cancer Prevention and Control, National Cancer Institute, National Institutes of Health, July.

Sullivan, C., and Bybee, D. 1999. "Reducing Violence Using Community-Based Advocacy for Women with Abusive Partners." *Journal of Consulting and Clinical Psychology* 67 (1): 43–53.

Swallen, K., Reither, E., Haas, S., and Meier, A. 2005. "Overweight, Obesity, and Health-Related Quality of Life among Adolescents: The National Longitudinal Study of Adolescent Health." *Pediatrics* 115 (2): 340–47.

Swinburn, B., and Egger, G. 2002. "Preventive Strategies against Weight Gain and Obesity." *Obesity Reviews* 3 (4): 289–301.

Szanton, S., Gill, J., and Allen, J. 2005. "Allostatic Load: A Mechanism of Socioeconomic Health Disparities." *Biological Research for Nursing* 7 (1): 7–15.

Tan, L. 2000. "Spending Patterns of Public-Assisted Families." *Monthly Labor Review* 123 (5): 29–35.

Tantisira, K., and Weiss, S. 2001. "Complex Interactions in Complex Traits: Obesity and Asthma." *Thorax* 56 (Suppl. 2): 64–74.

Tarasuk, V., McIntrye, L., and Li, J. 2007. "Low-Income Women's Dietary Intakes Are Sensitive to the Depletion of Household Resources in One Month." *Journal of Nutrition* 137 (8): 1980–87.

Taveras, E., Rifas-Shiman, S., Oken, E., Gunderson, E., and Gillmas, M. 2008. "Short Sleep Duration in Infancy and Risk of Childhood Overweight." *Archives of Pediatric and Adolescent Medicine* 162 (4): 305–11.

Teachman, B., and Brownell, K. 2001. "Implicit Anti-fat Bias among Health Professionals: Is Anyone Immune?" *International Journal of Obesity* 25: 1525–31.

Teachman, B., Gapinski, K., Brownell, K., Rawlins, M., and Jeyaram, S. 2003. "Demonstrations of Implicit Anti-fat Bias: The Impact of Providing Causal Information and Evoking Empathy." *Health Psychology* 22 (1): 68–78.

Teicher, M. 2002. "Scars That Won't Heal: The Neurobiology of Child Abuse." *Scientific American* 286 (3): 68–75.

Thompson, B. 2004. "'A Way Outa No Way': Eating Problems among African-American, Latina, and White Women." In *Feminist Frontiers* (6th ed.), ed. L. Richardson, V. Taylor, and N. Whittier. New York: McGraw-Hill.

Thompson, D., Edelsberg, J., Colditz, G., Bird, A., and Oster, G. 1999. "Lifetime

Health and Economic Consequences of Obesity." *Archives of Internal Medicine* 159 (18): 2177–83.

Thompson, D., Edelsberg, J., Kinsey, K., and Oster, G. 1998. "Estimated Economic Costs of Obesity to U.S. Business." *American Journal of Health Promotion* 13 (2): 120–27.

Thompson, J., Coovert, M., Richards, K., Johnson, S., and Cattarin, J. 2006. "Development of Body Image, Eating Disturbance, and General Psychological Functioning in Female Adolescents: Covariance Structure Modeling and Longitudinal Investigations." *International Journal of Eating Disorders* 18 (3): 221–36.

Thorpe, K., Florence, C., Howard, D., and Joski, P. 2004. "The Impact of Obesity on Rising Medical Spending." *Health Affairs* (Web Exclusive), Oct. 20. Available at *www.healthaffairs.org.*

Tjaden, P., and Thoennes, N. 2000. *Extent, Nature, and Consequences of Intimate Partner Violence: Findings from the National Violence against Women Survey.* Washington, DC: Department of Justice, National Institute of Justice.

Tolman, R., and Raphael, J. 2000. "A Review of Research on Welfare and Domestic Violence." *Journal of Social Issues* 56 (4): 655–62.

Townsend, J., and Wasserman, T. 1997. "The Perception of Sexual Attractiveness: Sex Differences in Variability." *Archives of Sexual Behavior* 26 (3): 243–68.

Townsend, M., Johns, M., Shilts, M., and Faran-Ramirez, L. 2006. "Evaluation of a USDA Nutrition Education Program for Low-Income Youth." *Journal of Nutrition Education and Behavior* 38 (1): 30–41.

Townsend, M., Peerson, J., Love, B., Achterberg, C., and Murphy, S. 2001. "Food Insecurity Is Positively Related to Overweight in Women." *Journal of Nutrition* 131 (6): 1738–45.

Trayhurn, P., and Beattie, J. 2001. "Physiological Role of Adipose Tissue: White Adipose Tissue as an Endocrine and Secretory Organ." *Proceedings of the Nutrition Society* 60 (3): 329–39.

Trifiletti, L., Shields, W., Bishai, D., McDonald, E., Reynaud, F., and Gielen, A. 2006. "Tipping the Scales: Obese Children and Child Safety Seats." *Pediatrics* 117 (4): 1197–202.

Trost, S., Owen, N., Bauman, A., Sallis, J., and Brown, W. 2002. "Correlates of Adults' Participation in Physical Activity: Review and Update." *Medicine and Science in Sports and Exercise* 34 (12): 1996–2001.

Trostel, P., and Taylor, G., 2001. "A Theory of Time Preference." *Economic Inquiry* 39 (3): 379–95.

Troutt, D. 1993. *The Thin Red Line: How the Poor Still Pay More.* San Francisco: Consumers Union.

Tucker, D., Palmer, A., Valentine, W., Roze, S., and Ray, J. 2006. "Counting the Costs of Overweight and Obesity: Modeling Clinical and Cost Outcomes." *Current Medical Research Opinion* 22 (3): 575–86.

Tucker, L., and Friedman, G. 1998. "Obesity and Absenteeism: An Epidemiologic Study of 10,825 Employed Adults." *American Journal of Health Promotion* 12 (3): 202–7.

Turner, R., and Lloyd, D. 1999. "The Stress Process and the Social Distribution of Depression." *Journal of Health and Social Behavior* 40 (4): 374–404.

Turner, R., Wheaton, B., and Lloyd, D. 1995. "The Epidemiology of Social Stress." *American Sociological Review* 60 (1): 104–25.

Unger, R. 2003. "Lipid Overload and Overflow: Metabolic Trauma and the Metabolic Syndrome." *Trends in Endocrinology and Metabolism* 14 (9): 398–403.

United Health Foundation. 2005. "America's Health: State Health Rankings: A Call to Action for People and Their Communities." Available at *www.unitedhealthfoundation.org.*

Uppot, R., Sahani, D., Hahn, P., Kalra, M., Saini, S., and Mueller, P. 2006. "Effect of Obesity on Image Quality: Fifteen-Year Longitudinal Study for Evaluation of Dictated Radiology Reports." *Radiology* 240: 435–39.

U.S. Census Bureau. 2007. *Statistical Abstract of the United States.* 126th ed. Washington, DC: Government Printing Office. Available at *www.census.gov.*

U.S. Department of Agriculture (USDA). 2006a. Food and Nutrition Service, Office of Analysis, Nutrition, and Evaluation. "Characteristics of Food Stamp Households: Fiscal Year 2005." FSP-06-CHAR. By Allison Barrett. Project Officer, Jenny Genser.

———. 2006b. Food and Nutrition Service, Office of Analysis, Nutrition and Evaluation. "Federal Costs of School Food Programs." Available at *www.fns.usda.gov.*

———. 2006c. Food and Nutrition Service, Office of Analysis, Nutrition and Evaluation. "School Breakfast Participation and Meals Served" and "National School Lunch Participation and Lunches Served." Available at *www.fns.usda.gov.*

———. 2006d. Food and Nutrition Service, Office of Analysis, Nutrition and Evaluation. *WIC Participant and Program Characteristics 2004.* Report WIC-03-PC. Alexandria, VA: U.S. Department of Agriculture.

U.S. Department of Health and Human Services. 2001. *The Surgeon General's Call to Action to Prevent and Decrease Overweight and Obesity.* Washington, DC: U.S. GPO.

———. 2002. *Healthy People 2010: Understanding and Improving Health.* Washington, DC: U.S. GPO.

———. 2006. Administration for Children and Families. "Characteristics and Financial Circumstances of TANF Recipients, FY2005." Available at *www.acf.hhs.gov/programs/ofa.*

Van Cauter, E., and Spiegel, K. 1999. "Sleep as a Mediator of the Relationship between Socioeconomic Status and Health: A Hypothesis." *Annals of the New York Academy of Sciences* 896 (1): 254–61.

Variyam, J. 2003. "Factors Affecting Macronutrient Intake of U.S. Adults: Looking beyond the Conditional Mean." USDA, Economic Research Service, TB-1901. Available at *www.ers.usda.gov.*

Vartanian, L., Schwartz, M., and Brownell, K. 2007. "Effects of Soft Drink Consumption on Nutrition and Health: A Systematic Review and Meta-analysis." *American Journal of Public Health* 97 (4): 667–75.

Vaughan, S., and Oldham, J. 1997. "Behavior and Adaptive Functioning." In *Psychiatry,* ed. A. Tasman, J. Kay, and J. Lieberman, 1: 549–62. Philadelphia: Harcourt Brace.

Ver Ploeg, M., Mancino, L., and Lin, B. 2006. "Food Stamps and Obesity: Ironic Twist or Complex Puzzle?" *Amber Waves* 4 (1): 32–37.

Ver Ploeg, M., Mancino, L., Lin, B., and Wang, C.-Y. 2007. "The Vanishing Weight Gap: Trends in Obesity among Adult Food Stamp Participants (US) (1976–2002)." *Economics and Human Biology* 5: 20–36.

Ver Ploeg, M., and Ralston, K. 2008. "Food Stamps and Obesity: What Do We Know?" USDA, Economic Information Bulletin Number 34.

Visscher, T., and Seidell, J. 2001. "The Public Health Impact of Obesity." *Annual Review of Public Health* 22: 355–75.

Von Mutius, E., Schwartz, J., Neas, L., Dockery, D., and Weiss, S. 2001. "Relation of Body Mass Index to Asthma and Atopy in Children: The National Health and Nutrition Examination Study III." *Thorax* 56 (11): 835–38.

Wakefield, S., Yeudall, F., Taron, C., Reynolds, J., and Skinner, A. 2007. "Growing Urban Health: Community Gardening in South-East Toronto." *Health Promotion International* 22 (2): 92–101.

Wang, F., McDonald, T., Champagne, L., and Edington, D. 2004. "Relationship of Body Mass Index and Physical Activity to Health Care Costs among Employees." *Journal of Occupational and Environmental Medicine* 46 (5): 428–36.

Wang, S., and Brownell, K. 2005. "Public Policy and Obesity: The Need to Marry Science with Advocacy." *Psychiatric Clinics of North America* 28: 235–52.

Wansink, B. 2006. *Mindless Eating: Why We Eat More than We Think.* New York: Bantam Books.

Wansink, B., and Huckabee, M. 2005. "De-marketing Obesity." *California Management Review* 47 (4): 6–18.

Wardle, J., Parmenter, K., and Waller, J. 2000. "Nutrition Knowledge and Food Intake." *Appetite* 34: 269–75.

Wardle, J., Rapoport, L., Miles, A., Afuape, T., and Duman, M. 2001. "Mass Education for Obesity Prevention: The Penetration of the BBC's 'Fighting Fat, Fighting Fit' Campaign." *Health Education Research* 16 (3): 343–55.

Wardle, J., Waller, J., and Jarvis, M. 2002. "Sex Differences in the Association of Socioeconomic Status with Obesity." *American Journal of Public Health* 92 (8): 1299–304.

Warne, J., and Dallman, M. 2007. "Stress, Diet and Abdominal Obesity: Y?" *Nature Medicine* 13 (7): 781–83.

Wechsler, H., Basch, C., Zybert, P., Lantigua, R., and Shea, S. 1995. "The Availability of Low-Fat Milk in an Inner-City Latino Community: Implications for Nutrition Education." *American Journal of Public Health* 85 (12): 1690–94.

Weiss, E., Longhurst, J., and Mazure, C. 1999. "Childhood Sexual Abuse as a Risk Factor for Depression in Women: Psychosocial and Neurobiological Correlates." *American Journal of Psychiatry* 156 (6): 816–28.

Whalley, L., and Deary, I. 2001. "Longitudinal Cohort Study of Childhood IQ and Survival Up to Age 76." *BMJ* 322: 819.

Whitaker, R., Phillips, S., and Orzol, S. 2006. "Food Insecurity and the Risks of Depression and Anxiety in Mothers and Behavior Problems in Their Preschool-Aged Children." *Pediatrics* 118 (3): 1242–43.

Wiecha, J., Peterson, K., Ludwig, D., Kim, J., Sobol, A., and Gortmaker, S. 2006. "When Children Eat What They Watch: Impact of Television Viewing on Dietary Intake in Youth." *Archives of Pediatrics and Adolescent Medicine* 160: 436–42.

Wiederman, M., Sansone, R., and Sansone, L. 1999. "Obesity among Sexually Abused Women: An Adaptive Function for Some?" *Women and Health* 29 (1): 89–100.

Wilbur, J., Chandler, P., Dancy, B., and Lee, H. 2003. "Correlates of Physical Activity in Urban Midwestern African-American Women." *American Journal of Preventive Medicine* 25 (3, Suppl. 1): 45–52.

Wilde, P., McNamara, P., and Ranney, C. 2000. "The Effect on Dietary Quality of Participation in the Food Stamp and WIC Programs." USDA, Economic Research Service, Food Assistance and Nutrition Research Report No. 9.

Wilde, P., and Peterman, J. 2006. "Individual Weight Change Is Associated with Household Food Security Status." *Journal of Nutrition* 136: 1395–400.

Wilde, P., and Ranney, C. 2000. "The Monthly Food Stamp Cycle: Shopping Frequency and Food Intake Decisions in an Endogenous Switching Regression Framework." *American Journal of Agricultural Economics* 82: 200–213.

Williamson, D., Thompson, T., Anda, R., Dietz, W., and Felitti, V. 2002. "Body Weight and Obesity in Adults and Self-Reported Abuse in Childhood." *International Journal of Obesity* 26 (8): 1075–82.

Wilson, D., Kirtland, K., Ainsworth, B., and Addy, C. 2004. "Socioeconomic Status and Perceptions of Access and Safety for Physical Activity." *Annals of Behavioral Medicine* 28 (1): 20–28.

Wilson, F. 2003. *When Welfare to Work Doesn't Work: Interlocking Problems of Low-Income Women.* Cincinnati, OH: Health Foundation of Greater Cincinnati.

Winicki, J., and Jemison, K. 2003. "Food Insecurity and Hunger in the Kindergarten Classroom: Its Effect on Learning and Growth." *Contemporary Economic Policy* 21 (2): 145–57.

Wolf, A., and Colditz, G. 1998. "Current Estimates of the Economic Costs of Obesity in the United States." *Obesity Research* 6 (2): 173–75.

Wolf, N. 1991. *The Beauty Myth: How Images of Beauty Are Used against Women.* New York: Morrow.

Wooley, S., Wooley, O., and Dyrenforth, S. 1979. "Theoretical, Practical, and Social Issues in Behavioral Treatments of Obesity." *Journal of Applied Behavioral Analysis* 12: 3–25.

World Cancer Research Fund/American Institute for Cancer Research. 2007. *Food, Nutrition, Physical Activity, and the Prevention of Cancer: A Global Perspective.* Washington, DC: World Cancer Research Fund/American Institute for Cancer Research.

World Health Organization. 2004. "Global Burden of Disease and Risk Factors." Available at *www.who.int.en.*

World Health Organization/Food and Agricultural Organization of the United Nations. 2003. "Diet, Nutrition and the Prevention of Chronic Diseases." Report of a Joint WHO/FAO Expert Consultation.

Wyatt, S., Winters, K., and Dubbert, P. 2006. "Overweight and Obesity: Prevalence, Consequences, and Causes of a Growing Public Health Problem." *American Journal of the Medical Sciences* 331 (4): 166–74.

Xue, Y., Leventhal, T., Brooks-Gunn, J., and Earls, F. 2005. "Neighborhood Residence and Mental Health Problems of 5- to 11-Year-Olds." *Archives of General Psychiatry* 62 (May): 554–63.

Yanovski, S. 2003. "Binge Eating and Obesity in 2003: Could Treating an Eating Disorder Have a Positive Effect on the Obesity Epidemic?" *International Journal of Eating Disorders* 34 (special issue): S117–S120.

Yen, I., and Kaplan, G. 1998. "Poverty Area Residence and Changes in Physical Activity Level: Evidence from the Alameda County Study." *American Journal of Public Health* 88 (11): 1709–12.

Yoshihama, M., Hammock, A., and Horrocks, J. 2006. "Intimate Partner Violence, Welfare Receipt, and Health Status of Low-Income African American Women: A Lifecourse Analysis." *American Journal of Community Psychology* 37 (1–2): 95–109.

Yusuf, S., Hawkins, S., and Ôunpuu, S. 2005. "Obesity and the Risk of Myocardial

Infarction in 27000 Participants from 52 Countries: A Case-Control Study." *Lancet* 366: 1640–49.

Zagorsky, J. 2005. "Health and Wealth: The Late-20th Century Obesity Epidemic in the U.S." *Economics and Human Biology* 3 (2): 296–313.

Zagorsky, J., and Smith, P. 2008. "Does the Food Stamp Program Contribute to Adult Obesity?" University of Michigan–Dearborn Working Paper No. 103.

Zatonski, W., and Willett, W. 2005. "Changes in Dietary Fat and Declining Coronary Heart Disease in Poland: Population Based Study." *BMJ* 331: 187–88.

Zenk, S., Schulz, A., Hollis-Neeley, T., Campbell, R., Holmes, N., Watkins, G., Nwankwo, R., and Odoms-Young, A. 2005. "Fruit and Vegetable Intake in African Americans: Income and Store Characteristics." *American Journal of Preventive Medicine* 29 (1): 1–9.

Zhang, L., and Rashad, I. 2008. "Obesity and Time Preference: The Health Consequences of Discounting the Future." *Journal of Biosocial Science* 40 (1): 97–113.

Zhang, Q., and Wang, Y. 2004. "Trends in the Association between Obesity and Socioeconomic Status in U.S. Adults: 1971–2000." *Obesity Research* 12 (10): 1622–32.

Zhu, S., Layde, P. M., Laud, P. W., Pintar, F., Nirula, R., and Hargarten, S. 2006. "Obesity and Risk of Death due to Motor Vehicle Crashes." *American Journal of Public Health* 96 (4): 734–39.

Zill, N., Moore, K., and Nord, C. 1991. "Welfare Mothers as Potential Employees: A Statistical Profile Based on National Survey Data." Washington, DC: Child Trends.

Zimmerman, F., and Katon, W. 2005. "Socioeconomic Status, Depression Disparities, and Financial Strain: What Lies behind the Income-Depression Relationship?" *Health Economics* 14: 1197–215.

Zimmermann, U., Kraus, T., Himmerich, H., Schuld, A., and Pollmächer, T. 2003. "Epidemiology, Implications and Mechanisms Underlying Drug-Induced Weight Gain in Psychiatric Patients." *Journal of Psychiatric Research* 37: 193–220.

Zins, J., Weissberg, R., Wang, M., and Walberg, H. 2004. *Building Academic Success on Social and Emotional Learning: What Does the Research Say?* New York: Teachers College Press.

Index